Sacred Space

Sacred Space:
Interdisciplinary Perspectives within Contemporary Contexts

Edited by

Steve Brie, Jenny Daggers and David Torevell

CAMBRIDGE SCHOLARS

PUBLISHING

Sacred Space: Interdisciplinary Perspectives within Contemporary Contexts,
Edited by Steve Brie, Jenny Daggers and David Torevell

This book first published 2009

Cambridge Scholars Publishing

12 Back Chapman Street, Newcastle upon Tyne, NE6 2XX, UK

British Library Cataloguing in Publication Data
A catalogue record for this book is available from the British Library

ISBN (10): 1-4438-0517-3, ISBN (13): 978-1-4438-0517-9

Contents

Introduction 1

1 The Monastery as Sacred Space *Mark Barrett* 9

2 Keeping a Balance: The Sacred Space of the Heart and the Modern University *David Torevell* 23

3 Liminality, Sacred Space and the Dirwan *David Weir* 39

4 Consumption, Sacred Places and Spaces in Profane Contexts: a Comparison between India and the UK *Jan Brown, John Phillips and Vishwas Maheshwari* 55

5 Could the Category of the "Sacred" Imply a Problematic Conception of the Contemporary World? *Pascal Mueller-Jourdan* 78

6 Shaping Women's Sacred Space: Christian Liturgy and Womanspirit Ritual in a Moment of Heightened Feminist Consciousness *Jenny Daggers* 87

7 Sacred Space and the Singing Voice *Robin Hartwell* 103

8 Consecrating the Body: The Sacred and the Profane in Performance Art *Rina Arya* 114

9 From Pilgrimage to Tourism: A Comparative Analysis of Kavadi Festivals in Tamil Diasporas *Ron Geaves* 127

10 Trial, Tribulation and Triumph: The Sacred Space of the Bulgarian Orthodox Churches *Pepa Grundy* 144

11 The Politics and Poetics of Sacred Ruins *Caroline Bennett* 157

12 Tracing Bodies: Jane Urquhart's *A Map of Glass* and Sacramental Geography *Mark Godin* 176

13 Wandering in the Wilderness: the Search for Sacred Space in Jack Kerouac's *The Dharma Bums* *Steve Brie* 187

Contributors 199

Index 203

ACKNOWLEDGEMENTS

The editors would like to thank all those who contributed to and ensured the success of the *Sacred Space: Contemporary Contexts* conference in September 2008 from which the chapters in this book emerged. Many staff at Liverpool Hope University and beyond contributed to the publication in a spirit of generosity – the book is a testimony to their efficiency and willingness to participate with enthusiasm in interdisciplinary conversations about sacred space. In particular, a special debt of gratitude goes to Fr. Mark Barrett OSB, who was the keynote speaker at the event and who has been highly supportive of the project since its inception. A final thank-you must go to Mark Ferguson for all his work and good humour and to Amanda Millar and Carol Koulikourdi from Cambridge Scholars Publishing who were a delight to work with throughout.

Picture credits

Alex Ramsay Photography/photographersdirect.com – page 170.
Tim Gurney/www.copix.co.uk – page 171.
Tony Thorogood Photography/photographersdirect. com – page 172.
Alex Segre Photography/ photographersdirect. com – page 173.

INTRODUCTION

This collection of essays is a contribution to an area of religious studies which has received surprisingly little attention to date and focuses on how sacred space is conceived and interpreted in a variety of contemporary contexts. Interdisciplinary in nature, it attempts to shed light on this phenomenon by grouping together a collection of papers delivered at a one day conference at Liverpool Hope University on September 16th 2008.

Contributors to this collection have reflected upon a broad spectrum of conceptions of sacred space, which are thrown into relief in their juxtaposition. As current formulations of what constitutes the sacred become dislodged from tradition-specific religious and theological conceptualizations, inevitably more fluid, amorphous and less easy-to-define understandings arise. As a consequence, the increasingly ambiguous relationships which are opened up between notions of sacrality and space call for a thorough discussion on how these two notions operate separately and in relation to each other in contemporary contexts. One might for example, make the point by contrasting twelfth century Christian Europe's understanding of sacred space, indelibly linked to experiences of divine power channelled through ecclesiastical structures, with postmodern understandings reflecting a vast range of conceptualizations, whereby notions of alterity and difference seem to sit equivalently alongside tradition-bound understandings of sacred space, for example, in liturgy and pilgrimage.

It may be helpful to the reader to make some further preliminary reflections on the provenance and predicament of sacred space in contemporary discourse. As all contributors are located in, or informed by, British – and in one case French – academic contexts, the provenance and predicament of sacred space within specifically *western* discourse is under scrutiny here. This observation is as relevant to David Weir's analysis of the Diwan in the Arab Middle East, as it is to Ron Geaves' 'Kavadi Festivals in Tamil Diasporas' or to Jan Brown *et al*'s reflections on the sacralizing of secular spaces in selected Indian and British contexts: western discourses frame these investigations, even when the research material throws up challenges to continued Eurocentrism.

Traces of the fate of Christian notions of the sacred – Catholic, Protestant and Orthodox – in post-Cartesian modernity and in post-Christian and post-modern western trajectories can be glimpsed within these essays; the rise of religious studies – at once infused with Christian world views and determined to reach beyond these – is also evident in perspectives offered from within Muslim traditions of the Middle East and the Punjab. Through the work of scholars gathered here, who responded to a "call for chapters", disparate "soundings" are taken concerning the provenance and predicament of the contemporary "sacred space".

The perfectly judged opening chapter by Mark Barrett of Worth Abbey demonstrates a clearly articulated and sophisticated awareness of the enduring value and relevance of the Catholic monastic tradition to many contemporary searchers after sacred space. In this inter-disciplinary presentation of the monastic life, the spiritual resources offered by the focal sacred space of the Abbey are presented as they appear to the spiritual seeker – many of whom "rarely if ever visit a church". The chapter is infused with the present day continuing of a Catholic tradition founded with the sixth century *Rule of St Benedict*, as a way of living the orthodox Catholic faith in the world, but yet this formative Christian commitment remains out of focus here. Rather, the experience of the seeker, who may discover "a deepened sense of what it means to be alive", is foregrounded.

There is little expectation that the seeker will opt more permanently for the "scripted space" of the Abbey, or even for the more diffused commitment of joining a Church congregation, in order to locate his or her own story in relation to the Christian story; while both seeker and monk should, in Barrett's closing words "discern in the monastic environment a way of 'Seeing Salvation', and having discovered it in one place begin to find it everywhere", in these unchurched times, this spiritual experience will not necessarily find its interpretation within the ancient orthodoxies of the Christian story. Catholic Christianity thus endures while being in danger of its spiritual sources being detached from any perceived necessity to commit to the "scripted spaces" where its focal Christian story is told.

This distinctively Catholic perspective towards sacred space offered by Barrett differs considerably from Protestant approaches. The former tends to emphasize the sacramentality of the world *and* specifically designated spaces and places of sacrality, where God's presence resides in a manner very different from those outside such designations. This Catholic attitude towards creation is underpinned by a strong doctrine of *analogia entis*, rooted in an incarnational theology – the sacred space of the cosmos really *is* the arena of God's ongoing revelation. Specific sacred spaces, like liturgical spaces, are always in relation to this broader picture of how God reveals himself in the world. There might be a differently experienced divine presence within these two spaces, but *both* are regarded as being sacred. Mark Barrett's opening chapter reflects this position strongly. He argues that the sacred space of the Christian monastery has recently witnessed a noteworthy revival in lay interest by offering itself as a venue for transcendence. One reason he is able to account for this is because he believes it offers a unique opportunity for divine encounter and transformation which is founded upon a strong theology of space; in other words, such an encounter is far more likely to take place in the monastery than in other contexts and settings.

Protestant understandings of the sacred are different and often emphasize the split between the sacred and the secular. Consequently, they are less inclined to argue for a sense of sacred space different from other spaces. Such formulations are more likely to guard against tendencies to produce idolatrous attitudes towards space than they are to encourage such spaces. Some sociologists, like Berger, have famously plotted how this kind of Protestant viewpoint resulted in "an immense shrinkage in the scope of the sacred in reality" (1980: 111) with the consequence that individuals started to inhabit a far more lonely universe than they did previously. This was one of the characteristics of the modern world, which, bereft of daily experiences of the sacred, allowed itself to become more easily susceptible to rational, empirical and secular investigations.

Whether we accept Berger's position or not, what is apparent is that an integrated social order based on a commonly agreed sacral and metaphysical system of meaning, became less easy to sustain. Consequently, more individual notions of what the sacred and its relationship to space might mean began to emerge. New understandings of space reflected many of the religious, social and political upheavals and presuppositions of modernity. It is worth remembering that before the Enlightenment space was believed to be symbolically constituted and consequently needed to be interpreted allegorically. The shift towards the autonomy of reason during the Enlightenment meant that space was no longer accepted as being linked to notions of the sacred. Those in power began to deny any claims about such relationships, as space became mathematically and empirically defined. Modernity, obsessed with origins, could see no reason for claiming space was determined according to a divine plan. Consequently, reformulated perceptions of space began to be divorced from traditional and historical patterns of understanding and, in turn, many began to float free from explicitly religious or theological contexts.

One of the consequences of this shift was that the relationship between the sacred and space became situated within a far wider net of meanings and interpretations, some religious, some not. Reformulated “modern” and “postmodern” understandings of the sacred up to the present day reflect a vast range of post-Enlightenment influences – intellectual, political, feminist, cultural, religious. For instance, contemporary conceptions are as likely to refer to human experiences of transcendence, self-fulfilment, authenticity and responsibility outside explicitly religious frameworks, as they are to concepts entailing an encounter with the God of classical theism. Emerging from an eclectic mix of such influences and sources, contemporary understandings of sacred space exhibit not only a more wide-ranging diversity of formulations, but at times point to conflictual barriers which seems to deny the possibility of any shared meaning. There really is no commonly agreed understanding of what constitutes sacred space any longer. However, on a more positive note, many disciplines previously divorced from the language of “spirituality” now wish to interpret aspects of their discipline in “religious” terms, even if that entails conceiving religion in new and perhaps idiosyncratic forms. Whether such reformulations overlap and satisfy readers’ own conceptualizations of sacred space can only be answered by the readers themselves.

What this book offers is an insight into a broad range of conceptualizations of sacred space which reflect shifting theological, post-Christian religious studies and postmodern understandings. What is noteworthy, in some cases, is how traces of the Christian tradition continue to influence and seep into apparently tradition-free formulations of the sacred; no approach reflected in the book is hermetically sealed from important historical, religious and cultural influences. One regret, however, is that the collection does not reflect sacred space in the practices of the many faith communities established in recent decades within western societies. Such perspectives would have enriched this project and might have begun a richer dialogue with the Christian and post-Christian perspectives represented in the book.

Those chapters which concern sacred space within the western world develop the themes opened by Barrett. Pascal Mueller-Jourdan returns this mode of seeing salvation everywhere to an explicit traditional Catholic position, wherein the ancient Stoic philosophy is deployed to argue for just such a homogeneity of sacred space: Mueller-Jourdan uses this Catholic version of the homogenous to challenge the reductive homogeneity of the post-Enlightenment modern scientific world view. David Torevell’s chapter introduces the interior “sacred space of the heart”, so investigating the spiritual formation of the nun or monk, the woman or man for whom the inner sacred space is more important than the outer, so linking monastic practice to apophatic theology. It is entirely consistent with the fascination of the contemporary unchurched searcher with the monastery that, in the monastic vision of Fitzpatrick – a key source for Torevell's reflection – "the heart of the monk purified by ascetism becomes the space where all creation enters into the silence of God and the solitude of adoration". The impetus outward from the sacred space of the monastic heart is traced in Torevell's challenge to the modern university, to recover the balance between active and contemplative that characterized its medieval origin, so that the monastic dimension in each person (Pannikar) might be nourished through participation in university life.

Two chapters explore tensions over control of the terms of women's access to the established sacred space of Anglican cathedral or church: Robin Hartley's reflections on anxieties surrounding the sound of the mature female singing voice within the cathedral music tradition, and Jenny Daggers' account of British Christian women's liturgies at a moment of heightened concern over the position of women within their churches. The latter poses the crucial question, as relevant now as it was in the late 1970s: how are Christian women who resist patriarchal control to inhabit denominational sacred spaces, "to be present to the divine–human encounter mediated therein, when they find themselves excluded, or included only on terms set out by a male tradition"? It will be fascinating to see how the legacy of Womanspirit Ritual plays itself out within the contemporary framework of world, rather than simply western, Christianity at the start of the twenty-first century. Both chapters issue a reminder that officially sanctioned sacred spaces are subject to human regimes of control, which mediate, and possibly restrict, the potential divine–human encounter.

The same tension found in Barrett's account between life-stories told within detraditioned secularizing narratives and the Christian story animates Rina Arya's negotiation of post-Christian performance art, wherein the Christian narrative throws the simultaneous desecration and consecration of the wounded body into stark relief, and Caroline Bennett's reading of the perpetuated sacrality of former sacred spaces, now put to use within the consumerist market economy. Similar themes emerge in a Bulgarian context in Pepa Grundy's exploration of the intertwining of Orthodox sacred space with narratives that sacralise nationalism, and the contemporary potential of orthodox sacred space turned museum for the healing of past and thus present ethnic and religious divisions. In all these instances, Christian sacrality persists as subtext in a secularized space; also sacrality reappears within spaces from which Christianity is considered to have been expelled. When Jan Brown *et al.* apply Hanlon's category of a belief system for an Age of Consumption comparatively in an Indian and British context, their thesis can be seen as an argument for the creation of yet another version of sacrality.

Several contributors refer to Durkheim's sociological approach to the study of religion, and to Eliade's universalized categories of the "sacred" and the "profane". These seminal thinkers have organised western understandings of sacred space in recent decades, but several contributors here seek to trouble this clear distinction. Thus, in his reassertion of a Catholic homogeneity, Mueller-Jourdan issues a direct challenge to Eliade's assertion of heterogeneity between sacred and profane spaces. For David Weir, "to define 'the sacred' in intercultural terms is a big task". With reference to the Middle Eastern Diwan, Weir seeks to destablize the "categorical essentialism" invited by Eliade's sacred/profane distinction: he deploys the concept of liminality – again a western concept, first coined by van Gennep – to argue that boundaries between sacred and profane are differently drawn in Muslim societies, so what is liminal between these categories must also be reconstructed.

Both Steve Brie and Mark Godin present interpretations of literary texts in order to facilitate discussions of the concept of sacred space. Both writers are interested in the relationship between physical and mental geography and religious experience. With subtle and imaginative cross referencing to Urquhart's novel *A Map of Glass*, Godin posits the idea that sacraments are "'maps of flesh' since they offer a 'graphy', a writing and tracing out of bodies". He shows how liturgical participants engaging in symbolic acts of baptism and the reception of the Eucharist, "write on each other and are written upon". The chapter offers an illuminating analogy between the novelist's use of map imagery and sacramental maps as "they trace out space in which people move in their habits of touching".Brie's chapter explores the way in which spirituality can become located within natural spaces upon which the quality of sacredness is conferred. His contribution contextualises this approach within a Buddhist framework, a spiritual stance adopted by Kerouac during an influential but transitional stage of his life.

In conclusion, to speak of sacred space is to invite reflection on the continuing vitality of Christian traditions and to extend the long engagement of Christianity with the resolute secularising tendencies of western modernity. But to speak of sacred space also focuses our attention on the "big task" of forging investigative tools for exploring sacred space in the multi-religious world beyond the confines and preoccupations of the western world, as shaped by Christendom. We offer this collection as a contribution to both projects.

Steve Brie
Jenny Daggers
David Torevell
(Editors)

Reference

Berger, P. 1980. *The Sacred Canopy: Elements of a Sociology of Religion.* New York. Anchor Books.

Chapter One

The Monastery as Sacred Space

Mark Barrett

A surprise hit of London's Millennium celebrations in 2000 was a relatively modest exhibition at the National Gallery. From a quiet beginning, *Seeing Salvation – the image of Christ in art* became one of the most talked about Millennium events in the capital, and certainly among the most visited. Some 350,000 individuals attended the Sainsbury Wing of the Gallery for this exhibition; a very large number by National Gallery standards. Such statistics suggest that, even in the extensively unchurched world of contemporary Britain, attendees were undeterred by an "overtly Christian depiction" (Davie, 2003: 29) of the life of Christ. I begin this exploration of monastic spaces here, away from the monastery, because an exhibition which concerned itself with the representation of the Christian message through a structured use of physical objects and spaces offers a perspective on my subject: how is a monastery to be understood as sacred space in the contemporary context?

The exhibition's curator, Neil MacGregor, explains in his introduction to the accompanying catalogue that the artefacts used in the National Gallery show were originally created to build up Christian faith through their use in public worship and private devotion. Subsequently removed from their original, faith-based, settings these works would usually hang today in secular galleries, organised around a chronological narrative of art history rather than a devotional journey into faith (MacGregor, 2000: 6). In *Seeing Salvation* MacGregor reversed this movement. In stark contrast to an art-historical chronology, the exhibition involved a scripted space articulated around the theological dimensions of the Christian faith story. The sections had titles such as "The Word made Flesh", "Praying the Passion", "The Saving Body", and "The Abiding Presence". This is the language of a confessional catechism; while the thematically organised spaces these titles denote would not be out of place in a cathedral.

After seeing the exhibition, an unusually high number of visitors took the time to write to Neil MacGregor. Their letters indicate that an atmosphere of reverence and devotion had been generated among the exhibition-goers by his organisation of the sacred objects. One correspondent writes that the exhibition "was far more devotional than many a sermon". Other letters explicate this remark, one commenting that entering the gallery "felt like going into a cathedral, and the atmosphere among the people was quite astonishing – we were all full of awe, sorrow and reverence" (quoted in Davie, 2003: 33). Sociologist Grace Davie, who has published a study of the letters, comments: "Over and over again, they admit to being profoundly moved by the 'experience' of 'Seeing Salvation', and for many the encounter was as much spiritual as cognitive" (Davie, 2003: 33). What light can the responses of visitors to a London exhibition throw on our understanding of the monastery as sacred space?

Significantly, MacGregor himself does not regard Christian artists as simply offering a window into the past, a record of what people used to think and feel, but as attempting a public depiction of a continuing truth, which intends to address a contemporary audience: "We the spectators have to become eye-witnesses to an event that matters to us now. Theological concepts must be given human dimensions". Paintings and sculptures created to bear witness to the devotional dimensions of Christian faith have an imaginative power that cannot be encountered in religious discourse alone, he argues: "If only words can tackle the abstract mysteries, paintings are uniquely able to address the universal questions through the intelligence of the heart" (MacGregor, 2000: 7). These universal themes of human living, such as the love of mother for child, innocence beset by violence or a love which endures through death, are at the same time profoundly significant topics in Christian theology. Here, in *Seeing Salvation*, they were localised in the public space of the gallery, and found speaking the symbolic languages of colour, shape, form and texture.

Two aspects of this exhibition and the visitors' responses to it strike me as important here: one is the fact that this was an event taking place in public, in a shared space where many individuals were able to participate together in an encounter with their physical environment, and with one another; the second is that this exhibition invited its visitors to enter the realm of the creative imagination, of symbolic memory and archetypal pattern. This was a public space where, as MacGregor puts it, universal questions engage the intelligence of the heart, so that our "interior spaces" and the exterior space we inhabit achieve a degree of congruence.

Monasteries are self-evidently different from exhibition spaces. But any monastery shares with this exhibition the conscious aim of building a physical environment which mediates a series of meanings, a cultural framework which speaks both of the interior values and of the interpersonal perspectives of the individuals who inhabit it. In the case of a monastery, this local culture, as we might term it, stands in contrast to the culture which prevails in the society around it. In the *Seeing Salvation* exhibition, gallery visitors were invited to sojourn within such an alternative culture for a shorter or longer time, and the letters they wrote to the curator reflect the varying results of their stay.

Christian monasticism, historically, has sought to achieve among those who follow its path a broad reorientation of thought and feeling, of moral and interpersonal perspectives, of internal awareness and aesthetic outlook; an extensive and demanding process which is intended to occupy a lifetime. The environment best suited to such a transformational process is unlikely to come about by accident. It is necessary for the sacred space to be more self-consciously constructed than even a millennium exhibition. However, like the National Gallery's millennial event, the sacred space of a monastery will be a shared space in which a number of people can encounter a self-consciously constructed culture together, a space characterised by the use of creative imagination, the engagement of symbolic memory and the deployment of archetypal pattern. When the effort is made to synchronise exterior and interior spaces the result is experienced as sacred space.

Historians and students of monasticism agree that the most striking feature of the monastic movement in Christianity has been a *fugar mundi*, a withdrawal or flight from society (Fry, 1981: 4). This has frequently involved a *physical* distance of the monastery from towns and cities but, whenever the monastic movement has been true to its ideals, it has always involved a *cultural* distance between the monastery and its surroundings. Although monastics do not withdraw from wider society simply in order to construct a cultural chasm between the monastery and the broader societal networks within which it exists, the distinctive local culture of a monastery requires, nonetheless, the provision of a sufficient distance from the "ways of this age" to allow for the generation, cultivation and sustaining of a way of living which contrasts with that of a secular society (Casey, 2003: 34–35). Specifically, a monastery exhibits a culture founded on and imbued with the Christian faith story, the sacred context within which we believe we are invited to "see salvation". And, like the designers of the "Seeing Salvation" exhibition, the builders of monastic spaces bring into being a context within which our encounters with the places we inhabit, and our encounters with one another within those places, will be qualitatively different from encounters which take place outside the monastery.

It is this understanding of the monastery as a space which allows for the cultivation of a special culture – one which foregrounds the sacred – that concerns me here. Before turning to examine four dimensions of sacred space in monastic culture in their own right, I wish to note the phenomenon of interest in monastic culture among non-monks, an interest which itself appears to be, at least in part, the product of a search for sacred space. Whether or not postmodern eyes view monasteries as, in some sense, sanctuaries of the human spirit or as places imbued with a promise of the transcendent, the distinctive culture that exists within their walls continues to exercise a widespread attraction. What are we to make of this phenomenon?

"Going on Retreat": Monastic Space as Sacred Space for the Visitor

A couple of years ago, the song of a nightingale in Berlin made front page news in the UK newspapers. It seems the constant din of city traffic is causing urban nightingales to sing so loudly that their melodies are technically breaking legal noise levels. Apparently, the nightingales in central Berlin are five times louder than their more laid-back rural cousins, generating decibels more usually associated with a motorbike on full throttle. One newspaper wryly commented that, under German safety laws, anyone encountering the song of a nightingale should require protective earphones.

The image of the hyper-aroused urban nightingale, attempting to out-sing an entire city, is powerful. Those of us who are or have been city dwellers are only too familiar with the need to shout our lives louder in an attempt to be heard over everyone else. The modern city is a total environment; its sounds, sights and smells are a constant stimulus to the senses. Nowhere, it appears, is urban culture to be found at rest. Thus, when city dwellers visit a monastery, the effect can be akin to stepping into a sensory vacuum. While the city moves at a breakneck pace, the monastic life moves slowly and values stillness; while the city involves continual change, the monastery prizes sameness and repetition; while the city invites ever-louder noise, the monastery is a place of silence.

In April of 2004, *The Times* correspondent, Andy Arkell, visited Worth Abbey, my own monastery, in Sussex. "Going from rush-hour London to a monastery feels almost dangerous," he writes. "If there were such a thing as 'psychological bends' this would surely be the way to get it." He comments that the change in pressure is so marked that it is "as if some crucial piece of elastic has snapped, dropping me back into just myself" (Arkell, 2004).

Arkell is right. Monastic culture is quite distinctive. At its heart is an environment consciously constructed to foreground a set of values which make monks into "strangers to the city", as Michael Casey puts it (Casey, 2005). The visitor discovers the natural sounds of the countryside, a rhythm of life much less hurried than that of a city centre, a sense of expansiveness and leisure, the space and opportunity to be alone: and all of these appear aspects of a rural idyll. But, in contrast to the exterior din of the metropolis, "all that inner noise that usually sits in the back of your mind, is suddenly in the foreground, loud and unnerving. It feels peculiar, these days, to be really alone" (Arkell, 2004).

Peculiar, perhaps. Nevertheless, monasteries continue to attract large numbers of guests, retreatants and visitors who want to encounter a different way of being, facing the challenge and opportunity of slowing down and finding time on their hands, in silence. My own community, in recent years, has witnessed a considerable growth in the number of retreat groups and individuals wishing to spend time doing – by secular standards – very little. And perhaps the most surprising dimension of this encounter between the monastic culture and the outside world is the extent of the interest in monastic communities among those members of our society who rarely if ever visit a church.

In May 2005 BBC 2 screened an unusual piece of what was, technically, reality TV. *The Monastery*, however, was about as far from *Big Brother* as would be possible to get. The three part documentary employed the reality TV convention of charting the journey of a group of "ordinary people" who set out into a situation which they had not previously encountered. Five men, from a variety of backgrounds, accepted the challenge of spending what the BBC's publicity department decided (perhaps understandably) to call "forty days and forty nights" living as retreatants alongside the monks of Worth: praying the Divine Office with us in the Abbey Church, eating in our monastery refectory, working in the grounds and receiving a basic formation in fundamental monastic values from the Abbot and the Novice Master. The show attracted 2.5 million viewers, and inspired similar programmes in the USA and Australia as well as follow up shows in the UK. The international success in the following year of the (very different) cinematic epic, *Into Great Silence*, filmed among the hermit monks of the Grande Chartreuse in the French Alps, confirms the impression that contemporary audiences of all persuasions are interested to see what happens behind monastery walls.

Some of the many hundreds of men who applied to take part in *The Monastery* were committed Christians and regular churchgoers, but most were not. I took part in the interviews of "short list" applicants: very little awareness of or even interest in formal religion was apparent in what most had to say, but all were intrigued to take part in a way of life about which they knew, perhaps, even less. Most had been attracted to the interviews by advertisements in the secular media, or by an email invitation circulated around the offices of central London media companies. Many potential participants appear to have believed that a monastery was a place which would enable them, in ways that were not entirely clear, to discover something about themselves which was not accessible to them in any other place.

Grace Davie has identified a phenomenon she terms "vicarious religion" (Davie, 1994; Davie, 2002). This is her term to describe a set of behaviours whereby members of our unchurched society can be understood as having effectively delegated to its religious institutions a task they themselves no longer intend personally to undertake but still wish, in some sense, to see maintained. I have no doubt that part of the fascination of the monastic way of life to contemporary society has this dimension to it: in a sense monasteries have always fulfilled a version of this role, being understood as the "praying class" in medieval society just as the knights were the "fighting class". Part of the contemporary interest in monasteries can also be understood as the manifestation of the natural curiosity we all feel about a way of life completely different from our own. There is also, inevitably, the hope we may well cherish that someone out there has answers to the questions which life has presented to us – this might be described as the image of the monk as *guru*, a perception encouraged, perhaps, by some media presentations of eastern monasticism.

But the experience of working with the participants in *The Monastery* was that none of these perspectives fully accounts for a willingness to spend time in a monastery, especially since partial or mistaken apprehensions quickly fall away when the living reality of a monastic community is genuinely encountered.

To borrow Philip Groning's *haiku*-like description of his film *Into Great Silence*, a time in a monastery offers for the retreatant "A meditation on life; a contemplation of time; silence, repetition, rhythm" (Soda Pictures, 2006: 1). Two experiences seem of particular significance to those who visit a monastery for a retreat. One is the experience of exterior silence, promoted by the lack of hurry, the freedom from time pressures and the strong rhythm of the day; the other is the accompanying awareness of interior noise, which stands out the more clearly in the context of the simplified patterns of monastic living. Such encounters are not encouraged by our secular society, perhaps because the discovery of this disjunction between interior and exterior worlds calls into question so many dimensions of the culture which promotes it. But this dis-comforting realisation has proven significant for those who come to monasteries as guests, hoping to explore within the sacred space of monastic culture a deepened sense of what it means to be alive.

The *Rule of St Benedict,* the short sixth century text which has guided monastic living in the western Catholic Church, begins by asking its readers: "Who among you seeks *life*?" (RB Prologue:14). (The *Rule of St Benedict* (abbreviated to RB) is available in many modern editions. References here are to Fry, 1981.) And this, of course, was the initial appeal of Christianity to its first practitioners, who called it *The Way* (of life). This remains the appeal of monastic culture for those who visit it as guests: the monastery functions as a sacred space, a sanctuary, where the tidal currents of their hearts, set swirling by crowded, noisy, busy lives, may find harbour. Paradoxically, perhaps, by stepping away from the regular trappings of everyday life, visitors find – like those viewing the "Seeing Salvation" exhibition – an enhanced sense of their own value and the value of others, a greater reverence towards their lives, and an awareness of something which goes beyond themselves.

The Monastery as Sacred Space

But a monastery is not, first and foremost, a guest house. If it is a sacred space for guests, it is so only because it is much more fundamentally a sacred space for the monks who inhabit it. A monastic community needs an environment which promotes and protects not simply geographical distance from society, but more importantly a cultural space for the distinctive monastic way of being, a space which allows the heart to breathe.

Four qualities of the monastic environment may be highlighted. When taken together, they constitute sacred space, a specifically monastic culture. These are: the monastic environment as (i) a purposive space which encourages recollection, (ii) a space ordered around regular routine, promoting a pattern or rhythm to the day and the week, (iii) a reflective, thoughtful space which foregrounds reading, the primary mode of Christian storytelling, and (iv) a space which summons isolated individuals into fellowship, and thereby sustains community. In each case we shall see that the distinctive quality of the monastic space is the self-conscious alignment of physical environment with interior aspiration. When this synchronisation is striven towards, the full beauty of the monastic culture manifests itself as sacred space where we can "see salvation".

Purposive Space and Purity of Heart

Look carefully around the apse of an ancient English cathedral and the chances are that you will find a small doorway discreetly placed alongside the choir, from which a well-worn stone staircase leads directly up to what used to be the common dormitory of a monastery. For centuries, monks worshipped in the choirs of these awe-inspiring buildings, and this was the "night stair", specifically placed to speed the monk's journey from his bed to the night office of vigils. Like the fireman's pole, the night stair was the quickest way from the dormitory above to the church below; a clear sign, we might say, of a purposive use of space! The night stair is a symbol from England's monastic past of the careful shaping of monastic buildings to monastic values.

The eastern monastic traditions, stemming from the teachings of the Buddha, stress the need for awareness, or "mindfulness". It is less well known in western society that the Christian monastic tradition cherishes a remarkably similar virtue, sometimes called "purity of heart" (see Luckman & Kulzer, 1999). This is in reality a singleness of focus, a disciplined recollection or awareness of God as the central reality of life. The first step towards this ideal is a mindful presence to ourselves and to others in each moment of our day. If, with the architect Le Corbusier, we were to say that a house is a machine for living in, the sacred space of a monastery is first and foremost a machine for focussing in, a place of awareness and recollection, an environment to promote and sustain purity of heart.

The *Rule of St Benedict* requires that the tools and goods of the monastery be treated with the same reverence as the sacred vessels of the altar (RB 31:10), thereby pointing towards this reality. The monk is altogether to shun forgetfulness (RB 4:48): which certainly involves arriving for things on time (hence the provision of details like the night stair), but more importantly requires that our steady, focussed awareness be centred upon God. All dimensions of the monastic environment tend to promote this virtue of awareness of the things of God, and thus, for example, monastic buildings are always oriented around an Abbey Church, the crucial symbol of that awareness.

As in many historic religious traditions, an awareness of death as a reality is encouraged in Christian monasteries rather than hidden, and many monasteries enjoy the privilege (no longer common in a society which tries to pretend that death does not happen, or at least not to us) of incorporating a cemetery for the deceased members of the community. A church and a graveyard – two powerful symbols of the boundaries set to our human independence and two signposts pointing towards the central realities of human living as understood within monastic culture.

The monastery as a whole is thus a scripted space, a purposive environment, within which everything is ordered to this one end: that in everything God may be glorified. Everything is structured towards this – times, places, patterns of living. The sanctuary of the monastery creates a space which constantly invites its inhabitants to return their attention to that which is at the centre of all things.

Rhythm of Life and Rhythm of Space

Such a patterning in our ways of using time and space has come to be regarded with suspicion in the modern world. The word "routine" has become a synonym for "depersonalized", "mechanical" or "thoughtless". Exploiting this fact, the Voluntary Service Overseas organisation advertises on the London tube with posters asking commuters: "Will you remember today for the rest of your life?" – contrasting the routine monotony of the day in the office with the heightened drama of a one-off decision to offer support to VSO as a volunteer. It is a perfectly valid strategy: the daily round can be precisely "one damn thing after another", routine can trivialise or dehumanise, producing a numbness and internal freezing which is the very opposite of life giving.

But the reverse can also be the case: more than anything else, human flourishing – especially in our crowded 21st century – is promoted by regular practices, recurrent events and established, familiar places, which establish a foundational sense of coherence to life. From these we derive our sense of who we are, making sense of our world and learning how it is possible to enjoy a degree of comprehensibility, manageability and meaningfulness. Where such a patterning underpins and permeates the day and the week there is a framework holding together even the busiest and most troubled day.

The *Rule of St Benedict* established a tradition of monastic building in which everything necessary for the orderly life of a self-sufficient community was to be found readily to hand within the space of the monastery (RB 66:6–7). Furthermore, the practices of monastic communities founded upon the Rule exhibit a sense of orderly, routinised, living. A monastery refectory is planned so that every monk has his specific place; a choir is similarly ordered. Thoughtfully constructed spaces for work, for sleeping, for reading, and for praying characterise the architecture of monastic communities. Above all, the relationship between these spaces has been considered. There is a rhythm to the patterning of spaces, just as there is a rhythm to the patterning of the day. To live within such a space is to be invited to reorder one's interior landscape to resemble the graceful rhythm of the monastery's environment. A harmony between inner and outer structures is the aim.

Public monastic prayer exhibits just such a rhythmic ordering, and is the model for interior prayer. The singing of psalms in church is cumulative, a rhythm arranged around certain times of day, week by week, with a structure of months and seasons, special times and ordinary times. There is a regular pattern, an iteration and reiteration which allows participants to be caught up completely into what they know so well that sound can be like silence. This is the experience of routine as a stream of life whose living waters can transport us to places we cannot achieve by our own striving.

And, like monastic praying, monastic living exhibits the same structures of patterned repetitions: times of work, and of rest; times of sharing and times of silence; times to eat and times to fast; times to pray together, and alone. A monastic space will derive the particular pattern of its buildings from the shaping of this rhythmic life, so that nothing seems left to chance. In this way, monastic buildings should be transparently carriers of purpose, shaped to function so that everything that is required to sustain the life of the community is easily to be found close at hand, while nothing that is present can draw the monk away from the focussed awareness to which he aspires.

Reflective Space and *Lectio Divina*

I have noted that a central dimension of the purposive space of the monastery is the orientation of all activities towards the Abbey Church, the symbol of the patterning of all monastic living around our engagement with God in prayer, public and private. Another such orientation of monastic space involves the role of reading, and especially sacred reading. Contemporary Christians have become more aware than was the case twenty years ago of the monastic tradition of *lectio divina*, holy reading, the prayerful exploration of the scriptures. Such reading goes beyond the simply distracting reading of thrillers or informational reading of guide books, to become transformational reading, in which – to adapt a memorable phrase of Rowan Williams – we do not so much interrogate the data on the page before us as recognise that the data interrogates us (Williams, 1979: 1).

In his classic study of medieval monastic culture, *The Love of Learning and the Desire for God*, Benedictine scholar Jean Leclercq beautifully evokes the actual practices associated with meditative reading of scripture as a "repeated mastication of the divine words" (Leclercq, 1961: 90), a deeply physical, embodied act of individual spiritual striving. As Michael Casey points out, this way of "chewing the text" is one we moderns have to re-learn as our information-driven society has taught us not to value practices which lead us to slow down, to activate our imaginations, and to enter the cave of the heart. "*Lectio Divina* is a technique of prayer and a guide to living. It is a means of descending to the level of the heart and of finding God" (Casey, 1995: vi).

A monastic culture thus requires the deliberate cultivation and promotion of slow, reflective reading of scripture, and the space of the monastery will be ordered in such a fashion as to make this fact obvious. At the centre of the life of the community stands an open Gospel book (perhaps a community might have the privilege of a beautifully hand-crafted edition), enthroned on a thoughtfully fashioned *Ambo* or formal public reading-desk. The recent exhibition of sacred texts at the British Library (North & North, 2007) gave some degree of insight into the vital role of the physical text in the Christian tradition (and, indeed, in Hebrew and Arabic tradition also). This is especially true in the monasteries. Reader's desks are also found in the monastery's refectory, and in the Chapter House where the community meets in formal assembly. The environment acts as a permanent public statement about the central role the reading of the text is to play in the life of each monk.

Because reading is a seamless activity in which the whole of what we do has an impact upon each part, monks tend to develop considerable reading resources, libraries, book collections, so that the reading of scripture finds its context in a wide programme of sacred and secular reading, sometimes in scholarship, and – in many cases – writing. As Casey notes: "the practice of solid reading gives the community a certain *gravitas*" (Casey, 2003: 39). The physical environment of the monastery will be geared to support this activity, with spaces both formal and informal, indoor and outdoor so arranged that reading is central to the life of the community and is clearly seen as such.

Community Space and Christian *Koinonia*

Finally, no monastery is complete without a shared space for eating, a shared space for relaxing together, and a shared space for formal discussion, learning together and decision making. This also is about more than simple practical convenience. It is one more example of the striving for congruence of interior and exterior in monastic living.

"New Testament authors expressed the essence of Christianity in one word. It is the Greek word *koinonia* usually translated as 'fellowship' . . . Fellowship with Christ leading to a fellowship with the Father, and fellowship with one another in Christ: there you have Christianity in one word." (Panikulam, 1979: 1). Monastic authors are clear that our way of living is founded upon this New Testament ideal: the sharing of a Christocentric life with others. From very early times, the term *koinonia* was employed as the technical term for "monastery", and St Pachomius, the third-century founder of monastic communities in Egypt, is remembered as teaching that "this *koinonia* . . . is the model for everyone who wishes to gather souls together for God's sake in order to help them become perfect" (Fry, 1981: 25).

The *Rule of St Benedict* views the *koinonia* as a dynamic process of incorporation into Christ, which takes places among the brethren: "No one is to pursue what he judges better for himself, but instead what he judges better for someone else . . . Let them prefer nothing whatever to Christ, and may he bring us all together to everlasting life" (RB 72: 7, 11–12).

In secular society, "home" is pre-eminently the space where one can "be oneself", as the home furnishing stores delight in endlessly reminding us: "It's all about *you*". But in a monastery, what the secular individual might expect to find in his or her own kitchen, dining room, living room and study, in a monastery is found in shared, communal spaces. This means that a monk does not, in the secular sense, have a "home": the environment of the monastery is not a place to "be oneself", but precisely a space in which one is constantly called towards the other, so that one can be transformed ever more fully into the image of Christ. The monk, in one sense, is called not to be himself but to become someone else.

The environment of the monastery is so designed as to invite the isolated individual to step into the nexus of relationships which is *koinonia,* fellowship or community, not simply in the social sense, but in the New Testament sense of a network of Christocentric relationships. Monks journey to God not as single travellers, but as a unified pilgrimage band.

Conclusion

These four elements go to make up the distinctive monastic way of organising space, which promotes and sustains a monastic culture. Its purpose is the Gospel purpose: to offer life in its fullest.

Every day, we breathe many of thousands of times and usually we do so without having consciously to advert to the process. It is one of those curious features of our bodily consciousness, however, that when something goes wrong and we do become aware of our breathing, we find we are having deliberately to choose to breathe and to remember to keep on doing so. We find ourselves taking breathing lessons! Luckily, for most of us, if this happens the process does not take long to return to automatic.

The function of the monastery is, perhaps, not too different. It draws our attention to practices which make us more human, which give us fuller life, but with which we have in some sense lost touch. Eventually, having been relearned, they can become internalised and natural, as they are intended to be. But at first they require the provision of external reminders, an environment that shapes us in particular ways, patterns of living which keep us aware of something which (did we but know it) was supposed to be automatic.

If the sacred space of the monastery is well-formed, the monk and the guest alike should be able to discern, in the monastic environment, a way of "Seeing Salvation," – and, having discovered it in one place, begin to find it everywhere.

References

Arkell, A. 2004. 'Far from the madding crowd', *The Times,* April 14.

Casey, M. 1995. *Sacred Reading: The Ancient Art of Lectio Divina.* Liguori, Missouri: Liguori/Triumph.

Casey, M. 2003. 'A Benedictine Decalogue: Ten Words from St Benedict.' [Paper read at the International Conference of Benedictine Women, Mount St Benedict, Pennant Hills, September 14]. Tarrawarra Abbey, Yara Glen. (Privately circulated)

Casey, M. 2005. *Strangers to the City: Reflections on the Beliefs and Values of the Rule of St Benedict.* Brewster, Mass: Paraclete Press.

Davie, G. 1994. *Religion in Britain since 1945.* Oxford: Blackwell.

Davie, G. 2002. *Europe: The Exceptional Case: Parameters of Faith in the Modern World.* London: Darton, Longman and Todd.

Davie, G. 2003. 'Seeing Salvation: The Use of Data as Text in the Sociology of Religion', in P. Avis (ed.), *Public Faith? The State of Religious Belief and Practice in Britain* (pp. 28–44). London: SPCK.

Fry, T. (ed.). 1981. *RB 1980. The Rule of St Benedict in Latin and English with notes* (I. Baker, T. Horner, A. Raabe, & M. Sheridan, associate editors). Collegeville, Minn: The Liturgical Press.

Hedley, D. 2008. *Living Forms of the Imagination.* London: T&T Clark.

Leclercq, J. 1961. *The Love of Learning and the Desire for God: A Study of Monastic Culture.* London: SPCK.

Luckman, H. A. & Kulzer, L. (eds). 1999. *Purity of Heart in Early Ascetic and Monastic Literature: Essays in Honour of Juana Raasch, OSB.* Collegeville, Minn: The Liturgical Press.

MacGregor, N. 2000. 'Introduction', in G. Finaldi (ed.), *The Image of Christ: Catalogue of the Exhibition "Seeing Salvation".* London: National Gallery.

North, P. & North, J. (eds). 2007. *Sacred Space: House of God, Gate of Heaven.* London: Continuum.

Panikulam, G. 1979. *Koinonia in the New Testament: A Dynamic Expression of the Christian Life.* Rome: Biblical Institute Press.

Sennett, R. 1974. *The Fall of Public Man.* London: Penguin Books.

Sennett, R. 1990. *The Conscience of the Eye: The Design and Social Life of Cities.* New York: Norton.

Sheldrake, P. 2001. *Spaces for the Sacred: Place, Memory and Identity.* London: SCM Press.

Soda Pictures. 2006. *Into Great Silence. A film by Philip Groning* [Production publicity notes distributed at a private showing of the film, December 2006] (Philip Groning, Cinematographer). London. (Privately circulated)

Williams, R. 1979. *The Wound of Knowledge.* London: Darton, Longman & Todd.

CHAPTER TWO

KEEPING A BALANCE: THE SACRED SPACE OF THE HEART AND THE MODERN UNIVERSITY

DAVID TOREVELL

In contrast to other contributions in the book, this chapter offers an alternative way of looking at sacred space by focussing on an interior, rather than exterior, location. Drawing from the Christian ascetic practice of the training of the heart (*askésis*), I claim that the modern university has something worthwhile to learn from this historical tradition. I suggest that that the creative integration of active *and* contemplative modalities of learning, as promoted in the medieval monastic and cathedral schools – sometimes refered to as the keeping of a balance between *scientia* (know-how) and *sapientia* (wisdom) – offers important insights into discussions about the educative task and that such integration is likely to result in the happiness and well-being of students. In addition to the array of pedagogical practices which encourage critical and analytical reading and thinking, contemplative and reflective pedagogy needs to find a firmer position through which to balance the sharpening of the intellect with *the cultivation of the heart* (Zajonc, 2006).

During an interview I conducted in September 2008 about the purpose of contemporary monasticism, Dame Andrea Savage, the Abbess of the Benedictine Abbey of Stanbrook, Worcestershire, England, emphasised that her community was there primarily to seek God by means of attentive listening. Referring to the *Rule of St. Benedict* which governed her community's way of life, she said: "The most important word is listen. And if you don't have silence you can't listen." Indeed, the opening words of the *Prologue* to the *Rule* encourage monks to "listen" and to incline "the ear of your (their) heart" (1981: 15) so that what is heard might bring about an inner transformation. Within monastic culture any such transformation is measured in terms of the expansion of the heart (a word denoting the innermost core or centre of the self) as it becomes formed (rather than informed) through attentive listening to the divine. Such encouragement to listen in silence reflects an ontological significance to the practice, a disciplined pursuit attuned to moments of revelatory insight and truth. As the Trappist monk Thomas Merton proclaimed, "Contemplation is an awakening to the Real within all that is real" (quoted in Shannon, Bochen and O'Connell, 2002: 83). Entailing a passive mode of receptive openness, this interpenetration of silence – listening as the heart is interwoven and changed with something outside the self – is at the very core of monastic spirituality and includes the operation of the spiritual senses – listening in silence to a revelatory voice which speaks to the "ear of the heart".

Certainly, the monastic strand of Christianity has always encouraged the search for God chiefly through silent contemplation. Watten's analysis of attentive silence in the *Rule of St. Benedict* hints that the practice encourages a serious pursuit – the contemplation of God. Listening in silence encourages a receptive mode of being and serves the goal of monasticism – the *gravitas* of the revelatory communication of God with His creation: "To keep silent for the sake of silence really means to keep silence because of the gravity and seriousness of monastic life ..." (1973: 30). Such seriousness is allied to "considering" oneself (understood by the Latin word *considerare* meaning "to lift up one's eyes or to get one's bearing from the stars") and therefore, as orientating oneself as part of something much greater (Torevell, 2006: 33). Rather than being weighed down by the drudgery of endlessly doing things, contemplation raises one up to look up beyond the self, a theme I shall pursue in more detail a little later.

Dame Andrea also emphasised the importance of balance in monastic living, referring to the tripod of prayer, *lectio divina* and manual labour; however, such balance was precarious at times. If the tripod is not maintained carefully, it can easily fall over. Things start to go wrong in the monastery when things get out of balance: "Keep to the balance of the *Rule* and you won't go wrong. Manual work takes over from *lectio* and prayer as the bustle of the day kicks in." Manual work is necessary so that we can feed and clothe ourselves, and not rely on others, but it needs to be kept in equilibrium with the other two constituents of the monastic life. Consequently, the monastic balancing of the active and contemplative pursuits which make up the routine of each day play a crucial role in maintaining community and encouraging a process of self-transformation. The two strands are not unrelated, she maintains, since one's approach to the active is always governed by the contemplative. However, it is important to stress not only the complementarity of activity and contemplation but the basic need to ensure *both* are spoken about and kept in some sort of balance. What this chapter attempts to do is recapture this emphasis on the cultivation of the heart in the modern university, a task not as extravagant as it might at first seem, since I shall outline how the emergence of the first universities grew out of this concern.

An Inclusive Space of the Heart

Monasticism, then, seeks by means of an externally enclosed space, the transformation of the heart, that inner space waiting to be recognised as the divine dwelling place. It encourages the heart to see itself as this sacred venue. Having set herself apart from the world, the monastic mystically prepares herself to embrace inwardly all things. In monastic life therefore, the "return of the *heart*" (*reditus ad cor*), the "life of the *heart*" and "finding the place of the *heart*" (Howe, 2005: 5) become central spiritual activities and foci. The real covenant, as the prophet Jeremiah noted, is always "written on the heart" (Jeremiah 1:31–34). Contemplation develops as the 'awakened heart is attuned to *being*' (Howe, 2005: 5) and changed by its encounter. The most important sacred space, therefore, is not the outer but the inner, and this is why it is wise to protect it from any potentially harmful external influences – the outer boundaries serve to protect the inner enclosure.

As the heart becomes changed, it learns to adore the One who addresses and resides in the heart. Fitzpatrick comments:

> The heart of the monastic purified by asceticism becomes the space where all creation enters into the silence of God and the solitude of adoration. The real cloister or enclosure is the heart of one dedicated to undivided love of God, not the enclosed space of the cloister. (2006: 151)

Such an inclusive space unites the whole of creation within the enclosure of the heart, especially those who suffer, as monastics develop a human and spiritual solidarity with all humanity. Although there are inevitable boundaries surrounding the outer and inner enclosures, these never serve as barriers but rather, paradoxically, as openings up to those outside the restraints:

> I have never experienced them as barriers or something imprisoning. Instead I have felt a deep union with people outside the enclosure, especially those who are suffering. (Fitzpatrick, 2006: 152).

Ascetical practices such as silence and solitude act as such boundaries and "as encounters and involvements are curtailed, one can go deeper into communion with others, and with God" (Fitzpatrick, 2006: 152). Freedom becomes the gift of this inclusive heart:

> Ideally, this solitude does not cause isolation from anyone or anything. Instead it gradually renders a person free, unencumbered, open to the Spirit and to the others in the community, finally embracing all people, all creation, in God (Fitzpatrick, 2006: 148).

As a consequence of its contemplative welcoming of silence and solitude monasticism becomes naturally allied to an apophatic theological framework. Silence more than language is attuned to the receptivity of the divine and within the silent space the attentive beholding of images and symbols becomes important (Carruthers, 2003) and acts as added transformational support.

> Images become an important means towards this transformation out of respect for the ineffable nature of God. As symbolic images of the reality to be adored become imprinted on an interior sacred space, they become contemplatively "painted" on the heart and mind, so that they . . . become a meditative icon of ascent (Torevell, 2007: 40).[1]

The natural impulse of the heart towards God encourages an expansive and profound space of receptivity. Howe calls this transforming space the 'deep *heart*':

> Perhaps because there is a vast interior space within the human person where the reality signified by the symbol or image can reverberate: this space is what we have been calling the deep *heart.* (2005: 73)

Any schooling which goes on in the monastery is, as a result, primarily directed to the heart, such that its *telos* is the creation of a pure heart, not the acquisition of intellectual ideas alone. Such silent attention to the transformation of the heart results in the experience of 'another order' which entails a changed way of being:

> This elemental spiritual life, which is ours, is a simple reality: a state of being, engaged in a continual yet imperceptible process of transformation – a spiritual transformation at the level of being. (Howe, 2005: 3)

It entails the discovery of the existence of *another order*. For Howe

> the external landscape of any particular monastic order with its distinctive charism must be transmuted into a personal venture seeking the frontiers of *another order!* (2005: 77)

Spiritual living within monastic cultures governed by a particular Order (in her case, Cistercian) encourages a journey within a journey – a unique journey within a common journey – what she calls the *soulscape* (Howe, 2005: 69). By moving within the Church's or Cistercian charism, "we make it our own, and a more subjective synthesis occurs" (Howe, 2005: 70). She goes on:

> An affinity exists between the soulscape and the landscape, this secret connection is undoubtedly present in seminal form at the outset of a monastic vocation but it requires cultivation throughout a lifetime. The soulscape is the secret connection between the depth of the person and the depth of the *milieu*. (2005: 71)

The interrelationship between the landscape and the soulscape is a creative one: "All this is merely a manner of transposing the principle of inculturation to a more personal level" and is a "mysterious union of landscape and soulscape, which far from attenuating the Cistercian experience, enhances and intensifies it" (2005: 71).[2]

It should now be becoming clear why the purification of the heart is so central to monastic culture. If this is the space where God communicates His presence and where God is heard, then obstacles of impurity prevent revelation from being heard and inclusiveness lived. All monastic communities are an extension of the experience of the Desert Fathers and Mothers who sought a place where purer forms of living could be experienced, outside cities and villages. These were places of purification involving intense fighting of demons which beset all Christians, but which were accentuated in the desert *and* simultaneously defeated. As Brakke highlights, "Only in the desert could the monk practice quietness, 'see the adversary' and 'overcome' him with divine assistance" (2006: 15). And once the battle started to be waged and signs of victory became apparent, revelatory moments occurred. Living in the space of the desert produced a thousandfold, as the veil of struggle between good and evil was removed and God's revelation experienced, moments of "illumination, insight, or wisdom" (Howe, 2005: 10). By entering into the Egyptian desert, not only were monks attentive to the Word which emerged out of God's eternal silence and which gave power to all those who listened, but they too learnt to speak out of silence for the good of the world (Nouwen, 1981: 57). In the desert environment of silence and solitude "monks and nuns pursue the ultimate goal for them and for all Christians: to attain purity of heart and thus to see God" (Fitzpatrick: 148). Silence prevented monastics from becoming entangled in world. The Desert Fathers and Mothers and all who followed in their footsteps knew that every conversation tended to make them interested in this world and to become "tangled in and polluted by the world" (Nouwen, 1981: 51). The way of being "in" the world was not through speaking, but by allowing the purified heart to be the dwelling place of the entire world through a life of prayer and contemplation.

The Russian Orthodox writer Paul Florensky sees the kind of contemplative asceticism I have spoken about as inextricably interwoven with beauty: "Asceticism produces not a good person but a beautiful personality" he writes (quoted in Ware, 1998: 3). Hans Urs von Balthasar reflects something of this position in his account of the Christological formation of the person through a contemplative seeing of beauty in the world. But he fears for the loss or marginalisation of beauty since once it loses its hold, *being* itself becomes under threat. The light of *being* becomes in danger of being snuffed out and its mystery consequently no longer able to express itself. In a remarkable passage from volume one of *The Glory of the Lord*, this twentieth-century Swiss theologian proclaims the inestimable importance of beauty. Although in later volumes he sets forth a strong Christological framework for his *theological* aesthetics, his earlier remarks in volume one refer to the banishment of beauty from society in more general terms. His advocacy of this particular transcendental interweaved inseparably with its siblings goodness and truth, offers the possibility of holding on to a contemplative vision and understanding of the world which the stirrings of secular modernity started to erode. That vision is none other than that spoken of by St. Thomas Aquinas when he recalls the "sure light" of *being* in his discussion of creation (1989: 19). Without the recognition of beauty, many are tempted to see life as little more than a "lump of existence" (1989: 19). Dangerous questions then start to be asked, such as why we should pursue goodness rather than its opposite, evil.

The last thing the intellect dare approach is beauty (1989: 18). Aware of beauty's greatness, the intellect recoils in fear, knowing its own capacities are limited in comparison. Balthasar is acutely aware that the traditional arguments for the existence of God, built around cognitive appeal and syllogisms, are unable to convince owing to their incapacity to capture the imagination of those who come into their ambit. Rotary presses and computers simply "spew out an exact number of answers" without any recourse to aesthetic considerations (1989: 19). By contrast, it was the ancients who knew and appreciated the importance of beauty. The Victorian Jesuit poet Gerard Manley Hopkins expresses this quality in the memorable first lines of his poem 'God's Grandeur':

> The world is charged with the grandeur of God,
> It will shine out like shaking from shook foil.

In some mysterious manner, this "shining out" of God's beauty in the world has the result of swallowing up others in its attraction and taking hold of them without their knowing why. There is no rationally motivated movement here, but rather a humble acquiescence of the self to be transported upwards beyond the intellect. We become enraptured and entranced by the beautiful. Beauty is irresistible and inestimable; we find ourselves drawn into its splendour. And we go on being attracted since its power is never exhausted. Like art itself, there are no limits to its attraction for us. We desire to live in its presence and to be transformed by it. But there is more to this movement towards beauty. Once the movement occurs, we are nudged towards the *contemplation* of the world and start to behold its significance, even to the point of adoration. Beauty has thus created a sacred space in which the heart can rejoice as we learn to see the world as gift.

Knowledge through Beholding and Looking

Dame Andrea was keen to stress the historical connections between the early formation of the university, and the medieval monastery and cathedral schools:

> Monasteries were spaces where monks educated boys. The most striking visible instance of this influence is in the retention of the academic gown based on the monastic cowl.

The medieval university developed from the monastic and cathedral schools of the early Middle Ages (Louth, 2004: 70) and continued a strong tradition of combining the active with the contemplative. Monastic culture clearly influenced the development of Western universities and their philosophy of education. But, significantly, the Latin word for school was *schola* which means leisure, so the University was to be a space of "leisure". Leisure did not have the same meaning in the Middle Ages as it does today, but described the learning process when students reflected and pondered on the nature of the universe, the self and the divine. The inclusion of the liberal arts assisted this "occupation" where free arts as opposed to servile arts (simple making and knowing how to do things) were encouraged. Universities made possible through such "leisure pursuits" this exercise of freedom through the arts and prepared the student "to rise to the life of contemplation" (Louth, 2004: 73). In this, students sought to gain access to the divine by entering into those educational practices which allowed human nature to transcend itself. The self's transformation was the goal of such endeavours and contemplation the gift and means. It entailed a passive receptivity and humility to be open to that which could not be precisely articulated and which allowed students to feel a presence of something beyond the toil and labour of the day. The balance between the active and contemplative life was maintained.

Louth's encouragement for the modern university to regain something of this balance is articulated in his contrast between two modes of knowledge and learning: He writes:

> Contemplation is, then, knowledge, knowledge of reality itself, as opposed to knowing how: the kind of know-how involved in getting things done. To this contrast between the active life and contemplation there corresponds a distinction in our understanding of what it is to be human between reason conceived as puzzling things out, solving problems, calculating and making decisions . . . and reason conceived as receptive of truth, beholding, looking. (Louth, 2004:71)

St. Augustine of Hippo expressed this contrast by using *scientia* for the kind of knowledge attained by ratio and *sapientia*, wisdom, for the kind of knowledge received by *intellectus*. Aristotle, too, shares this view in Book 10 of his *Nicomachean Ethics* when he argues that the realm of the *intellectus* fulfils what it is to be human since it is the exercise which is highest in our human nature and entails our involvement with the divine. "Human nature finds its fulfilment in transcending itself," adds Louth (2004: 72).

One example of this kind of receptive openness is reflected in the monastic practice of *lectio divina* (divine reading) which encourages a slow, meditative rumination on a short text, sometimes scriptural, sometimes early Christian, sometimes accounts of the lives of holy women and men. It entails four things: reading (*lectio*), meditation (*meditatio*), prayer with words (*oratio*), and contemplation (*contemplatio*). The classical expression of these given by the twelfth-century prior of the Grand Chartreuse, Guigo II, suggests that the first three are different from the fourth since they are concerned with our doing and our initiative. The fourth, *contemplatio*, is something God does to us, taking us out of our realm of doing things and allowing us to be in the presence of God. It is a gift which comes to us when we are prepared to receive it. The emphasis given to this kind of reading is not on the consumption of information but on allowing the heart to be changed. This contemplative pursuit is not about reading for the acquisition of knowledge but in order that the moral and spiritual self might be formed. The sacred space of the listening heart becomes attuned to the words and images reflected upon which involves an interior purifying of the heart. Spiritual texts have always fulfilled this aim of allowing the words and images to transform the inner depths of a person. Reading becomes transformative formation.

Of course, it was not Christianity which sought this kind of balance between the contemplative and the active first. Greek and Roman culture understood well the importance of these two components. Hadot has shown how the ancients' education entailed a training which encouraged students to be both contemplatives and women and men of action and doing (Hadot, 2002). Peiper's work, too, on the ancient philosophers' pursuit of wisdom and their concern for "higher knowledge" endorses the later monastic and cathedral schools' position and reminds us that classical understandings of philosophy as *a way of life*, rather than a series of abstract and discursive reasonings, entailed a revelatory knowing not possible by virtue of our humanity, but by our capacity to transcend ourselves through receptive openness (Peiper, 1998). It was crucial that a balance be kept between activity and passivity. What Peiper's work calls attention to is that frenetic activity prevented the person from *receiving revelatory truths.* The opposite of calm receptivity is "'absolute activity' . . . the hard quality of *not-being-able-to-receive*" (Peiper, 1998: 14). Indeed, it was the passive receptivity of the person which was the central means of achieving a sense of well-being and happiness. For the Greeks, "not-leisure" was the word for work on a daily basis and the Greek language (ά-σχολία) like the Latin (*neg-otium*) had only this negative word. Consequently, leisure in its fullest and most creative sense, was the most important "occupation" in which human beings could engage, a time for humanity to investigate and reflect on the meaning and goal of life. This pursuit was associated with learning to encounter something Other, outside the self brought about largely through a passive beholding of the "real" which lies beyond the world of ordinary sense experience. It was associated with a sense of happiness or well-being. Education was eudaemonic.

This receptive openness to being is reflected again in Pope John Paul II's *Fides et Ratio* (1998), an encyclical critical of modernity's attempts to destroy the balance between the active and contemplative. When the balance between *scientia* (know-how) and *sapientia* (wisdom) became distorted and the contemplation of *being* became marginalised, things started to go wrong. Knowledge seen as an instrumentalist, skills-based gaining of information was a one-sided affair. The consequences were, and are, alarming; knowledge rather than freeing and lifting up began to oppress and flatten the mind and became transmuted into an oppressive 'occupation'. The consequences are significant since the mind 'weighed down by factual knowledge has instead turned back on itself, so that almost every day it becomes less able to lift its eyes to higher things and so courageously pursue the truth of existence' (*Fides et Ratio*, 95). Modern philosophy, instead of 'exalting the capacity given to man for recognizing the truth' has 'preferred to accentuate his limits and conditions' (*Fides et Ratio,* 5). This encyclical is echoed in Pope Benedict XVI's September 2008 address at the Collège des Bernadines Paris, in which he claimed that monastic culture was about the search for what was ultimately valid and lasting. Monks wished to go from the inessential to the essential; it was a contemplative search for the ultimate and the true.

Regaining the Balance

What I want to suggest now is that thosse working in the modern university, although clearly not willing or able to reflect the religious aspirations of the monastic culture, might learn from its historical roots, in particular, its keeping of the balance between *scientia* and *sapientia.* Although not explicitly theological in their analysis, many questions and concerns about what a university is for in the twenty-first century are starting to emerge. This chapter has offered one possible way forward in relation to the balance which needs to be recaptured between the active and the contemplative. Panikkar's work on the monk within all of us is a good way of introducing just two examples of how this might be done:

> The monk is the expression of an archetype which is a constitutive dimension of human life . . . Not everyone can or should enter a monastery but everyone has a monastic dimension that ought to be cultivated. (1982:13)

The monk becomes a monk not to do or to acquire anything but through a wish 'to *be* (everything, yourself, the Supreme being, nothing . . .)' (1982: 12). *Being* is as important as achieving.

But how might this notion of *being* rather than achieving occur when suspicions are raised towards the taking of religious approaches to what goes on in the modern university? I shall use just two examples. The first is from Zajonc's understanding of contemplative pedagogy and the second is from Docherty's notions of democracy and aesthetics to show how this might take place. Zajonc argues for a re-imagining of knowing in relation to loving and shows how contemplative practice can become contemplative inquiry (2006: 2). In contrast to the monastic lifestyle which encourages a creative *monos* (being alone with God), Zajonc shows how much modern education in the academy stimulates an unhealthy solitude:

> Solitude is the mirror side or inevitable correlative of an increasingly strong development of self and personal identity. . . . If left to go on indefinitely, we logically end up with a collection of selfish monads. (2006 : 2)

What is needed is an intentional stance to counter this spiritual and psychological malaise. It won't happen automatically. Contemplative pedagogy is one way of realising this through more empathetic and affective human relationships with the objects we come to know.

He explains how this might come about by suggesting certain qualities the educator might foster. For example, "Gentle intimacy leads to participation by the contemplative inquirer in the unfolding phenomenon before one" (2006: 2). It is necessary to move and feel with the natural phenomenon, text, painting, or person: "Respectfully and delicately, in meditation we join with the other, while maintaining full awareness and clarity of mind" (2006: 2). Contemplative inquiring is centred on the other, not ourselves as we move towards authentic participation in the object before us. This leads to what in the German language education is about: *Bildung* – formation. In turn this stimulates insight, those moments when we come to know something beneath the surface of things and glimpse what Buddhists refer to as the way things really are – a direct apprehension of the nature of being. He quotes Emerson's essay on 'The Poet' to extend his explanation: "The path of things is silent. Will they suffer a speaker to go with them?" (2006: 3). The condition of true naming, for a poet, is "his resigning himself to the divine aura which breathes through forms and accompanying that" (2007: 3).

As one specific example of contemplative inquiry he refers to a course he co-taught with an art historian at Amherst College in the USA entitled "Eros and Insight". To begin the course he handed out on the first day two key passages – one from Henry David Thoreau's *Walden:* "I went to the woods today because I wished to live deliberately, to front only the essential facts of life, and see if I could not learn what it had to teach" (quoted in Zajonc, 2006: 4). By asking students to reflect on this passage, Zajonc wants to assist students in seeking a place apart, their own "wood", in which they can do the same – live deliberately and to help students be awake to this experience. The second passage is from Weil's *Gravity and Grace*: "Grace fills empty spaces but it can only enter where there is a void to receive it" (quoted in Zajonc, 2006: 7). Gravity is everywhere and orders everything except grace but it needs certain conditions in which to appear. This quotation is used to point to the importance of silence, emptiness and open spaces which allow moments of grace to appear. By the end of the course the students will have learnt

> to embody virtue not only legislate for it, to engender creativity and the capacities for insight, not only memorise formulae and works of art . . . They will have learned to love. (2006: 6)

My second example is from Docherty's work. He raises his concerns about modern higher education and, although, like Zajonc's, not couched in explicit theological terms, many of his ideas stem from his dissatisfaction with the modes of learning and teaching encouraged in the Academy.

In contrast to this kind of prescriptivism, he suggests that the teaching of aesthetics might correct this imbalance. Indeed, it is the very basis of democracy and freedom. For example, he argues that aesthetics actually determines social formation and enables people to be true citizens and participants of a polity. His claim is that students should be encouraged to become subjects of perception and be given opportunities for "becoming". Here we notice a clear emphasis on *being* rather than achieving. A democracy that is keen to establish and further the freedom of subjects who know themselves always to be conditioned by the alterity to which art opens them is the most fundamental form of democracy. Culture should be defined as

> an event of perception – the root sense of "aesthetic" (*aisthanomai*) – that calls a human subject to differ from itself, and to define or to constitute its very identity precisely through the specific mode of that differing. (2006: xiii)

For Docherty, the usual interpretation of the word "democracy" is as a form of consumer choices; this needs to be replaced with a notion that celebrates students' identity as "citizens". Drawing from Baudrillard's insights, he suggests that human beings have sunk into defining themselves in relation to objects consumed and then, due to a logic of seduction, become victims of the objects they seek. What is worse is the growing mercantilisation of the university accompanied by "the mercantilisation of the aesthetic disciplines of the arts and humanities, where our practices are construed and legitimated in almost entirely instrumentalist terms" (2006: xv).

As in monastic culture, he draws from classical Greek understandings of what constitutes good education. For the ancient world, says Docherty, knowledge was always eudaemonic and formed its citizens in well being and happiness. Drawing from David Simpson's notion of "situated" knowledge, he claims that a relativist knowledge has seeped into the university that eschews any possibility of "absolute knowing" or of a truth that transcends the relative. A more "contemplative" approach to the formation of the self drives his vision. Aesthetics ought to focus on "eventful" thinking which entails "the forming and informing of a self in the spirit of growth, development, and imagining the possibility that the world and its objects might be otherwise than they are" (2006: 74). He argues for a way of teaching literature which defies the "crude philistinism of a British educational system that has become increasingly Gradgrindian in its concentration on education as pure instrumentality" (2006: 74).

Docherty's notion of aesthetic education complements my previous consideration of contemplative approaches to knowledge. Although not referring explicitly to the religious language of the heart, his hopes for the teaching of aesthetics is grounded in the belief in the potential transformation of the person through an encounter with alterity and otherness. There is a "becoming" by "our condition of being-with-otherness" (Docherty, 2006: xiii). One of the foundations on which contemplation is built is that subjects become the recipients of a knowledge outside themselves by their disposition of attentive openness. The contemplative receiving of knowledge leads to freedom and happiness through an expansion of the self. Docherty's understanding of what the arts might achieve has similarities with the approach taken by *lectio divina.* A dynamic of transformation takes place as disturbing but creative encounters with the alterity of aesthetics begins. Art, he suggests, should be able to change us through its unsettling nature. Instead of saying that "Plato banishes the poets" we should say "Plato dramatically banishes the dramatic" since it is the latter which is "unsettling to the self who speaks it, even as it constitutes knowing as such" (xviii).

For Docherty, any instrumentalist model of education is nothing less than a giving up of truth, only to be replaced by an ideology; as such, it is so often understood as what is taken for granted by a community, or what people will in a popularist market. He writes:

> For those condemned to live and work in such a polity, knowledge indeed

> becomes a celebration of the ordinary as such, a celebration of the pre-existing identities of its students . . . It follows . . . no one is ever called to change, to extend or to expand the self into something different. (2006: xvi)

The balance has tipped in favour of consumption rather than contemplation.

Conclusion

What I have attempted in this chapter is to outline the importance of the formation of the heart in monastic culture from its earliest days to the present. This emphasis enabled the monastic and cathedral schools to keep a balance between the contemplative and active dimensions of learning which influenced approaches to learning in the universities. I also plotted how this balance emerged out of Greek culture. Then, using the insight from the *Rule of St. Benedict* articulated by Dame Andrea, I suggested that things start to go wrong when this balance is not kept. Although there is no easy reversal of this at a time when explicitly religious approaches to learning are viewed with suspicion, I referred to Zajonc's contemplative pedagogy and Docherty's notion of aesthetics and democracy to argue that a retrieval of this balance is possible in the modern University. But it requires a willingness and confidence to be engaged in learning activities with students which seek to foster a transformational, rather than simply a consumptive, self. There is, I think, much wisdom in the monastic notion of the sacred space of the heart.

Notes

1 See my book, 2007, *Liturgy and the Beauty of the Unknown: Another Place*, Aldershot: Ashgate, especially pp. 39–43 on the Victorines.

2 Mark Barrett, 2001, takes up a similar theme in relation to an internal landscape of lifelong renewal with reference to the Divine Office in *Crossings: Reclaiming the Landscape of Our Lives*, London: Darton, Longman & Todd.

References

Balthasar, Hand Urs von. 1989. *The Glory of the Lord. Volume 1, Seeing the Form*. Edinburgh. T&T Clark.

Barrett, M. 2001. *Crossings: Reclaiming the Landscape of Our Lives*. London. Darton, Longman & Todd.

Benedict XVI. 2008. 'Christian worship is an Invitation to sing with the angels', *Address of His Holiness Benedict XVI* <http://www.zenit.org/article-23606?/=english> – accessed 18 November 2008.

Brakke, D. 2006. *Demons and the Making of the Monk: Spiritual Combat in Early Christianity*. Cambridge, Massachusetts. Harvard University Press.

Carruthers, M. 2003. *The Craft of Thought: Meditation, Rhetoric, and the Making of Images, 400–1200*. Cambridge. Cambridge University Press.

Docherty, T. 2006. *Aesthetic Democracy*. Stanford. Stanford University Press.

Fitzpatrick, G 'Enclosure: The Heart of the Matter' in Hart, P. (ed.), *A Monastic Vision for the 21st Century: Where do We Go From Here?* Michigan. Cistercian Publications. 145– 164.

Fry, T. (ed.). 1982. *The Rule of St. Benedict in English*. Collegeville. The Liturgical Press.

Hadot, P. 2002. *What is Ancient Philosophy?* (trans. M. Chase). Cambridge, Mass. Harvard University Press.

Howe, J.-M. 2005. *Secret of the Heart: Spiritual Being*. Michigan. Cistercian Publications

John-Paul II. 1998. *Fides et Ratio* (Faith and Reason), London. Catholic Truth Society.

Louth, A. 2004. 'Theology, Contemplation and the University', *Studies in Christian Ethics*, 17(1): 69–79.

Muers, R. 2004. *Keeping God's Silence: Towards a Theological Ethics of Communication,* Oxford. Blackwell.

Nouwen, H. 1991. *The Way of the Heart: Desert Spirituality and Contemporary Ministry*. New York. HarperSanFrancisco.

Panikkar, R. 1982. *The Monk as Universal Archetype*. Seabury Press

Peiper, J. 1998. *Leisure as the Basis of Culture: St. Augustine's Press.*

Scruton, R. 2007. *Culture Counts: Faith and Feeling in a World Besieged*. New York. Encounter Books.

Shannon, W., Bochen, C., O'Connell, P. 2002. *The Thomas Merton Encyclopedia*. New York. Orbis Books.

Torevell, D. 2006. 'Circles of Meaning: The Christian Dynamic of Contemplation, Meaning and Purpose', *Journal of Christian Education,* 49 (3): 33–42.

Torevell, D. 2007. *Liturgy and the Beauty of the Unknown. Another Place*. Aldershot. Ashgate.

Ware, K 1998. 'The Way of the Ascetics: Negative or Affirmative?' in V. Wimbush and R. Valantasis (eds), *Asceticism*. Oxford. Oxford University Press.

Watten, A. 1973. *The Meaning of Silence in the Rule of St. Benedict*. Michigan.

Cistercian Publications. No.22.
Zajonc, A. 2006. 'Love and Knowledge: Recovering the Heart of Learning Through Contemplation', *Teachers College Record,* 108 (9): 1742–1759.

Chapter Three

Liminality, Sacred Space and the Diwan

David Weir

The "sacred" is a complex concept and not easy to define. Webster offers the following alternatives:

> 1 a: dedicated or set apart for the service or worship of a deity <a tree *sacred* to the gods> b: devoted exclusively to one service or use (as of a person or purpose) <a fund *sacred* to charity>
> 2 a: worthy of religious veneration: holy b: entitled to reverence and respect
> 3 of or relating to religion: not secular or profane <*sacred* music>
> 4 *archaic*: accursed
> 5 important <a *sacred* responsibility>

Our definition of what is "sacred" leans more centrally on the definitions familiar to social anthropologists from Frazer onwards that are based on the concept of the sacred as a *human universal*. In its turn this concept is related to that of myth, defined as that which, in Scruton's terms "does not describe what happened in some obscure period before human reckoning, but what happens always and repeatedly. It does not explain the causal origins of our world, but rehearses its permanent spiritual significance" (Scruton, 2007).

Scruton's analysis also relates to the insights of Eliade (1957) and Girard (1972). For Eliade "that which is essentially human is the relation of man to the sacred" (Eliade, 1982: 148), that "Consciousness of a real and meaningful world is intimately linked with the discovery of the sacred" (1982: 153) and more generally that it is the human quest for meaning that creates the "sanctification of the mundane" (1969). In much of the writings within these traditions, to identify a space or spaces as "sacred" appears to imply a dualism in which the "sacred" is opposed to the "secular" or "profane". But this distinction is by no means always as obvious in other cultural settings as in the post-Cartesian Western consciousness. In particular, in Islamic cultures the attempt at the unique identification of specific spaces with sacred practices may bring its own analytical problems.

Spatial deconstruction is a significant theme in organisation analysis more generally (Kornberger and Clegg, 2004; Weir, 2005). Filkin and Weir attempted a classification of the various ways in which sociologists and social anthropologists have used these notions in contemporary field research and doubtless this work needs to updated to take account of more recent empirical studies (Filkin and Weir, 1974). More recently, Maruyama has been especially concerned to characterise the generic spatial constraints on social processes (Maruyama, 1969; Maruyama, 2005) and formalises an account based on some aspects of complexity theory (Maruyama and Reniker, 1991). This formulation contrasts types of management logic in ways that may be relevant to our concerns by distinguishing two core types:

> Type H: Homogenising, Hierarchical, Classificatory, Competitive, Zero-sum, Sequential
> Type S: Heterogenising, Interactive, Pattern-oriented, Cooperative, Positive-sum, Parallel. (Maruyama, 1994).

These dimensions may be relevant to other behavioural settings than those of management; in particular to characterisations of sacredness and secularity.

In the Christian tradition special places are associated with sacred practices. The cruciform shape of the Christian church embodies a dense network of sacred and symbolic understandings. The shape of the mosque may not be so easily deconstructed. The nature of prayer and its relation to special "sacred" spaces and times are equally different. But rectangular space, devoid of ornament and available for human activity, occupies a special place in Islamic cultures in both "sacred" and "secular" contexts.

The styles of decision-making in the Arab Middle East are different in structure and process from those traditionally favoured in Western management and organisation. Their history and evolution are likewise different and yet it would be highly dangerous to portray them as aspects of deviant types or as evidence of earlier stages of a common process of development.

Status, position and seniority are more important than ability and performance in business and management in the Arab world. And decision making is located in the upper reaches of the organisational hierarchy, with authoritarian management styles predominating. Subordinates tend to appear deferential and obedient, especially in public. Autocratic decision-making styles are favoured. Nonetheless autocratic decision-making is tempered with an emphasis on consultation, typically practised on a one-to-one but sometimes a group basis. Decisions emerge rather than issue explicitly from formal decision making processes. Prior affiliation and existing obligation are more influential than explicit performance objectives (see, for instance, Al-Faleh, 1987). But these summary characterisations need to position decision-making in these cultures in their characteristic spatial setting. Chief among these are the social spaces known as "Diwan".

The organisation of space known as "Diwan" can be construed as a place of decision as well as of social intercourse. Here, decisions are the outcome of processes of information exchange, practised listening, questioning, and the interpretation and confirmation of informal as well as formal meanings. By informal in this context we imply the ambiguity and ambivalence that are central to the operation of the Diwan so that it may in practice be difficult, if not impossible, to ask for a formal record of events either before or after, even though participants in a Diwan may sense informally what the outcome may have been.

Thus decisions are enacted by senior people but, after enactment, may be owned by all, ensuring commitment based on respect for both position and process. Seniority and effectiveness are significant but, to be powerful, the concurrent consent of those involved has to be sought, and symbolised in the process of the Diwan. In this paper the "swirl" of the Diwan is described and interpreted.

Liminality as an Interpretative Concept

The intellectual history of the concept of liminality is well-understood and will be only briefly sketched out here. The term comes from the Latin word *lîmen*, meaning "a threshold". Van Gennep introduced the concept in his work *Rites de passage* (1908) to explain the process of social role transformations and individual lifestyle changes. A limen is seen as a necessary feature of any type of role-transition and expresses a dichotomy between "stable" and "transitory" structures in that, to pass from one phase to another, some threshold has to be overcome.

Each process transition is characterised by three phases: isolation or separation; marginality or liminality; incorporation or reaggregation.

Separation implies the isolation of a chosen individual, the "initiant", from an existing fixed social or cultural structure. Liminality expresses the initiant's ambivalent state and its passage to the intermediate ambivalent social zone, the so-called "limbo". The final phase of incorporation corresponds to the initiant's return to the society with a new social status or "reaggregation". According to van Gennep, it is socially essential for all three stages of the ritual to be completed, otherwise participants can be left stranded in the potentially transformative, but behaviourally "dangerous", liminal space.

Liminality became a central term in the theoretical concerns of Turner who used the concept in his studies of role-transformation in adolescent boys in the Ndembu tribes (Turner, 1957). For Turner, the liminal phase is construed as an "interstructural situation" existing among different positional structures as an individual becomes free from pre-existing social expectations before adopting those appropriate to a new role (Turner, 1964).

For some scholars, the concept of social actors existing in a liminal state has constituted a sort of essentially structural problem and the liminal role itself has created specific difficulties for its occupants because it may give rise to experiences of social marginality, ambiguity, openness, feelings of indeterminacy, disorientation and lack of acceptance. But these presumptions are not necessarily essential to Turner's formulation, though these considerations evidently pose issues for heavily structural concepts of social identity (Turner, 1962). At the time that Turner introduced the term to explain role-transitions among the Ndembu, he was using an essentially structural-functional interpretive schema and it is only in later work that this framework is expanded into the symbolic arena and generalised to incorporate the universalising notion of *communitas* (Turner, 1972). In our subsequent discussion we lean towards Turner's earlier formulation (see Deflem, 2002 for a thorough account of the evolution in Turner's thinking on these points).

Similar issues arise in the discussion of the spatial determination of the sacred. Spaces may be sacred in essence or as locational identifiers of activities that are themselves sacred. It is important also to consider these as folk categories in the sense that they "are the terms used by ordinary people to give meaning to their environment and thus to distinguish between localities" (Filkin and Weir, 1972: 143). This distinction lies at the heart of some characteristic differences between Christian and Islamic versions of "sacred space". In the former, a church or any consecrated space is sacred in essence, as indeed a mosque is as a place of prayer, but in the Muslim world any place may become sacred by becoming the locus of prayer that can take place anywhere. Of course it is in no way logically or behaviourally impossible for Christians to constitute a place as sacred by virtue of the nature of the activities hosted there (see for example Hooker, 1821: 265). Nonetheless, in Western culture, these binary distinctions are quite generally made or implied, but this is not necessarily so in other cultures. Where ambiguity is not construed as a threat to identity, the dangers perceived in liminality are much diminished. Thus the questions implied in the distinctions between "empty and full space(s), open and closed, public and private, intimate and expansive, negative and positive, narrative space and production space" (Deflem, *op. cit.*) are limited in scope and effect. Space as such can be any of these things and partake in all or some of these interpretations, depending on what is happening there.

It is true, however, that Turner did seek to identify certain performances with spaces that are defined as liminal, and with the presumed social identities that may be found there, when he wrote that "prophets and artists tend to be liminal and marginal people, 'edgemen,' who strive with a passionate sincerity to rid themselves of the clichés associated with status incumbency and role-playing and to enter into vital relations with other[s] in fact or imagination" (Turner, 1995: 127). It is clear that this interpretation rests for its effect on the structural-functional schema, and some assumptions about roles as relatively fixed and behaviours as more or less appropriate to certain contexts. Thus ambiguity and lack of definition themselves constitute, at the least, issues to be resolved if not intrinsically problematic; but these may be schematic and interpretative rather than behavioural problems.

Bauman offers a general account of the centrality of liminality in the post-modern project when he states that "the post-modern state of mind is the radical . . . victory of modern (that is an inherently critical, restless, unsatisfied, insatiable) culture over the modern society it aimed to improve through throwing it wide open to its own potential" (Bauman, 1992: viii–xi).

Likewise, in the field of post-colonial studies, since the work of Said and others the term "liminality" has become a term of art. Sometimes this category is strongly related to the concepts of cultural hybridity and "linguistic multivocality" that are presented as having the potential to reinterpret political discourse. Werbner, though, criticises the over-general use of transcultural explanation in much of this discourse (Werbner, 2001).

Other contemporary uses of the concepts of liminality can be found in transgender research, urban structures and post-modernist society more generally (Zukin, 1991; Bauman, 1996). Thus Ratiani and Bradford relate the liminal concept to contemporary literary studies (Ratiani, 2007; Bradford, 2007). More applications of the concept are found in Kay et al (2007) who explore the relevance and significance of the limen or threshold from a variety of critical and theoretical perspectives on culture across a broad range of historical periods. Navon and Morag explore the experience of liminality in a study of patients with advanced cancer (Navon and Morag, 2004).

Tempest and Starkey extend the concept of liminality to the terrain of organisational learning using examining individual and organisational learning in the context of organisational re-composition, where learning increasingly occurs at the limits of organisations within networks and teams that cross organisational divides (Tempest and Starkey, 2004).

Cornis-Pope postulates the dynamic possibilities in liminality in cultural systems claiming that

> as with a natural system, which needs . . . heat regulation, cultural systems also need a regulating balance in order not to collapse or disappear. This regulating balance is manifested in the stratificational oppositions. The canonized repertoires of any system would very likely stagnate after a certain time if not for competition from non-canonized challengers, which often threaten to replace them" (Cornis-Pope, 1997: 27).

The dangers of some kind of categorical essentialism, even of ethnic or gender as well as structural role-essentialism in such formulations, is evident, as it is in Mircea Eliade's concept of a necessary division of human experience into the sacred and the profane (see for instance Otoiu, 2003). This is so even in cases where the disturbance evoked by the experience of liminality is positively regarded either for individuals or for larger social collectives.

Management Practices in the Arab Middle East

The profession of management involves different formal practices in the Middle East from those with which we are familiar in the West. We have previously identified these practices as together constituting a "fourth paradigm" of management values, styles and behaviours (Weir, 1998; Weir, 2000). Al Rasheed has argued that the designation as a "paradigm" overstates the differences and underemphasises the similarities with management practice in other cultures (but see also Al-Rasheed, 1994).

While there is a growing body of empirical research on management in the Arab Middle East, much of the contemporary literature suffers from an attempt to explain the organisational practices of this milieu in terms of Western models and modes of explanation that are inappropriate to the physical and spatial structures as well as the cultural framework. This critique applies equally to the spatial dimensions of analysis where Western models of structure may implicitly underpin explanations.

Muna claims that the typical form of decision making in Arab organizations is consultative. Loyalty is prized above all other organizational values, even efficiency. Loyalty can be guaranteed by surrounding the executive with subordinates whom he can trust (Muna 1980).

Arab managers have a more flexible interpretation of time than Western management, and often seem able to run several meetings, perhaps on quite unrelated topics, simultaneously. The basic rule of business with Arab managers is to establish the relationship first and only come to the heart of the intended business at a later meeting, once trust has been achieved. This process may, and often does, take considerable time. Verbal contracts are absolute and an individual's word is his bond. Failure to meet verbally agreed obligations may be visited with dire penalties and will certainly lead to a termination of a business relationship. Al-Faleh identifies the importance of status, position and seniority as more important than ability and performance. Decision-making is located in the upper reaches of the hierarchy and authoritarian management styles predominate. Subordinates are deferential and obedient, especially in public in the presence of their hierarchical superiors. These consultations occur however, on a one-to-one, rather than a team or group basis (Al-Faleh, 1987). The typical form of decision-making styles preferred by Arab managers is neither "autocratic" nor "democratic" as these extreme ideal types are found in the Western world. But neither are they "consultative" nor "participative", as defined in Western studies of leadership. In each of these distinguishing characteristics of style, we see in the Muslim world a greater tolerance of ambiguity and ambivalence.

The Spatial Swirl of the Diwan

Said is widely cited in respect of his contentions about the "subtle and persistent Eurocentric prejudice against Arabo-Islamic peoples and their culture" and his references to "the aggressiveness necessitated by the colonial expansion of the European powers" (Said, 1995). These prejudices also comprise those induced by certain discourses relating to space.

Thus the Diwan is an idea that is familiar in many depictions of the Orient, often for the wrong reasons. In the Western literature of the Orient, as pictorially represented in "Orientalist" tradition, the "divan" is portrayed as a type of low couch, a sofa without a back on which partly-clad females loll in languorous poses while richly dressed Sultans feast their eyes on the concupiscent scene. The dimly lit chamber is sweet with the perfumes of nargileh-smoke and an air of decadence pervades. But the "Diwan" is much more, and much more deeply rooted in its cultural traditions than would be imagined from all this "Orientalist" symbolism.

The connotation of the word "Diwan" has undergone much change and evolution in the history of the Muslim worlds. Umar, the second khalifah of Islam, first introduced the Diwan and made an elaborate system of granting pensions to the Muslims. The pension roll and the office for this account was called the Diwan. In the sultanate period of Delhi, the Diwan stood for a department of administration, much the same as the present ministry. For example, Diwan-i-Arz (military department in charge of recruitment and payment of salaries) etc. These uses survive to this day.

In the Mughal period in India, the term "Diwan" identified the head of the revenue department, the diwan-i-aam was the assembly or court for ordinary matters and people and the diwani-khaas formed the court or assembly for special matters and people. So, historically, a Diwan could be an individual or collective term, as well as describing a process and the results of – or the structure of – a system of administration.

This use of Diwan to denote a governmental department is common throughout the region (Library of Congress, 1993). Thus the administrative offices of the ruler or Emir in Kuwait is the Amiri Diwan and can consist both of the core administrative support for high-level strategic decision-making and also as the repository of various projects and activities in which

Fig. 3-1. A Diwan in a grand home in Morocco

the ruler and his family take a special interest.

A Diwan can thus signify a couch, a room, the holder of an office of state, a place, an organisation, and a style of decision-making. It can also be a historical account or a mode of literary production. Its multiplicities and connotations are understood by practically everybody in the Arab and Islamic worlds and by virtually no-one outside of this milieu. To understand Diwan is to penetrate to the heart of decision-making as a fundamentally different social process from that in Western organisations. This helps us appreciate why strategy and implementation are different, and why the rhythms and pace of management are distinct and irreducible to the abstractions of Western management theory.

Thus Diwan can, in principle, occur in any type of spatial context but is most characteristically associated with a room with low seats around the walls found in one guise or other in every Arab home and in public and private spaces alike. Within this space, the movements of people tend to describe characteristic patterns.

The Diwan in Space and Time

Diwan is common throughout the Middle East region. In Iran it may be described as a "Majlis", in the Yemen, where Qat may be chewed, as a "Chew". It is found in Judaic tradition throughout the Mediterranean world. According to the Jewish tradition of the Middle Ages in Spain, it was common for Jews to meet outside the synagogue or house of study. Following holy prayer or study, they would create culture in the space between sacred and secular time. They would integrate spiritual search, their yearning for the "Shechina" (the divine presence) and for the return to Zion. These encounters in Spain, Egypt, Morocco and Yemen were called "Diwan". The musical repertoire of Yemenite Jews, the sum of their devotional poems, sung and intoned outside the synagogue, is called Diwan. This title is also used for a contemporary journal published in the Balkans (Diwan 2002).

Essentially any place of meeting can be a Diwan. It may be the whole building or a room within a building. The Diwan-I-Khass, for example, is one of the grandest buildings in the Indian sub-continent. And it may be an open space or a courtyard. The space in which the event is celebrated is also a Diwan, as is the event itself. If records, verbal or pictorial, are made of the occurrence, this is also a Diwan.

The same elements may be present in both family and business situations as well as in sacred and secular contexts. The dynamics are similar.

The space is used in a way that is quite different from a Western meeting-room or board-room. But in this space movements are far from random and rules of order apply. There is a precision to the movements and a structure to the timings as participants move through the space. The movement of people is generally counter-clockwise and central players are located near the apex of the Swirl.

Hierarchy is a feature of the Diwan. It can be clearly noted in the layout of the Diwan and in construing the purposes of those who move through the space. Arguably the hierarchy is modified by fluid movement, what Bauman calls "liquidity" (Bauman, 2005). This is a highly-ordered interactional event. In the Diwan, we observe a characteristic pattern of social networking that characteristically reinforces existing strong bonds of religion, family and kinship.

These patterns of social networking are not of course restricted to the Arab Middle East and they appear in differing forms in the Arab and Chinese business worlds (Hutchings and Weir, 2005 and 2006). But in a specific cultural milieu we also see the operation, in a precise and well-understood framework, of an activity that creates the spatial manifestation of a method of managing and generating social knowledge that can lead to business and political opportunity. The Diwan is a matrix for knowledge-management that embodies an openness to the possibility of new knowledge that can emerge as the Diwan progresses. Within the Diwan, ideas can be reviewed and positions checked without the formalities of official reporting or precise financial announcement.

Similar uses of space and time occur in family as well as in business and managerial settings. The Diwan is a knowledge-management device that permits both openness and closure. Agendas are not issued, nor minutes taken. But what has happened is transparent. By participating in the Diwan, those present become members of a more extensive Diwan that persists through space and time to create social obligation and permits the generalised basis for more specific encounters with more focussed purposes.

The ongoing spatial swirl of the Diwan defies some conventional types of organisational analysis because decisions can be summarised despite never having formally been taken. And participants in Diwan are self-consciously taking part in a ritual that has evolved through historical time. In the Diwan, decisions are the outcome of processes of information exchange, practised listening, questioning and the interpretation and confirmation of informal as well as formal meanings. Decisions of the Diwan may be enacted by the senior people, but they have eventually to be owned by all participants as bases for action. This ensures commitment based on respect for both position and process. Seniority and effectiveness are significant but, to be powerful, the concurrent consent of those involved has to be sought, and symbolised in the process of the Diwan.

What identifies the Diwan uniquely and makes it of particular interest for theorists of managerial and business behaviour is that the Diwan provides a context for a particular type of decision-making. It is non-linear, and non-hierarchical, discursive and recursive, self-limiting but co-extensive with the range of interactional possibilities available. The swirl of the Diwan permits an order to emerge that is not rigid and pre-imposed but creates potential, reinforcing existing social categories. The swirl is a temporary structure that can be persistent as long as the activity lasts.

Several anthropologists have been unhappy about the western tendency to create dichotomies. Indeed Geertz (1980) urges the western anthropologist not to try to fit every experience they have in a different part of the world into the dichotomies to which they appear so attached. This advice may be equally relevant to the use of the dichotomy between "sacred" and "secular".

While decision making is located in the upper reaches of the organisational and family hierarchy, with authoritarian management styles predominating and subordinates expected to be deferential and obedient, especially in public, the implications of power are quite different from what they might be in the West. These characterisations of authority omit to position decision-making in these cultures in their characteristic spatial settings. The structures of social, family and political life are replicated in managerial settings because a common matrix unites them all.

Seniority and effectiveness are significant but, to be powerful, the concurrent consent of those involved has to be sought and symbolised in the process of the Diwan. The spatial swirl draws participants in, assures the marginal participants that their voice may be heard and their interests and needs are attended to in a context that assures equality of access and equivalence of respect.

To define "the sacred" in inter-cultural terms is a big task. In Maruyama's terms these dimensions may be pre-endowed (Maruyama, 1994). For Scruton "the intellectual enterprise is that of showing the place of the sacred in human life, and the kind of knowledge and understanding that comes to us through the experience of sacred things" (Scruton, 2007). He goes on to relate this characterisation explicitly (as many have done) to the Graeco-Roman tradition and avers that "by calling these moments 'sacred,' we recognise both their complex social meaning and also the respite that they offer from alienation" (Scruton, 2007).

The study of ritual performance is central to the distinction between what is to count as sacred or secular. But, because the boundaries between the secular and the sacred in behavioural terms are drawn differently in Muslim societies, what counts as liminal between these organising categories has itself to be reconstrued.

The Diwan is a form of social structure in which ambiguity and ambivalence are of the essence. This gives it strength rather than weakness. Its existence through centuries of evolution has been emphatic, while other forms of spatial organisation have been challenged or withered on the bough. This fact may cast doubt on formulations like those of Beck and Bauman for whom ambivalence and ambiguity have been identified as central elements of modernity (Beck, 1992; Bauman, 1993). This is not an issue in "first" or "second" modernist or post-modernist framing of these questions but one about whether the discourse of modernity is appropriate in the context of the interpretation of these social practices.

I have attempted to demonstrate that the imposition of classical Western models of the decision-making spaces available to managers is limited and requires to be extended to comprehend Diwan processes. Post-Cartesian western minds appear to be unhappy with ambiguity. Moreover, as these spaces encompass behavioural phenomena that are common to both the sacred and secular realms, it is necessary to be careful in applying binary distinctions to the "sacred" and the "secular". Liminality is not here to be construed as a problem because, while roles may be fixed, openness and closure, status and access alike are preserved in the spatial swirl of the Diwan. Ambiguity is of the essence. Ambivalence rules OK – at least until it becomes clear what outcomes have occurred. Processes are at work that encourage emergent decisions which are not pre-formed by hierarchical or periodic structures.

References

Abuznaid, S. 1994. 'Islam and management', in *Proceedings of the Second Arab Management Conference,* University of Bradford Management Centre.

Ahmed, A. 1992. *Postmodernism and Islam.* London. Routledge.

Akbar S. Ahmed. 1993. *Living Islam.* London. Penguin Books.

Al Fahim, A.R. 1998. *The 200th Hadith.* Makkah, Saudi Arabia. Ministry of Information.

Al-Faleh, M. 1987. 'Cultural influences on Arab managerial development', *Journal of Management Development,* 6(3): 19–33.

Al-Hashemi, I. and Najjar, G. 1989. 'Strategic choices in management education: the Bahraini experience', in J. Davies (ed.), *The Challenge to Western Management Development.* London. Routledge.

Bauman, Z. 1992. *Mortality, Immortality and other Life Strategies*. Cambridge. Polity Press.

Bauman, Z. 1993. *Modernity and Ambiguity*. London. Polity Press.

Bauman, Z. 1996. 'From pilgrim to tourist: or a short history of identity', in S. Hall and P. Du Gay (eds), *Questions of Cultural Identity.* London. Sage.

Bauman, Z. 2005. *Liquid Life*. London. Polity Press.

Beck, U. 1992. *Risk Society: Towards a New Modernity.* London. Sage.

Bhabha, H. 1994. The Location of Culture. London. Routledge.

Bradford, C. 2007. Unsettling Narratives: Postcolonial Readings of Children's Literature. Waterloo, ON. Wilfrid Laurier University Press.

Cornis-Pope, Marcel. 1997. 'Rethinking Postmodern Liminality: Marginocentric Characters and Projects in Thomas Pynchon's Polysystemic Fiction', *Symploke* 5(1–2): 27–47.

Dake, K. 1992. 'Myths of nature: culture and the social construction of risk', *Journal of Social Issues*, 48:21–37.

Deflem, M. 2002. 'Ritual, Anti-Structure, and Religion: A Discussion of Victor Turner's Processual Symbolic Analysis', *Journal for the Scientific Study of Religion,* 30(1): 1–25.

Dench, G. 1986. *Minorities in the Open Society: Prisoners of Ambivalence*. Oxford. Blackwell.

Diwan. 2002. http://www.diwanmag.com.ba/arhiva/diwan9_10/sadrzaj/sadrzaj0E.htm.

Douglas, M. and Wildavsky, A. 1982. *Risk and Culture.* Berkeley, CA. University of California Press.

Eliade, M. 1957. *The Sacred and the Profane.* Trans. from the French by Willard Trask. New York. Harcourt Brace.

Eliade, M. 1969. *The Quest: History and Meaning in Religion*. Chicago. University of Chicago Press.

Eliade, M. 1982. *A History of Religious Ideas, vol. II, from Gautama Buddha to the Triumph of Christianity* (trans. W. Trask). Chicago. University of Chicago Press.

Filkin, C. and Weir, D.T.H. 1972. 'Locality', in Gittus, E. *Key Variables in Social Research*. Heinemann and British Sociological Association.

Geertz, C. 1980. *Negara: The Theatre State in Nineteenth Century Bali.* Princeton, NJ. Princeton University Press.

Girard, R. 1972. *La Violence et le Sacré*. Paris. Grasset. (Trans. *Violence and the Sacred.* Baltimore. Johns Hopkins University Press, 1977.)

Gole, Nilufer. 2002. 'Islam in Public: New Visibilities and New Imaginaries', *Public*

Culture 14(1): 173–190.

Hitti, P.K. 1949. *History of the Arabs.* 4th edn revised. Oxford. Oxford University Press.

Hooker, R. 1821. *The Works of Mr. Richard Hooker*. New York. Bumpus.

Hutchings, K. and Weir, David. 2005. 'Cultural Embeddedness and Contextual Constraints: Knowledge Sharing in Chinese and Arab Cultures', *Knowledge and Process Management* 12: 89–98.

Hutchings, K. and Weir, David. 2006. 'Guanxi and Wasta: A review of traditional ways of networking in China and the Arab World and their implications for international business', *Thunderbird International Business Review: Special Issue: Journeys Along the Silk Road.*

Karim, A. 1963. *Murshid Quli Khan and His Times*. Dhaka.

Kay, L. Kinsley, Phillips, Z. Terry and Roughley, A. (eds). 2007. *Mapping Liminalities: Thresholds in Cultural and Literary Texts.* Bern. Peter Lang.

Kornberger, Martin, and Clegg, Stewart R. 2004. 'Bringing space back in: Organizing the generative building', *Organization Studies* 25: 1095–1114.

Library of Congress. 1993. *A country study: Saudi Arabia.* <http://lcweb2.loc.gov/frd/cs/satoc.html> – accessed 26 January 2009.

Maalouf, Amin. 1988. *Leo the African*. London. Abacus.

Maalouf, Amin. 2000. *In the Name of Identity: Violence and the Need to Belong.* Translated by Barbara Bray. New York. Arcade Publishing.

Maalouf, Amin. 2002. *Balthasar's Odyssey*. London. Harvill.

Maruyama, Magoroh. 1969. 'Epistemology in Social Science Research: Exploration in inculture researchers', *International Review of Philosophy of Knowledge* 23: 229–280.

Maruyama, Magoroh. 1994. *Mindscapes in Management: Use of Individual Differences in Multi-cultural Management.* Aldershot. Dartmouth Press.

Maruyama, Magoroh. 2006. 'Architectural Configuration', in *APROS 11: Asia-Pacific Researchers in Organization Studies: 11th International Colloquium, Melbourne, Australia, 4-7 December 2005,* 248–255. Melbourne: Asia-Pacific Researchers in Organisation Studies. <http://search.informit.com.au/documentSummary;dn=305803731502744;res=IELBUS> – cited 9 September 2008.

Maruyama, Magoroh and Reniker, S. 1991. *Context and Complexity: Cultivating Contextual Understanding*. Berlin. Springer-Verlag.

Naipaul, V.S. 1998. *Beyond Belief, Islamic Excursions among the converted peoples*. London. Little, Brown.

Navon, L. and Morag, A. 2004. 'Liminality as biographical disruption: unclassifiability following hormonal therapy for advanced prostate cancer', *Social Science and Medicine* 58(4): 2337–2347.

Otoiu, A. 2003. 'An Exercise in Fictional Liminality: the Postcolonial, the

Postcommunist, and Romania's Threshold Generation', *Comparative Studies of South Asia, Africa and the Middle East* 23(1&2): 87–105.

Qureshi, I.H. 1971. *Administration of the Sultanate of Delhi*, 5th edn. New Delhi. Oriental Books Reprint Corporation.

Rahman, F. 1979. *Islam*. Chicago. University of Chicago Press.

Ratiani, I. 2007. 'Theory of Liminality', *Georgian Electronic Journal of Literature* 1(1). Rustaveli Institute of Georgian Literature.

Said, Edward. 1995. *Orientalism: Western Conceptions of the Orient*. Revised edn. Penguin, 1995. (Original edn Pantheon, 1975.)

Schutz, A. 1943. 'The Problem of Rationality in the Social World', reprinted in Schutz, A. *Collected Papers* vol. 2 (hereafter cited as "CP2"), pp. 64–88. Amsterdam. Martinus Nijhoff, 1964.

Scruton, R. 2007. 'The Sacred and the Human', *Prospect Magazine* 137(August).

Siddiqui, A. 1997. 'Ethics in Islam: Key Concepts and Contemporary Challenges', *Journal of Moral Education* 6(4): 423.

Simmel, Georg. 1950. *The Sociology of Georg Simmel*, trans. Kurt Wolff. New York. Free Press.

Simmel, Georg. 1979. 'Digressions sur l'étranger', in *L'Ecole de Chicago: Naissance de l'écologie urbaine*, ed. Yves Grafmeyer and Isaac Joseph. Paris. Editions du Champ Urbain.

Sulieman, M. 1984. *Senior Managers in Iraqi Society: Their Background and Attitudes*. Unpublished PhD thesis. University of Glasgow.

Tempest, S. and Starkey, K. 2004. 'The Effects of Liminality on Individual and Organizational Learning', *Organization Studies* 25(4): 507–527.

Thompson, M., Ellis, R.J. and Wildavsky, A. 1990. *Cultural Theory*. Boulder, Colorado. Westview.

Thompson, M., Warburton M. and Hatley, T. 1986. *Uncertainty On A Himalayan Scale*. London. Milton Ash.

Turner, V.W. 1957. *Schism and Continuity in an African Society: a study of Ndembu Religious Life*. Manchester. Manchester University Press.

Turner, V.W. 1962. *Chihamba The White Spirit: a Ritual Drama Of The Ndembu*. Rhodes-Livingstone Paper no 33. Manchester. Manchester University Press.

Turner, V.W. 1964. 'Betwixt and between: The liminal period in rites de passage', in *Symposium on new approaches to the study of religion: Proceedings of the 1964 Annual Spring Meeting of the American Ethnological Society*, edited by J. Helm, pp. 4–20. Seattle. American Ethnological Society.

Turner, V.W. 1972. 'Passages, margins and poverty: Religious symbols of communitas', *Worship* 46: 390–412, 482–494.

Turner, V.W. 1995. *The Ritual Process: Structure and Anti-Structure*. New York. Aldine de Gruyter, 1995. (Originally published 1969.)

Van Gennep, A. [1909] 1960. *The rites of passage.* London. Routledge & Kegan Paul.

Weir, D.T.H. 1998. 'The Fourth Paradigm', in A.A. Shamali and J. Denton (eds), *Management in the Middle East.* Kuwait. Gulf Management Centre.

Weir, D.T.H. 2000. 'Management in the Arab world', in Warner, M. (ed.). *Management in Emerging Countries: Regional Encyclopedia of Business and Management.* London. Business Press/Thomson Learning.

Weir, D.T.H. 2003a. 'Human Resource Development in the Arab Middle East: a 'fourth paradigm', in Lee, Monica (ed.), *Human Resource Development in a Complex World.* London. Routledge.

Weir, D.T.H 2003b. 'Management Development and Leadership in the Middle East: An Alternative Paradigm'. Paper presented to the Leadership in the Management Theory at Work Series Conference, June 2003. Lancaster. Lancaster University.

Weir, David 2005. 'The Diwan as a spatial context for decision-making in Arab organisation'. Presented to the 11 APROS (Asian and Pacific Researchers in Organisational Studies) Conference, Melbourne, Australia, 4–7 December 2005.

Werbner, P. 2001. 'The Limits of Cultural Hybridity: On Ritual Monsters, Poetic Licence and Contested Postcolonial Purifications', *Journal of the Royal Anthropological Institute* 7(1): 133–152.

Wildavsky, A and Dake, K. 1990. 'Theories of Risk Perception: Who Fears What and Why?' *Daedalus* 119: 41–60.

Zukin, S. 1991. *Landscapes of Power*. Berkeley. University of California Press.

Chapter Four

Consumption, Sacred Places and Spaces in Profane Contexts: A Comparison between the UK and India

Jan Brown, John Phillips and Vishwas Maheshwari

It may be that in an affluent, materialist and consumerist world, one of the unspoken assumptions is that matters relating to consumption are matters of the profane. By consumption is meant not just the purchasing transaction of products or objects, but the involvement in and consuming of experiences, moving consumption out of things and into thoughts, beliefs, and emotions. Labelling consumption as profane distinguishes it from the sacred. It may be helpful therefore to remind ourselves that the term "profane" derives from the Latin *pro*, in front of, and *fanum*, the temple, and so anything in front of or outside the temple was contrasted with that which went on inside or was reserved for the "sacredness", the special and exclusive apartness, of the temple. The contrast has been reduced to simple, and more than likely simplistic, oppositions. The sacred was that characterised by godliness, holiness, other worldliness, by the transcendent, rising above the here and now and the limits of worldly matter; to the profane was left the tangible here and now, the ordinary transactions of human intercourse, and the goods and chattels that mediated those exchanges. As such, consumption is self-evidently profane.

In *The Sacred and the Profane,* the Romanian, Mircea Eliade, argued that

> man becomes aware of the sacred because it manifests itself, shows itself, as something wholly different from the profane . . . a reality that does not belong to our world. (1959: 12)

He introduced the term "hierophany" to describe the way in which the sacred expresses itself. Consumption then, according to these derivations, should be a study of the profane, a study of earthly behaviours and experiences, concerned only with earthly goods and with earthly values. However, in the last couple of decades, some consumption theorists (for example, Beck, Wallendorf and Sherry, 1989; Holbrook *et al.*, 2001; Hanlon, 2006), have argued that apparently earthly behaviours and actions in pursuit of mammon, rather than being "profane", and so setting themselves apart from being "sacred", have the same characteristics and features as those religious and "sacred" behaviours expressed in the search for, and worship of, gods and transcendent values beyond people's material being. In this matter, therefore, the opposition of the "sacred" to the "profane" may not be helpful as the human behaviours around both are common.

We suggest here that certain consumption experiences have seen the transference of the profane to the level of the "sacred". In Eliade's terms, "they are worshipped precisely because they are hierophanies, because they show something that is no longer stone or tree but the sacred" (1959: 12). Similarly, Durkheim's (1915) *The Elementary Forms of the Religious Life,* setting out the separation of the sacred and the profane may not adequately explain the distinction. We wish to argue that the domains of the "sacred" and the "profane" have shared, or parallel systems and structures. Consumer and religious relationships and meanings are both expressed through symbols, rituals, language and myths. Objects and experiences are desired and consumed, and "gods" searched for and worshipped. The processes are similar, and it is held that the "profane" are as much underpinned by a value system as the "sacred". The "sacred" behaviour is, like the "profane", reified through objects and experiences, which may be used or consumed. However, it is further argued by some, that not only are the behaviours similar but the reasons for them also mirror each other. Maslow (1943, 1987) in his studies of motivation set out an increasingly sophisticated hierarchy of individual needs that placed basic physiological and security needs at the bottom, but topped off the hierarchy of motivators by suggesting that self-actualisation and transcendence moved people to their fulfilment. For Herzberg (1959) the intrinsic achievement and personal growth and recognition are similarly consistent with patterns of consumption directed at self and social esteem, and self-fulfilment.

It is further suggested that the contexts in which both these behaviours are exhibited are essentially "sacred". As Hanlon (2005) argues,

> Once you think of a brand as a belief system, you automatically get all the things that enterprise spends billions of dollars trying to obtain: trust, relevance, vision, values, leadership.

Around both behaviours, those of religious practice and consumption, can be constructed the same framework to identify either the primal religion or the primal brand. These signifiers in a "primal code" can constitute a belief system for the twenty-first century, the marketers' "Age of Consumption", just like a belief system for the Age of Religion in centuries before it.

The framework, or code, of such belief systems, it is suggested (Hanlon, 2005), contains seven elements: the myths and stories, most notably the creation story; the creed or basic tenets of belief; the totems, symbols and icons associated with that belief; the words and language that legitimise the belief; the believers and non-believers; the faithful and the faithless; and, the leaders, and key players and actors. The theatre where these actors play out their beliefs do not need to be inside the temple to be called "sacred": the places and spaces bring their own special and apart "sacred" validity to the belief system. Consequently we can begin to observe and to understand places of consumption as "sacred spaces and places", and to ask whether or not it is helpful to either religious behaviour or consumer behaviour to so do.

Place Branding and Rebranding

The phenomenon of branding, "a name, term, design, symbol, or any other feature that identifies one seller's good or service as distinct from those of other sellers", as defined by the American Marketing Association (2008), is well known. For some, it quickly reached into the cult of religion. As Hanlon (2007) puts it, it has its

> evangelista . . . For decades marketing types have talked about how some brands have a soul . . . The importance is transcendent. It becomes more and more obvious that brands of the future will be those who are able to surround themselves with communities of customers. And whether we call them evangelists . . . or just plain good customers, marketers require enthusiasts.

Currently there is an increase in the phenomenon of countries, regions and cities attempting to differentiate and (re)brand themselves from each other, and from what is ordinary across the globe. The process by which products and services were branded and from which marketing strategies emerged to sell them, has been translated to places (Zukin, 1995; Sassen, 2001).

For example, in the UK, Liverpool is currently undergoing a rebranding exercise to reposition itself in the twenty-first century. Its status in 2008 as the European Capital of Culture was instrumental in this process. Part of a place branding strategy is often to use sacred places and spaces in secular contexts. An illustration of this is the Northwest Multi-Faith Tourism Association which works with those responsible for sacred sites – cathedrals, churches, synagogues, mosques, temples and gurdwaras – throughout the northwest region. Its purpose is to encourage these sites to be open, in order to help the growth of understanding between the faith groups, and to enrich the experience of holiday makers and tourists in an understanding of different spiritual perceptions and the role of faith in a community's "story".

Consistent with its business or consumer culture, the Association awards the Marque of Excellence to sacred spaces in the northwest of England that reach the Association's standard in welcoming visitors. These places of worship share their cultural heritage and collections with the community and visitors alike. They are not only sacred to those who worship in them, but they are also buildings which showcase a variety of stories about their communities.

The rebranding process is also to be seen in India, in Varanasi (often referred to as Benaras), one of the oldest cities in the world. For Mark Twain, "Benares [*sic*] is older than history, older than tradition, older even than legend and looks twice as old as all of them put together" (1996: 480) The city has its own claim to be the cultural capital of India, and is described on its own website <http://www.varanasicity.com/> as "the city of temples". It has been a great centre of learning and a centre of civilisation for over 3000 years, but it is currently undergoing redevelopment to enhance tourism. The sacredness of the city is regarded as the key to this rebranding so that it is being marketed as a centre for spiritualism and mysticism. This contrasts with its reputation for fine silk ware, or its brass goods and jewellery, and moves far beyond the consumption of Hindu or Buddhist masks and artefacts, as memorabilia or souvenirs.

Both these examples bring into open tension some of the issues in the management and use of sacred places and spaces. For some the holy sites are exactly that: sites holy and sacred, part of a living and lived faith system, to be respected and protected as elements of a religious experience. For others, tourists, they are sites of attraction and casual interest, sites to be observed and visited, but not for any religious experience. So, simple issues such as when the cathedral or temple is open for worship and when it is open for visitors become problematic. It is not obvious that the sacred experience and the profane experience can live side by side in the same place at the same time.

Consumption and Sacredness

The process of consumption has given rise to a field of study that takes the act of consuming beyond the transactional, the simple purchasing or consuming of an object that brings particular attributes and benefits, as in an economic perspective. A consumption object can be a thing, a product, or an experience, like going to a sports event or a museum or art gallery. Different people consume it in different and multi-faceted ways. They construct different meanings around the process, and attach different values and significance to it. Belk, Wallendorf and Sherry have suggested that "for many, consumption has become a vehicle for experiencing the sacred" (1989: 1). They argue that the concept of the "sacred" operates beyond belief in a god, to include, they suggest, a belief in the nation. Likewise, in line with Durkheim's notion that "the totem is the flag of the clan" (1915: 220), they hold that consumers set certain things, from national parks to works of art, for example, as "sacred", that is as "set apart", and "revered, feared, and treated with the utmost respect" (Belk *et al.*, 1989: 2).

They have constructed their version of a primal code, properties of sacredness, tying belief and consumption together. This model is based around six features or domains: Places; Times; Tangible Things; Intangible Things; Persons and other beings; and Experiences.

The meanings of these domains are briefly thus. Places are those locations invested with a very special significance because of their history, because of what continues to happen there, because of what they are, places of pilgrimage, places of great natural beauty, or a homeland.

Times are moments and periods of particular significance, such as initiation and induction, coming of age, the passing of the seasons. Tangible things are artefacts, icons, relics, totems, special objects, rare or otherwise, and memorabilia of significant events in life histories.

Intangible things are the values embedded in rituals, or knowledge known only to the few, such as the way things are done in this place, family, or house. Persons and other beings are those sacred by being special, or set apart, and encompassing a variety of levels and special powers, and including animals. Experiences capture moments out of the ordinary, moments in the pursuit of the "other" and the sacred, attended by rituals and myths which sacralise the experience.

The religious manifestations of the domains are obvious. Places can be mosques, churches, shrines; times are those of services, sacramental ceremonies, rituals; tangible things are icons, idols, statues; intangible things may be hymn singing, adoration, worship; persons or other beings could be Allah, Christ, or Buddha; and experiences can be fasting, church-going, and pilgrimage.

Similarities between "Sacred" Practice and Profane Consumerism: Examples from the UK and India

We consider here how patterns of consumption and consumer behaviour can first of all be said to be similar to the "sacred", to the behaviour of those engaged in religious practice or exhibiting a belief system underpinned by the values of a primal religion. To evidence the shifting process in the UK, three well-worn examples of consumerism are chosen as quasi-hierophanies that manifest the sacred-like qualities of consumption: following and engaging in sports, and being a football fan in particular; going shopping, and experiencing the shopping cities and malls that are the "temples" of the consumption age; and the manifestations and expressions of the youth culture, going partying or clubbing. To illustrate this sacralisation drawing on the process in India, a similar sporting analogy is suggested, a cricketing one; an Indian model of "sacred" consumption, in the way that sacred values underpin purchasing transactions, is offered ; and, finally, a representation as sacred, of the recreational phenomenon of Bollywood is suggested.

Sport

UK: Football a consuming passion

The drawing of parallels between sport (and watching sport) and religious practice is not recent. Guttmann's (2004) first edition in 1978 showed how going to a sports stadium was like going to a church, how the players were revered and worshipped, how sports fans were willing to "die for the team", and how they came away with memorabilia that they cherished as sacred relics. Tomkins (2004), a writer on church affairs, has argued that we are increasingly deserting the church in favour of the pitch. Players are "gods", the stands are the pews, football is the new religion. Supporting a football team is not a matter of rational choice, but a matter of faith. But this is not just a British obsession. The *Jakarta Post* carried an article 'Comparing football to religion' (Makin, 2008) when the 2008 European football championships coincided with the second World Peace Forum in Jakarta.

India: Cricket the 'first religion that unites all in secular India'

Similarly to the passion for football and its equivalent 'religious' practice in the UK, the game of cricket and its national cricket team drive approximately 1.2 billion Indian people into a state of near frenzy. Kaiser (2007) contends that although the Indian sub-continent has a wide variety of people following different religions, the real India has one religion followed by almost all, and that is cricket. Cricket, it is argued, is the biggest "religion" in India. According to Mehta (2004), editor of the Indian weekly magazine *Outlook India*, the whole country comes to a stop when a cricket match is being played: the roads are deserted and weddings are postponed, operations in hospitals are rescheduled, and parliament goes in for early recess. It becomes like a holy day of obligation, or of abstinence: the obligation to abstain from anything but watching cricket. There are cases where an Indian might not know the name of the current Prime Minister or even the President of India, but Indians can readily recite, like a litany of the saints, the names and figures of their national heroes, their high priests, their gods, or Krishna, the Indian cricket team players.

Belk *et al.*'s (1989) domains of football and cricket as religions can thus be aligned as follows:

Domains	Football	Cricket
Places	football grounds and stadia	Cricket grounds
Times	fans' pre and post match rituals, outside the stadium as well as inside it	Match-days, often considered as national holidays and as religious festivals
Tangible things	the purchase of replica kits, scarves, and programmes	attendance, special rituals for cricketers
Intangible things	chanting, club anthems and theme songs	cricket anthems and songs
Persons & Other Beings	home side stars, opposition villains, referees	stars and legendary cricketing heroes, a litany of 'saints'
Experiences	collective euphoria, or dismay	huge home coming receptions for victorious teams

Shopping

UK: Shopping a passionate consumption

Greider (2000) described the phenomenon of "a booming, modernizing industrial system [that] expands so robustly that it's described as a 'miracle'". Expressions of wealth and standards of living are found in the act of shopping. For some it has become compulsive. There is even a term, "oniomania" (from the Latin *onos*, or "price"), for the addiction, and in the United States it is estimated that one in twelve people manifest symptoms of compulsive shopping.

Shopping in the UK moved into a new dimension in the 1990s with the opening of extensive shopping malls or cities, like the Trafford Centre in Manchester, with 235 stores and up to 140,000 visitors a day, nearly 30 million annually <http://news.bbc.co.uk/1/hi/england/manchester/4308332.stm>; the Metro Centre in Gateshead, with 339 stores and over 24 million visitors a year <http://www.capital-shopping-centres.co.uk/shoppingcentres/metrocentre/pdf/press_releases/metro_retail_park.pdf>; Meadowhall in Sheffield, with 285 retailers and averaging about 30 million visitors a year <http://www.geographypages.co.uk/meadow.htm>; and in late 2008 Europe's biggest inner city shopping complex, Westfield Shopping Centre, opened in White City, London, covering an area of thirty football pitches and having 265 retail units. These become as sacred temples; entry into them and behaviour inside them is managed or controlled by "priestly" wardens or security guards, to ensure order and respect.

This does not make it a religion or like a religion, but the shopping and consumption experience lies deep nevertheless within many people and reaches the consumer society, to levels of the fanatic or zealot. It can be said to lie deep within the individual's basic assumptions, as Schein (2004) would have it, assumptions about oneself, about what to do, and about how to do it. Or, as Bourdieu (2005) would have it, consumption through shopping has become a deeply embedded social construction, whereby individuals engage in symbolic constructions which provide profound meaning and value to the things, experiences and places they consume. At the marketing end of the shopping spectrum, Ind's (2007) work *Living the Brand* suggests by its very title, a management of values and behaviours beyond simple acquisition, and a transformational experience in which one's life is subsumed by the process of consumption.

India: Consumption and communalism

One body of research explores an interesting area of conjecture thrown into focus by the processes of globalisation, that is, how far developing-world consumers mimic the pattern of western consumption. Those selling their products worldwide need to know if there are differences between one place and another in what excites consumers to purchase. Belk (1995) and Ger and Belk (1996) have shown contrasting strands in both homogeneous and heterogeneous patterns of purchasing. This acts as a backdrop to considering the way in which consumers in India express a similar passion for spending to those in the west, but attend that passion with distinct "cultural value orientations" regarding matters of quality, price, consistency, and branding (Sethna, 2006: 267). In all this the influence of the community can become key.

The context for consumption in India becomes communal, as opposed to individualistic. Purchasing is oriented around "religious" or faith-like qualities: brand loyalty; integrity in relationships between sellers and buyers; values based over time, like dealing with the known, and the reliable; and contracting between partners bonded by notions of trust, dependability, and accountability. There is a group, or communal, dimension, whether it is the family, or ethnic factors, that places a premium on the soft areas of relationships and unwritten codes of practice, alongside the hard ones of price and quality. These value orientations bear a real influence on consumer behaviour and consumption (Rugimbana and Nwankwo, 2003). In this sense they become matters of faith, as in a religion.

Therefore, the domains of consumption as sacred are characterised as:

Domains	**Shopping centres**	
Places	shopping malls, metros, outlet villages	the marketplace as expressions of integrity of relationships
Times	shopping expeditions, January sales	interactions between seller and buyer
Tangible things	'shopping city', brands, fashion accessories	products and services
Intangible things	window shopping, browsing	brand loyalty, trust, quality, reliability, relations

Persons & Other Beings	life style gurus	retailers, traders, entrepreneurs, salespeople
Experiences	'living the brand', 'being cool'	tradition, communal integrity

Recreation

UK: Partying

"Mass" is a nightclub and live music venue in south London set in the old St Matthew's church there. On the fourth Sunday of every month there is "Latin Mass", the music flavoured by South America. Its promotional literature <http://www.mass-club.com/> promises that "a night out here is a truly religious experience, where you'll be taken out of this earth by big music and big beats". It is not unique. Liverpool has the Alma de Cuba, a converted church in Seel Street. In seeking a wider audience it invites people to "bring your family and friends along and enjoy a great Sunday Brunch whilst listening to our amazing live Gospel choir" <http://www.breakfastandbrunch.com/venues2.php?venueid=1420>.

A music group, Faithless, have achieved success with a number called "God is a DJ". The relationship between religion, clubs and music is explicitly signed for young people.

India: Bollywood

The Indian film industry has come to be represented by the phenomenon of Bollywood. It is a misrepresentation. Bollywood is only part of it, but it is the largest part, based in Mumbai, and essentially Hindi or Hindustani. Productions coming out of Bollywood tend to be multimillion dollar films, with mass appeal, not only in India and the subcontinent, but also to the Indian diasporas in the rest of the world. However their appeal has extended beyond India's cultural and language limits to being dubbed across all continents.

The popularity as a recreational pursuit of these films has no accidental alignment to religious practice. In the 1920s and 1930s the physical proximity of the sacred and the profane was represented by early travelling film shows being set up in tents beside the temples. Indeed Ostrowski (2007) actually inverts the relationship; "religion", he argues, "is nearly synonymous with the Indian film industry". There are explicit cultural and historical influences on Bollywood films which suggest aspects of the "sacred". These include ancient and mythological epics, the dance-drama stylistic conventions of Sanskrit drama, and regional folk theatre traditions. They tell simple stories of good and evil, glorify the family, offer values of self-sacrifice, and respect tradition and authority. They are modern parables and act as extensions of 5000 years of religious practice.

So the domains can be set out accordingly:

Domains	**Partying**	**Bollywood**
Places	nightclubs, music places	cinemas, film theatres, film tents
Times	weekends mostly	cinema showings, tours
Tangible things	dressing up	dancing, music, action, comedy
Intangible things	drinking, dancing, socialising, music	triumph of good over evil
Persons & Other Beings	clubbers, disc jockeys, bands	Bollywood film stars, producers
Experiences	group/gang image, 'beautiful people', release in the music	three hour festive or 'ceremonial' ritual

From the Profane to the Sacred: The Shifting Process of Consumption

Having drawn out some obvious similarities between behaviour categorised as residing in the "sacred" and that which has been for most of the twentieth century regarded as belonging to the domain of the "profane", it is a short step for some consumption theorists to suggest that it is more than a matter of similitude between the sacred and the profane, and that it is not just that there might be an overlap between the two, but that there might be a linguistic conflation of the two, that, for example, watching a football match is spoken about as if it actually were a religious experience.

We again take the sporting illustration to suggest how this might be so. In respect of football it can be argued that the domains have more than a shared commonality, that they need more than simile and metaphor with which to compare and contrast the sacred and the profane. As the marketing of Nevada Smith's bar in New York has it: "Nevada Smiths – *Where Football is Religion*. The planet's most famous live Football venue. Experience the legendary matchday atmosphere in the place the hardcore call the Church. Showing over 100 live matches per week from the world's top leagues plus all the cup and International action" <http://www.nevadasmiths.net/>.

Sacred consumption in the UK: Football is "God"

In the language of some, football is no longer like a religion, nor is it a quasi-religion: it is a religion. Metaphor and simile seem to be dispensed with. Such a view can appear from quite unexpected quarters. Rt. Rev. Derek Worlock, Archbishop of Liverpool at the time of the Hillsborough football ground disaster in which ninety-six football supporters were killed in 1989, recalled, in the aftermath, meeting Lord Justice Taylor who had been appointed to lead the enquiry into the tragedy. "Archbishop", the judge asked him, "aren't you jealous of football as a rival religion?" (1991: 119). Alan Edge's (1999) *Faith of our Fathers* mediates his life as a football supporter through chapters entitled "baptism", "indoctrination", "confirmation", "communion", "confession", and "penance". The association of football and religion has become unavoidable.

Taking Belk *et al.*'s (1989) domains of sacred consumption, we can place the consumption of the football spectators into a quasi-religious experience. They can be set out thus:

Places: Football grounds as shrines, and memorials

Church attendance in the UK may be declining: football attendance is not. Furthermore the latter has moved beyond attending the local ground. Football was played across the globe throughout the twentieth century, but those who supported football largely stayed at home except for international tournaments like the World Cup when a few travelled to follow their national team. A modern phenomenon in Europe, stimulated significantly by cheap air travel, has seen the growth of overseas supporters' clubs, devoted (and the term is significant here) to following a particular club, not a national team. Budget airlines take supporters to a football fixture at the ground of their devotion: on a pilgrimage. Rogan Taylor, a lecturer at Liverpool

University School of Management and a founder of the Football Supporters Association, in a radio interview about the European Champions League Final in Athens in 2007, referred to the vast numbers of football fans making the journey, as being on "a secular hajj . . . it's a pilgrimage".

For such supporters the grounds are their cathedrals, places of veneration and pilgrimage, their medium for transportation to the transcendent, their way out of the world. The very names of the stadia reinforce this transcendence: Manchester United's Old Trafford stadium is called "The Theatre of Dreams", Sunderland Football Club's ground, like Benfica's in Portugal, is termed "The Stadium of Light", and fans who go to Glasgow Celtic's Parkhead stadium are "Welcome to Paradise". Stephen Done, Curator of the Liverpool FC Museum, posed the question at a recent conference, "Anfield: the third cathedral?" (2008), citing an ex-player, John Aldridge, who said, "I always thought Anfield was a place more beautiful than heaven".

More profoundly, football grounds can be places of death and loss, and memorials to the dead assume a religious significance. Three British football grounds have memorials to those who died at their club's football matches: Glasgow Rangers have their Ibrox Disaster Memorial in memory of those killed in accidents there in 1902 and 1961; Bradford City has a memorial to the victims of the 1985 fire at their Valley Parade ground; and Liverpool FC has the Hillsborough memorial at a corner of their ground. In Done's terms, here is a sacred memorial, not a profane object, and as such it is excluded from the official tour for visitors to the ground (2008).

Before and after each game, candles burn perpetually at the Hillsborough memorial; the memorial itself is bedecked by scarves offered by home and opposing fans; supporters stand in silence, and in prayer with bowed heads. Each year the ground hosts the Hillsborough Memorial Service; the fans form the congregation; the team emerges from the sanctuary of the changing room; the players and officials of the club lead the liturgy, before the high altar of The Kop, the renowned bank of seats behind one of the goals. The service is grounded in the stadium, the fans' cathedral.

Times: Festivals and feasts

As religious calendars are punctuated by feast days, and periods of abstinence or denial, and periods of celebration, so the football calendar has its own religious patterns and rhythms. Cup Final day, World Cup championships, the process of relegation to a division or league below, and the hope of promotion to one above, even the "close season" when no games are played but reserves of energy are built up in preparation, all unfold to the pace of religious seasons of birth and rebirth, death, and resurrection. Kelly's (2008) oral histories of fandom on the Kop trace fans' accounts of their life rhythms through initiation rites, instigated by the father taking the child to the football match, then being in the care of an older brother, and having their own area or pen, before joining the main congregation in a rite of passage from adolescence to manhood.

Tangible things: Sacred relics, goods and chattels

The signs and symbols of football fervour, of clan loyalties, are not the preserve of children. They are not confined to places where the game is played: they are brought into the home. In the way that statues and sacred pictures adorn mantelpieces and walls, so the memorabilia and totems of a particular club adorn the homes of fanatical supporters. A plethora of football goods from replica shirts to club logo embossed bed covers is available for consumption, and club shops inside or beside football grounds have taken the place of the repositories of religious objects so often a part of churches in the past, to which the faithful went at the end of the service.

Intangible things: Hymns and anthems

The English FA Cup Final is prefaced by the singing of the time-honoured hymn "Abide with me". All clubs have their own hymns and anthems, invoked throughout the game to express collective solidarity, or to abuse the opposition. Some tunes, like a song from Rodgers and Hammerstein's 1945 musical *Carousel*, "You'll never walk alone", have assumed mythical proportions in Glasgow and Liverpool. These arouse and inspire, and are called upon at key moments in an act of mass singing, to express the hearts and minds of the faithful. These are more than rituals. They deeply reflect the values of the worshipping congregation. They invoke the club's history and place in community. They bind fervent supporters together. The tangible and the intangible meet in the not infrequent occurrence of a fan wishing for his ashes to be spread on the field of play after death. This is his link with eternity, reaching beyond this life in time, but staying firmly in it in place. Here is football's sacred world, extending from earth to eternity, through the spirit of the fan's ashes.

Persons and other beings: more than human

Religious leaders are often endowed with charismatic qualities. Media focus and attention cast the personalities of footballers, managers, and those engaged in the sport, under a perpetual spotlight, and present the followers with their leaders. In a text coming out of Liverpool it is not inappropriate to quote the legendary Liverpool Football Club manager's oft-cited but also oft-misunderstood dictum: "Some people believe football is a matter of life and death. I'm very disappointed with that attitude. I can assure you it is much, much more important than that." Bill Shankly was mocking himself. A truer statement of his belief came when he hesitated to visit a local children's hospital in case expectations were too high. "I am not God. I do not work miracles", he said (quoted in Kelly, 1996: 248). But this did not stop him from being viewed in a very particular messianic light. In 2008 Newcastle United Football Club declared on the appointment of its new manager, "Geordie messiah to return – Kevin Keegan is returning to Newcastle United as manager" <http://www.guardian.co.uk/football/2008/jan/16/newsstory.newcastleunited4>.

Footballer Robbie Fowler was known as "God" to many Liverpool supporters. Here was a player set apart, sacred because of his talents. Don Revie, a manager of England and Leeds United, described the Liverpool and Celtic talisman player Kenny Dalglish as "blessed by God" (Done, 2008).

Experiences: "Kissing the shirt"

The football match is capable of moving out of the ordinary those who attend it. The sacralisation of the rituals is most apparent at moments of success, when the awe and wonder of victory can reach into sublime ecstasy for some. Fans depart the earth and go "onto a cloud" of joy and euphoria. For Durkheim, "dying for the flag" (1915: 220) was an act of self-sacrifice totally beyond the significance of the piece of cloth. The flag had become more than symbol: it represented and effectively became the embodiment of the country. Football fans talk of "dying for the shirt", or more accurately expecting the players on the field to do so. Footballers regularly kiss their shirt and club crest upon scoring a goal or registering a victory. The brand logo embossed shirt, which so many wear, transforms the experience from the ordinary to the extraordinary, and allows the fan to reach beyond the here and now into the transcendent. The primal brand has become the primal religion. Loyalty, keeping the faith, is all. The French manager of

Liverpool FC in 2000, Gérard Houllier, met with great hostility, as did the player, when he signed Nick Barmby from fierce city rivals Everton. "Are we talking about a change of religion here?" asked Houllier <http: //www.guardian.co.uk/football/2000/jul/20/newsstory.sport1>.

Sacred consumption in India: Cricket is a religion

The parallel of cricket in India to football in the UK applies equally in the transference of the profane to the level of the sacred.

Places: Cricket grounds as temples

Passion for cricket in India is unrivalled anywhere else in the world, the sport being observed with the fervour of a religion. Whether it is a one-day match or a test, stadiums in India are teeming with lively spectators, cheering and hooting with great enthusiasm, no matter in which part of the stadium they are, either in VIP seating or in open seating facilities under scorching heat. Spectators will wait all day if it is raining and the match has been called off or abandoned, because they just want to feel the atmosphere of the cricket ground, and to have a glimpse of their cricketing heroes, members of the Indian cricket team. The cricket ground is the temple: importance lies in being in it – nothing has to happen in it. This is not watching: it is worshipping.

The "temples" exert a gravitational pull, the focal point of a "call to worship" for the "believers", the large crowds, or congregations. These grounds vary in size and the facilities they have, but binding them all are the ubiquitous banners proclaiming their cricketing heroes, and the ability of the noise, the choral liturgy, to resound throughout the entire ground with the spectators' or worshippers' cheering. Almost every cricketer who visits India to play matches has admitted that those moments of electrifying atmosphere in the Indian grounds are some of the most memorable moments in their cricketing careers, elevating the experience to a transcendence. The South African cricketer Gary Kirsten recalls that on achieving the dismissal of the Indian hero Sachin Tendulkar,

> it was a surreal experience and very quickly I began to realise the immense pressure these Indian cricketers are under when they "cross the ropes". The passion for the game of cricket is seen everywhere you go. (Kirsten, 2008)

Times: Match-days often considered as national holidays or "religious" festivals

In the same way as the football calendar and various leagues have their own "religious" patterns or "liturgical" calendar in the UK, so the various cricket tournaments such as the Asia Cup, India–Pakistan cricket series, India–Australia and India–England series are followed and observed as a religious calendar, with the festivals recurring annually or every two or three years.

Attendance at matches, like attendance at religious services, is a duty, and part of a practising responsibility. For example, the recent Twenty 20 Cricket World Cup 2007 in South Africa, the India–Australia Test series 2007 (Gavaskar-Border trophy), and the India–Australia and New Zealand–Commonwealth Bank Series 2008 saw unprecedented support not only from Indians residing in India and travelling with the Indian cricket team, but from the attendance of Indians travelling from all over the world. In addition, the International Cricket Council (ICC) World Cup in 2007 in the West Indies saw a tremendous loss in millions of dollars of advertising revenue to the TV broadcasters and media companies that were live telecasting to India and the cricket world, because the India cricket team was eliminated in the early qualifying stages of the tournament. Spectating and viewing are part of a religious practice in India, fuelled by the religious fervour of its cricket fans.

Tangible things: Rituals and icons

Indian cricket fans performed rituals in front of posters of Indian cricketers during a prayer ceremony in support of the Indian team for the 2007 cricket World Cup in the West Indies. They offered special prayers for the team's victory and made supplication to their God for a triumph. Furthermore, devotional practice came not only in terms of prayers, and the performing of "religious" rituals but also through the use of art and craftsmanship, and the use of symbols and artefacts embedded in their culture. A combination of 115 kites displaying the pictures of Indian cricket players was made by one of the worshippers to show his devotion towards the national team. In addition, icons were displayed everywhere. College and university students across the country signed on giant cricket bats during a signature campaign in support of the team. Streets and main roads in various cities are plastered with pictures and posters depicting the country's popular cricket stars. These icons make the worship explicit.

Intangible things: National anthem and cricket songs

No matter who the opposition is, or where it is that "Team India" is playing, in an international league or in the final match of a high profile tournament, each game starts with the congregation in hearty salute to the unifying icon, the Indian national flag. Patriotism merges into religious certainty, "dying for the flag". This is that intangible notion that unites each member of the team to perform for that tri-colour and make their nation and fans proud. On the other side of the literal fence, the support and enthusiasm of the fans, the faithful assembly of believers, make it a moment of true love, and a form of religious ecstasy, for the game.

Moreover, a recent Bollywood film about a hockey team launched an anthem, "*Chak de*" (meaning "Common India"), which, in cricket, has now become second to the national anthem as a hymn of praise. It is sung before, after and during the games by fans and supporters of the team to boost their beloved cricketing heroes, to sing their praises to their "gods".

Persons and other beings: Stars and legendary cricketing heroes

With their international success Indian cricketers have achieved tremendous publicity in the media, both on and off their sacred turf, and their public and personal exploits are quite often on the front page. Indian cricket blogs such as <http://blogs.cricinfo.com/meninwhite/archives/2007/03/indias_slip_is_good_for_cricke_1.php> continually express sentiments like "if cricket is the religion for the die-hard cricket fans in India then all time legendary Indian cricketer 'Sachin Tendulkar – master blaster' is the God, who rules the hearts and minds of the fans". One website, in a bizarre conjunction of the sacred and the undeniably profane, declares that "Cricket is not only a sport in India but a religion and criccontest.com is all set to redefine online cricket coverage with the launch of the world's first ever live cricket gaming during the India–Lanka Test series" <http://www.prlog.org/10091677-criccontestcom-to-launch-worlds-first-ever-live-cricket-gaming.html>.

More recently, the Indian one-day cricket team captain Mahendra Singh Dhoni had his hair cut, and it led to thousands of people gathering outside that salon to have a glimpse of him or possibly to greet him. The salon where he had his haircut is now considered to be a most sacred place, a shrine to their "god". This is the behaviour of a celebrity-worshipping community of believers.

Experiences: Kissing the ground

Pope John Paul II often kissed the ground when visiting foreign lands. This ritual of appreciation and acceptance of an invitation, an expression of shared faith and hospitality, became a behaviour exciting much discussion within the Roman Catholic Church <http://romancatholicblog.typepad.com /roman_catholic_blog/2006/05/why_did_pope_jo.html>). In a similar gesture of religious significance, Indian cricketers were seen kissing the pitch when they won the Twenty-20 World Cup in September 2007. Success and defeat bring with them the ceremonies of thanksgiving and mourning, attended by their own customs and practices, offering prayers to their gods for a victory delivered in the face of powerful odds, or burning effigies to purge the loss. As far as the Indian cricket fans are concerned, the patterning is that of a primal religion.

Conclusion

It has been suggested here that there is in process a paradigmatic shift in how sacred places and spaces are viewed in the Age of Consumption. An initially clear distinction between the sacred and the profane allowed the categorisation of consumer behaviour to be considered only in terms set apart from the sacred. It concerned itself with earthly things, and earthly goods and chattels. It was bounded by the here and now.

That distinction has been blurred by the willingness of social analysts, marketing theorists amongst them, to search for distinctive metaphors to describe and explain consumption behaviour (Holt, 1995). It has moved on from drawing out the similarities in the behaviour between those intent on the pursuit of "god", and those interested only in mammon. The comparisons and parallels are many. Consequently it could be said that the profane is in several respects like the sacred. Primal branding, in many instances, has the same characteristics as primal religion.

It has not stopped there however. Belk *et al.* (1989) represent a growing school of thought amongst consumption theorists who are not satisfied by holding the profane to be like the sacred, but instead they argue that the profane and the sacred are as one; that the binary is a false one and unhelpful in understanding consumer behaviour. Hill *et al.* explore the relationships of humans with their pet animals presented as "transcending the ordinary consumer behaviour domain of possessions/possessors to that of sacred and spiritual consumption" (2008: 554). Holbrook *et al.* are quite explicit in this matter:

> Without excessive sentimentality, we can infer that pets are *part* of consumption experiences for many people but that these experiences are *above* the domain normally explored by marketing and consumer research. In that sense, pets occupy hallowed ground. They belong to the sphere of *sacred consumption* (2001: 3).

In this way of looking at things, consumption, whether consumers realise it or not, is conceived in sacred terms and ways, as a sacred behaviour, taking place in a sacred space, and lived in a sacred experience.

Some, if not much, of this rests on simplification, both of consumption and of religion. There are different levels of consumption experience. Not all who visit the Manchester Trafford Centre actually shop; their experience of window gazing or whatever is a different one from that of those who purchase. Similarly there are different levels of religious experience. And the significance of these experiences is not easily or readily discernible to the individual or to society. As Wilson has suggested,

> it is conceivable that many of those who are religiously committed, who attend church, make donations, have their children baptized and confirmed . . . do not seek a larger role for religion in the organization and operation of society . . . There are other areas of voluntaristic commitment, some of which elicit response no less fervent than that of most churchpeople; which command larger audiences; which pay their professionals vastly higher stipends; but which none the less exert no great influence on the social system. Football would be one of them (1992: 200).

The argument, for some, will be neither complete nor convincing. What is clear is that Durkheim's defining heterogeneity, which marked the sacred from the profane, is not, for some, a final or total distinction.

> It is absolute. In all the history of human thought there exists no other example of two categories of things so profoundly differentiated or so radically opposed to one another (1915: 38).

In these terms, consumption by definition is profane, but in wrestling with what might constitute "sacredness" in consumption, the language of metaphor and simile might inadequately describe the phenomenon. The supposed sacralisation of consumption is an argument that challenges both its theorists and its critics to clarify and to find a common ground for the essential characteristics of the sacred. Sri Aurobindo, the Indian spiritual guru, for one, mapped out his territory when he wrote:

> Money is the visible sign of universal force, and this force in its manifestation on earth works on the vital and physical planes and is indispensable to the fullness of outer life. In its origin and its true action it belongs to the Divine (1995: 14).

References

American Marketing Association. 2008. 'Brand definition'. <http://www.marketingpower.com/_layouts/Dictionary.aspx?dLetter=B> – accessed 30 October 2008.

Aurobindo, S. 1995. *The Mother*. Twin Lakes. Lotus Press.

Belk, R.W., Wallendorf, M. and Sherry, J.F. 1989. 'The Sacred and the Profane in Consumer Behavior: Theodicy on the Odyssey', *Journal of Consumer Research,* 16(June): 1–38.

Belk, R.W. 1995. 'Hyperreality and globalization: culture in the age of Ronald McDonald', *Journal of International Consumer Marketing*, 8(3/4): 22–38.

Bourdieu, P. 2005. *The Social Structures of the Economy*. Cambridge. Polity.

Done, S. 2008. '*Anfield: the third cathedral?*' Unpublished paper for the Centre for Liverpool and Merseyside Studies Conference *Culture and Merseyside,* November 2008.

Durkheim, E. 1915. *The Elementary Forms of the Religious Life.* London. George Allen and Unwin.

Eliade, M. 1959. *The Sacred and the Profane: the nature of religion.* Orlando. Harcourt.

Ger, G. and Belk, R.W. 1996. 'I'd like to buy the world a Coke: consumptionscapes of the "less affluent world"', *Journal of Consumer Policy,* 19(3): 271–304.

Greider, W. 2000. *Shopping till we drop*. <http://www.thenation.com/doc/20000410/greider> – accessed 20 October 2008.

Guttmann, A. 2004. *From Ritual to Record: the Nature of Modern Sports*. 2nd revised edn. New York. Columbia University Press.

Hanlon, P. 2005. *Primal branding.* <http://www.allaboutbranding.com/index.lasso?article=405> – accessed 20 October 2008.

Hanlon, P. 2006. *Primal Branding.* New York. Free Press.

Hanlon, P. 2007. *Evangelista! – creating customer evangelists when nobody really gives a crap* <http://www.allaboutbranding.com/index.lasso?article=457> – accessed 20 October 2008.

Herzberg, F. 1959. *The Motivation to Work.* New York. Wiley.

Hill, R.P., Gaines, J. and Wilson, R.M. 2008. 'Consumer behavior, extended-self, and sacred consumption: An alternative perspective from our animal companions', *Journal of Business Research,* 61(5): 553–562.

Holbrook, M.B., Stephens, D.L., Day, E., Holbrook, S.M., and Strazar, G. 2001. 'A Collective Stereographic Essay on Key Aspects of Animal Companionship: The Truth about Dogs and Cats', *Academy of Marketing Science Review,* 1: 1–20 – accessed 24 November 2008 at <http://www.amsreview.org/articles/holbrook01-2001.pdf>.

Holt, D.B. 1995. 'How Consumers Consume: A Typology of Consumption Practices', *Journal of Consumer Research,* 22(June): 1–16.

Ind, N. 2007. *Living the brand.* 3rd revised edn. London. Kogan Page.

Kaiser, A. 2007. *Cricket is a religion in India.* <http://diarist.com/abhinav-kaiser/cricket-religion-india> – accessed 20 October 2008.

Kelly, S.F. 1996. *Bill Shankly: It's Much More Important Than That.* London. Virgin Books.

Kelly, S.F. 2008. *'You'll Never Walk Alone': Tales of the Kop.* Unpublished paper for the Centre for Liverpool and Merseyside Studies Conference *Culture and Merseyside,* November 2008.

Kirsten, G. 2008. *Gary Kirsten's Indian journey begins.* <http://www.moneyweb.co.za/mw/view/mw/en/page72234?oid=186718&sn=Blog%20detail%20back%20button> – accessed 17 November 2008.

Makin, A. 2008. *Comparing football to religion* <http://www.thejakartapost.com/news/2008/07/04/comparing-football-religion.html> – accessed 23 October 2008.

Maslow, A.H. 1943. 'A Theory of Human Motivation', *Psychological Review,* 50(July): 370–396.

Maslow, A.H. 1987. *Motivation and Personality.* 3rd edn. New York. Harper and Row.

Mehta, V. 2004. *Letter: India's cricketing religion* <http://news.bbc.co.uk/1/hi/programmes/3734038.stm> – accessed 20 October 2008.

Ostrowski, A. 2007. 'Found in translation: From Hollywood Hits to Bollywood Blockbusters', *Journal of Religion and Film,* 11(2), at <http://www.unomaha.edu/jrf/vol11no2/OstrowskiHollyBolly.htm> – accessed 21 October 2008.

Rugimbana, R. and Nwankwo, S. 2003. *Cross Cultural Marketing*. London. Thomson Learning.

Sassen, S. 2001. *The Global City.* 2nd edn. New Jersey. Princeton University Press.

Schein, E. 2004. *Organizational Culture and Leadership*. San Francisco, CA. Jossey Bass.

Sethna, Z. 2006. 'An investigation into how individual and organisational consumption is affected when dealing with SME organisations from emerging economies'. *Asia Pacific Journal of Marketing and Logistics*. 18(4): 266–282.

Taylor, R. 2007. Interview. <http://www.liverpoolecho.co.uk/videos-pictures/liverpool-audio/liverpool-sport-audio/2007/07/29/rogan-taylor-part-3-100252-19548717/> – accessed 21 October 2008.

Tomkins, S. 2004. *Matches made in heaven*. <http://news.bbc.co.uk/2/hi/uk_news/magazine/3828767.stm> – accessed 10 October 2008.

Twain, M. 1996. *Following the Equator: and anti-imperialist essays.* New York. Oxford University Press. First published in 1897.

Wilson, B.R. 1992. 'Reflections on a Many Sided Controversy', in Bruce, S. *Religion and Modernization*. Oxford. Oxford University Press.

Worlock, D. 1991. *Bread Upon The Waters*. Middlegreen. St Paul's Publications.

Zukin, S. 1995. *The Cultures of Cities*. London. Blackwell.

Chapter Five

Could the Category of the "Sacred" Imply a Problematic Conception of the Contemporary World?

Pascal Mueller-Jourdan

As implied in the title, in this chapter I suggest that problematic conceptions of the world result from the use of the concept of the sacred, as distinct from the concept of the profane, to qualify differences between spaces. But before considering some of these problems, we can admit that there is a wide and complex range of ways to think the world and its degrees of spatiality.

The history of western thought, either religious or theological or philosophical, shows that there are at least two major antithetical ways of conceiving the world. The first is the traditional religious conception or, let us say, the romantic conception of the world which echoes a possible secret sacrality of the world. The second is the modern scientific view of the world, which necessarily implies a positive explanation of the natural phenomena. Note that I do not speak here of the scientist as a person, but of the scientific as a type of attitude towards the world. Indeed, it is absolutely obvious that a scientist, even if not a believer, may pay a careful attention to the mystery of life, and may be fulfilled by a sort of respectful perception of the secret and mysterious laws of the nature of the world.

In this paper, I intend to develop this dialectical approach towards the world;[1] a dialectic between the subjective or intersubjective approach and the objective one. I will examine a selection of some Greek philosophical approaches leaving aside the complex history of religious behaviours among the ancient Greeks (rites, observances, devotions, even magic).[2] In particular, I would like to point out the evolution of the use of religious language to speak about issues of physics.[3] This is, in my opinion, a particular characteristic of the history of Greek philosophy, long before the mutation we observe today. But before examining some philosophical reflections upon the world, the space and the sacred, it will be useful to pause and to take into account an important outcome of recent inquiries into the history of comparative religion concerning the structuration of the world's spaces, that is, to take into account a kind of religious topography of the ancient world.

Religious and Non-religious Approaches of the World

Mircea Eliade, leading Romanian scholar and chair of the department of History of Religions at the University of Chicago, wrote many years ago a major study in French, *Le Sacré et le Profane* (translated into English under the title *The Sacred and the Profane*).[4] He suggests that the main difference between the experience of space as understood within basic religious society, and secular experience, which is not considered to be religious, such as the experience of the world of physicists and naturalists, as well as of many modern scholars, is the fact that for the former – the basic religious society – the world is lived and experienced as essentially "non-homogeneous" and for the latter – the scientist – it is on the contrary considered to be a "homogeneous" world.

Indeed, for the traditional religious society, assuming that such a type of community has specifically existed, the world seems to be composed of spatial sectors. Those sectors are not of the same kind, and have neither the same precise value, nor the same precise function.

For the traditional religious society, at the highest level there is a divine and celestial space, devoted to gods and spiritual beings. At the opposite, beneath, are many terrestrial spaces, which are intended for living natural beings, although those spaces – considered, in their former state, to be unorganised – need to be ritually "cosmicized" (this neologism used by Eliade comes from the Greek verb *kosmo-poieô* [see Eliade, 1959: 29–31]). There is a third level between them. It is an intermediate space, which is considered as a passage or a meeting point by which the human can enter into a relationship with superior realities and by which the divine can manifest itself to the human. This type of place or space, which is intermediate, often surrounds a sort of centre, an *axis mundi*, such as a sacred pillar, a mountain, a stone, or other symbolic objects from which and around which the human living place is organised, in a word "cosmicised". We can add that for popular religious beliefs there frequently is an extra place, a partially chaotic space, located underground, a space which seems to have been commonly conceived as the realm of the half-life (i.e. the space of an inferior degree of life). Eliade called such a general conception of the world non-homogeneous, because of the different levels of the spatial organization of the world that he identified and studied in his inquiries into many different religious societies.

For Eliade, in opposition to this non-homogeneous conception of the world, stands a contrasting conception of the world, which is accepted today as the modern one. However, we can note in the history of western philosophy a "pre-modern" attempt, troubling for the religious consciousness, which has been pretending to explain natural phenomena through physical causes. The pre-Socratic philosophers seem to have been tempted to break with the theological (i.e. religious) explanations of nature. They seem to have been the first to create the basis of a sort of monism. For them, the world, its movement and the concatenation of causes and effects, is no longer explicable by the actions of gods. Probably for the first time in western history, the naturalist explanation of phenomena is trying to eradicate religious views as a possible explanation of the universe. Thus we can note and certainly admit that the so-called modern and post-modern attitudes towards the world, which is definitely explainable without the help of theological discourses, is already in fact an ancient pre-modern philosophical position.

In this opposite case, the world is homogeneous. This means it is composed of spaces and places which do not differ qualitatively one from the other. I have spoken above about qualitative differences in a religious context, which confer a sort of value-added "sacredness" to places which are basically neutral. Indeed, the homogeneous world is radically considered as being made of the same basic elements whichever place is under inspection. Hence there is no possibility of classifying spaces by the qualitative distinctions between sacred and profane as used in a religious context, where one place is designated as being sacred and, by exclusion, another is deemed to be profane. But this radical denial of distinctions between spaces seems to have been quite rare, even among scientists and contemporary non-believers, given the fact that they themselves, as human beings, find the need to classify and so to distinguish between living spaces, as for instance, private space, public place, social domain and so on. As Eliade (1959: 24) wrote:

> Yet this experience of profane space still includes values that some extent recall the nonhomogeneity peculiar to the religious experience of space. There are, for example, privileged places, qualitatively different from all others – a man's birthplace, or the scenes of his first love, or certain places in the first foreign city he visited in youth. Even for the most frankly nonreligious man, all these places still retain an exceptional, a unique quality; they are "holy places" of his private universe, as if it were in such spots that he had received the revelation of a reality "other" than that in which he participates through his ordinary daily life.

Indeed, it seems very difficult, historically speaking, to deny the relevance of the persistent and strong concept articulated in classical anthropology, namely that the dualistic polarisation of the world as "sacred and profane" corresponds to a major phenomenon which emerges autonomously within the history of the beliefs, behaviours and practices of all human societies.

The Emergence of a Philosophical Point of View

First of all, it is certainly correct to note that the dichotomy between the sacred and the profane is not only a religious topic but fundamentally a philosophical problem. Indeed, in a philosophical context, applied to the world, such a dichotomy implies a sharp dualism usually interpreted as a recurrent opposition between form and matter, pure and impure, good and evil, beauty and ugliness, the noble and the depraved, power and weakness . . . the pairs of opposites always go together.

What does "sacred" mean in a philosophical context? We well know that, generally speaking, "sacred" means "separated from . . .", pointing to something which does not belong to everyday life, something which seems clearly to be situated at a superior level. But for a philosophical use, the meaning of the term "sacred" needs to be absolutely precise. We know that for the history of religions, as shown by Mircea Eliade, "sacred" qualifies the experience of the highest degree of reality which is indifferently named "divine". This metaphysical experience contrasts with the common experience of the things, which are experienced in everyday life, in the ordinary, mundane and transitory (i.e. impermanent). Thus we can admit that "sacred" is akin to "divine" in the more general sense. They are both attributes for the highest degree of reality and can be used in a non-specific religious way. However, we note in the history of philosophy a profound mutation in the use of religious vocabulary.

After the pre-Socratic philosophers broke the predominance of theologies of the Homeric age, "divine" became a qualitative category used to express the transcendence of the principles and the causes of all visible phenomena (i.e. moving, changing, generation, corruption and so on). It certainly still conserves some religious connotations, but it no longer implies either accepting religious beliefs such as dogma or a particular catechism, or becoming a member of a specific religious community. The attribute "divine" as well as the attribute "sacred" is about to lose its traditional, strictly religious, meaning.

I propose now to examine briefly some cases of a major current of thought of the Hellenistic age, which seems to be reactivated today in the postmodern concept of self-fashioning, or "Care of the Self" (this concept is the English translation of the *souci de soi* of the French philosopher Michel Foucault [Foucault, 1988]). I would like particularly to concentrate my inquiry upon Stoicism, leaving aside today the very special case of the dialogues of Plato wherein, through the voice of Socrates, he criticises the mythical beliefs of his contemporaries. The Stoics often use religious concepts but in a non-specifically religious way. And this point deserves close scrutiny in the case of our contemporary context.

The doctrine of the Stoics, called Stoicism, was established by Zeno of Citium in the third century before Christ. Chrysippus, the third instructor of the new Athenian school, was particularly influential in development of the new doctrine. Unfortunately, only fragments of his monumental works and researches on physics remain. However, the most popular figures among the Stoics have certainly been Roman philosophers like the slave Epictetus and his famous pupil the Emperor Marcus Aurelius Antoninus, during the first centuries of the Christian era. We can also observe a very strong influence of Stoicism on other streams of Greek philosophy, even, astonishingly, upon its opponents, such as the first-century Roman statesman Cicero and Plutarch, a famous Middle Platonist well known for his moral writings (*Moralia*).

We must underline that the Stoic aim was not the creation of new theories on physics but the strong intention of promoting the individual human life to the rank of the life of universal Nature by connecting the particular to the universal. Their purpose was definitely ethical involving a changing of perspective, a changing of mind, and thus a changing of life, therefore a changing of behaviour. For the Stoics, the highest value of life was virtue and virtue always expresses the power which actualises all human potentialities in accordance with the profound nature of man. The aim of philosophy was the perfect life. That is why the study of Nature, in other words the study of physics (space, time, form, matter, motion and rest, natural laws), should result in the good life, in right behaviour – in a word, ethics.

For the Stoics, the world is one, divine, eternal and rational, a sort of universal living being ruled by a divine logos. As Marcus Aurelius (2006: IV.40) says:

> Think always of the universe as one living being, comprising one substance and one soul: how is all absorbed into his own consciousness; how a single impulse governs all its actions; how all things collaborate in all that happens; the very web and mesh of it all.

For this reason, the universe naturally enters into the category of the sacred, for it is directly related to the divine logos although this world seems to be experienced, most of the time, by most human beings, as non-sacred, i.e. as "desacralised". Note that the Stoics rarely use the word *hieros*, sacred, but an accurate reading of their writings seems clear to me: "sacred" is a synonym of "divine" and can be used to qualify a thing related to the divine. If the world must be held to be sacred by the fact that it is inhabited, pervaded say the Stoics, by the divine logos, and, if the sacred has to do with things which are linked with the highest degree of reality, therefore "sacred" becomes an essential attribute conferred by the perpetual presence and the permanent action of the divine logos, which is not god in the conventional sense,[5] at least for the Stoics. It is clear that the pantheon of the Stoics is expressing diverse aspects of the rationality of Nature, in contrast with traditional religious beliefs. In his *Lives of Eminent Philosophers*, Diogenes Laertius (1925: vol. II: VII.147–8) wrote:

> The deity is . . . the artificer of the universe and, as it were, the father of all, both in general and in that particular part of him which is all-pervading, and which is called many names according to its various powers. They give the name Dia [*Δία*] because all things are 'due to' [*διά*] him; Zeus [*Ζηνα*] in so far as he is the cause of life [*ζην*] or pervades all life; the name Athena is given, because the ruling part of the divinity extends to the aether; the name Hera marks its extension to the air; He is called Hephaestus since it spreads to the creative fire; Poseidon, since it stretches to the sea; Demeter, since it reaches to the earth. Similarly men have given the deity his other titles, fastening, as best they can, on some one or other of his peculiar attributes.

Thus, for the Stoics, when a man, having lost the sense of the self, no longer lives in accordance with the rules of his own nature nor with the rules of the Nature of the Universe, which are both rationally structured andsorganized, he breaks with the universal Nature of which he is only a part. He breaks also with the divine, immanent,[6] rationality[7] of the Universe which is his origin, and so doing, he also breaks with its natural living space which is for him a sort of original, rational and harmonious biotope. This break with the logos of Nature creates temporarily a new state of life, an irrational state, an unnatural state, in a space which consequently becomes unnatural, therefore inhuman, for himself first and, in the Stoic view, without any doubt, this new state extends to others. For the Stoics, philosophy is a way of life, which proposes exercises of mind to restore the relationship of man to a former state of nature, which is for each part of the universe the true state of Nature.[8] In reality, Nature never changes in substance. But, for the Stoics, man can produce a paradoxical unnatural state, and thus a paradoxical unnatural space that we can call a "desacralised" space. Once more, the space, which is the three-dimensional extension of universal Nature pervaded by the logos, remains in substance what it is, even if the rational being, man, has the astonishing power to create individually, and sometimes collectively, a major paradoxical situation. Philosophy as a way of life must therefore be a way of reintroducing the human into a natural living space, sacred because it is naturally structured and inhabited by the divine logos.

In admitting the sacrality of the whole universe, in so far as the world is a three-dimensional body pervaded by the divine logos and the rational *pneuma*, we can now understand that this philosophical view is comparable to the view I have described before, a view of a world as naturally homogeneous. We might say such a world is "one" and that would be true, at least for the conception of the world of the Stoics, but certainly also for Neo-Platonists such as Plotinus and Proclus.

We have seen that rational living beings who live in opposition to their own nature, and consequently in opposition to the unique universal Nature, have the power to produce personal disaster and large collateral damage. Thus rational beings can paradoxically create a fractured world, by their denial, albeit temporarily, that the world is fundamentally "one", sacred because divine. A world broken like this is, in fact, "desacralised".

Conclusion

For the ancient philosophical tradition, man, as a rational and free agent, seems to have lost his natural link with the world, in fact with himself. This is why philosophy is always viewed by the Stoics as a necessary therapy, the only one able to reintroduce the human into its own rational capacity. In the contemporary context, wherever spaces are intersubjectively qualified as sacred, this designation can help humankind to pause, then to come back to the fundamental nature of things, to its own fundamental human nature.

But, from the point of view argued in this chapter, it could be time today to think of replacing the dichotomy of the sacred and the profane with a vision of a more unified world and thus of a more unified conception of the human vocation. For such a task, the vision of the world proposed by Stoicism, its sense of the common destiny of mankind because of common Nature offers a possible first outline of a sane globalisation. The universalism of the Stoics is not based on the international market, but on a strong sense of the continuum between the universal and natural sympathy of all things (i.e. a natural affinity, and a mutual – reciprocal – influence), with the common good and the notion of virtue – in sum, with universal reason. Both, religious posture and non-religious posture, are the concern of such a proposal, which exceeds the ancient divisions between civil and religious societies, although, it is quite clear that ancient philosophy, first attends to the fundamental relationship that man has with himself, with the world and with others (see Marcus Aurelius, 2006: VIII.27). Unfortunately, the philosophical posture proposed by the Stoics gives little information about the practical realisation and the real consequences of such a relationship; except, perhaps, in their proposal of a strong educational and self-educational system based upon fundamental common values determined by common and universal reason.

The fact of rethinking today the sacred in general and the sacred space in particular, implies, in my opinion, the necessity of going beyond the radical dichotomy of the ancient cleavage; and the necessity of reconsidering the world (i.e. the human cosmos) in its fundamental unity and in its coherence, and thus, of reconsidering human life in its coherent unity with itself, with others and with the Universe.

Could the category of the sacred imply a problematic conception of the world today?

Probably, yes and no! Yes, if such a conception leads us to fracturing the qualitative continuum of human life. No, if such a conception helps humans to make the necessary break with the relentless overstimulation of modern life. No, if sacred space helps humanity to become more naturally human.

Notes

1 Note that I use the term "world" here in the old sense, meaning the whole domain of physical reality.
2 See Dodds, 1951 and Dodds, 1965.
3 See the quotation below (p. 85) from Diogenes Laertius.
4 See Eliade, 1959.
5 It is not a particular being who might be entering into a personal relationship with humanity but rather the cause explaining the laws and the rules which are organising the world. In this sense, it could be called "meta-historical reality".
6 In fact, a rationality both transcendent and immanent.
7 I understand "divine" rationality as (1) the highest degree of rationality, and (2) the cause of rationality.
8 See the works of Pierre Hadot, particularly Hadot, 1995.

References

Diogenes Laertius. 1925. *Lives of Eminent Philosophers* vol. II. transl. R.D. Hicks. London. Harvard University Press.

Dodds, E.R. 1951. *The Greeks and the Irrational.* Berkeley and Los Angeles. University of California Press

Dodds, E.R. 1965. *Pagan and Christian in an Age of Anxiety: Some Aspects of Religious Experience from Marcus Aurelius to Constantine.* Cambridge. Cambridge University Press.

Eliade, Mircea. 1959. *The Sacred and the Profane: The Nature of Religion.* Orlando, Florida. Harcourt.

Foucault, Michel. 1988. *The History of Sexuality, Vol. III: The Care of the Self.* New York. Vintage Books.

Hadot, Pierre. 1995. *Philosophy as a Way of Life: Spiritual Exercises, from Socrates to Foucault.* Oxford. Wiley-Blackwell.

Marcus Aurelius. 2006. *Meditations*, ed. M. Hammond and D. Clay. London. Penguin.

CHAPTER SIX

SHAPING WOMEN'S SACRED SPACE: CHRISTIAN LITURGY AND WOMANSPIRIT RITUAL IN A MOMENT OF HEIGHTENED FEMINIST CONSCIOUSNESS

JENNY DAGGERS

The year 1978, exactly three decades ago, was a significant year in the life of a British women's movement that had been emerging in fragments within and at the edges of the Christian churches. It was a year in which a range of existing groups and initiatives came to visibility and new groups were formed; women involved in these small enterprises became aware they were part of a larger rising current of concern over the position of women in the churches. For many of those involved, their participation in the regular rhythm of liturgy or meeting in the sacred spaces of their respective denominations was marked by alienation or ambivalence. As some among them turned to print to give voice to these newly-articulated perceptions, the women described themselves as "dispossessed daughters of Eve", as cartographers of a "new country", or as "mirror" to their church (Dowell & Hurcombe, 1987; Maitland, 1983; Furlong, 1988).

Amid the diversity of the movement, the issue of the ordination of women in the Anglican and Catholic churches was creating a widespread sense of shock at the misogyny revealed, for example in the letters pages of the Church of England newspaper, the *Church Times* – a sense of shock felt even by women who themselves opposed women's ordination to the priesthood. For women whose feminist consciousness had already been sharpened by participation in the Women's Liberation Movement, this misogyny provided confirmation of the patriarchal nature of Christianity. And how are Christian women who resist patriarchal control to inhabit denominational sacred spaces, to be present in the divine–human encounter mediated therein, when they find themselves excluded, or included only on terms set by a male tradition?

A powerful response to this dilemma arose in the form of distinctive women's liturgies and rituals, in which sacred space is actively shaped to reflect Christian feminist concerns and explorations of the divine in the context of the British Christian Women's Movement of the 1970s and 1980s. Many of those involved perceived their experimental liturgy as a gift to the churches, a work of the people worthy of inclusion within the sanctioned sacred spaces of their respective denominational traditions.

This paper examines how these "celebrating women" shaped sacred space, with occasional reference to the feminist spirituality rituals of the post-Christian Womanspirit movement. The paper is in two main parts with a brief conclusion. The first part argues the significance of creative liturgy within the wider movement. Widespread liturgical activity shows that this shaping of sacred space was as important as the political activity by which the diverse groups challenged their respective traditions to transform long-standing attitudes and practices: a full inclusion of women would involve changes to liturgical use of traditional sacred spaces. The second part looks in more detail at the shaping of sacred space in representative liturgies and rituals and at what these Christian liturgies shared with the Womanspirit movement emerging in the same period, with its reconstruction of the ancient pre-patriarchal tradition of the Goddess. The final part of the paper evaluates the legacy of these ephemeral and provisional sacred spaces in contemporary liturgical and ritual life.

The Importance of Liturgy and Ritual within the Christian Women's Movement

The British Christian Women's Movement comprised groups across the denominations, as well as of ecumenical "Christian feminist" groups and projects. Catholic, Anglican, Quaker and Unitarian denominational groups were prominent, while many women with free-church affiliations were active within ecumenical ventures.[1] (See the appended table of groups.) At the Catholic end of the spectrum, liturgical experiment by women and men together, or in women's groups was one aspect of wider Vatican II renewal. Ianthe Pratt of the St. Joan's International Alliance was central in collecting and publishing these liturgies from the late 1970s (Pratt, 1987). When the Catholic Women's Network was founded, members continued this tradition, and Pratt herself was to play a leading role in the Association for Inclusive Language (AIL).

In the Anglican context, Una Kroll, founder of the Christian Parity Group – a precursor of the Movement for the Ordination of Women – made a significant intervention in the life of the broader movement. During 1974 in Philadelphia, bishops of the Episcopal Church of the USA (ECUSA) who were in favour of women's ordination had conducted "illegal" ordinations of women to the priesthood, which ECUSA retrospectively recognised. Kroll strongly opposed similar tactics being used within the Church of England. In the recently launched *Christian Parity Group Newsletter* (*CPG NL*), she exhorted campaign groups to make full use of existing opportunities for developing and experimenting with liturgy, including the ministry of women (*CPG NL*, Nov 1978). Liturgies had already played an important part in the life of the Christian Parity Group, and the timing of her exhortation, in the year in which the wider movement took shape, led to a wider spectrum of groups heeding her call.

Liturgical or ritual experiment was to become a hallmark of the British Christian women's movement. Taking place in marginal and ephemeral spaces, in public space as witness to the cause of women's ordination or of world peace, and sometimes in cathedrals, churches or meeting houses, women sought ways of integrating their feminist consciousness with the Christian liturgical tradition, in whatever form they had inherited it.

The Movement for the Ordination of Women

The (Church of England) Movement for the Ordination of Women (MOW), formed in 1978, included an active feminist minority among its wide spectrum of support. From its inception, liturgies were important within the life of MOW. Gradually, through the initiative of a minority, including Susan Dowell and Linda Hurcombe, it became MOW practice to mount vigils during ordination services, and soon liturgies were to become incorporated within these vigils.[2] In this vigil context a form of 'wilderness liturgy' evolved, where parallels were drawn between the Exodus experience and the current wilderness experience of Anglican women with a felt call to ordination, which could not be tested (Rees, 1983; MOW, 1984). Juliantide 1983 provided an occasion for MOW-organised liturgical gatherings at locations across the country. In January 1984 a Eucharist of thanksgiving was celebrated at Westminster Abbey to mark the fortieth anniversary of the ordination of Li Tim Oi, attended by Li Tim Oi herself and by women already ordained in the Anglican Communion outside the Church of England.[3]

For Christian feminists in MOW, liturgical experiment was extended in offshoots which grew from MOW during the 1980s, notably a programme of "Hartlebury weekends" entitled *In the Image of God*, hosted by Diana McClatchey during 1982 and 1983 and the formation of Women in Theology (WIT) in 1983 and of the St. Hilda Community in 1987. Liturgical experiment was one means of women involved exploring the issues in their own terms, over against the stasis of the Anglican women's ordination debate.

Women in Theology

The process begun during the Hartlebury weekends was continued in the ongoing life of WIT. For Janet Morley, who advertised the Hartlebury programme in the *Christian Feminist Newsletter*, one aim of the weekends was to explore women's spirituality and the female imagery hidden within the Christian tradition (*CF NL* 17:17). WIT's first publication, *Celebrating Women*, was a collection of liturgical material (Morley and Ward, 1986). These liturgies arose from the life of a bi-monthly WIT Liturgy Group in London, and from local WIT groups, who shared their liturgies through a regular WIT mailing. The currency of such experiment is demonstrated by the fact that the booklet sold 2,500 copies in two months and is still in print now with a mainstream publisher (Ward, Wild & Morley, 1995). By the beginning of the World Council of Churches Ecumenical Decade for Churches in Solidarity with Women in 1988, WIT's established reputation in creation of liturgy inclusive of women led to an invitation to prepare liturgical material for its launch. In the same year, Morley published a collection of her own liturgical writing, *All Desires Known*, where she places her writings within a neglected tradition of female imagery evident in the Psalms and the writings of medieval mystics (1988a).

The St Hilda Community

The St. Hilda Community was formed to continue MOW liturgical experiment, and to create a location for MOW members to experience the ministry of women, using to the full the available scope, to which Kroll had previously drawn attention. Like MOW, but unlike WIT, the St Hilda Community was open to men as well as women. The community took the name of Hilda of Whitby – whom Bede had likened to a jewel enlightening the Church – as a symbol of the spiritual gifts of contemporary women. It was to be a further five years before the Church of England Synod would eventually decide to ordain women: from its inception the St Hilda Community had a high profile within the Church of England, the national secular press and internationally (Furlong, 1991a: 5–8). From an Anglican initiative within MOW, St. Hilda's soon became an ecumenical venture, open to lay ministry and to the ministry of women ministers of other denominations, as well as to the ministry of Anglican women "lawfully ordained abroad". Publicity in the wider Christian feminist network contributed to this ecumenical broadening, and women active in a range of Christian feminist groups contributed to shaping the liturgies and to the St. Hilda collection of liturgical material, *Women Included* (Furlong, 1991).

The Oxford Christian Women's Group

A variety of women's groups in Oxford operated within a broad forum, the Oxford Christian Women's Group (OCWG), which included monthly liturgies as a central focus. These emerged from a monthly women's mass, initiated by Catholic women's groups arising from Newman Association events organised in the early 1970s. The radical nature of the women's mass in its early years lay in women's preaching and participation in Eucharistic celebration, rather than in liturgical experiment. A publicity leaflet of 1982 described the mass as open to both women and men, with the support of the Dominican community at Blackfriars, aiming to create an opportunity for lay Christians to fulfil their baptismal obligation to preach the gospel (OCWG, 1982). From its inception, attendance was ecumenical with a significant Anglican and Quaker presence: gradually the mass became known as eucharist and then as liturgy, reflecting a growing experimental approach. As in the MOW context, a theme emerged of a specific women's spirituality, expressed in the liturgy, of women's exclusion "from the language, liturgy and lawmaking of the Church", as one OCWG member put it in her talk scheduled on Radio 4 (Campbell, 1984). As with MOW liturgies, the OCWG liturgy was a significant example of the liturgical experiment advocated by Kroll.

Catholic Women's Network

Liturgical experiment was one of three founding concerns of the *Catholic Women's Network* (*CWN*) at its inauguration in 1984 (*CWN NL* 1:2). CWN formalised a network that had grown in strength since 1978, drawing together activity arising in the Catholic Renewal Movement, the longstanding St. Joan's International Alliance and newer Christian feminist groups, such as the Roman Catholic Feminists and the Oxford Christian Women's Group. From its inception, it worked closely with its sister Anglican group, WIT, and its members were also active in various local ecumenical Christian feminist initiatives. Reports in the *CWN NL* show that liturgy was a regular component in local CWN group meetings, and in 1990 a liturgy group was formed in South London (*CWN NL* 26:6–7).

Unitarian Women's Group and Quaker Women's Group

In comparison with the marginal position of Christian feminists in other denominations, the work of the Unitarian Women's Group fed directly into Unitarian policy and practices. There was a general willingness to adopt inclusive language, and UWG members shaped an anthology of Unitarian worship material, published in 1987 (*UWG NL* 15:2, 22:4), having also contributed to a working party in feminist theology set up by the Unitarian General Assembly in the year UWG was formed.

Newsletters for the UWG and for the Quaker Women's Group (QWG) show an openness to the British Womanspirit movement that had emerged from the Women's Liberation Movement, and was growing in tandem with the Christian women's movement.

Greenham Common Liturgies and Rituals

The establishment of a women's camp at the Greenham Common US nuclear base in 1981 created a visible feminist presence within the broader peace movement. Christian and Womanspirit feminists met at Greenham and, for both, liturgy and ritual was an important aspect of their life in the camp. Accounts of liturgies appear in the *CF NL* (6:1,16:12–13,20:8–9), and from August 1984 a monthly vigil was established at the Blue Gate, with local groups maintaining the vigil in solidarity elsewhere. A tradition of Holy Week liturgies began in 1985; a *Greenham Peace Vigil Newsletter* (*GPV NL*) records over fifty women participating in a Maundy Thursday and Good Friday watch (Summer 1987:1). In the same year, a group of WIT members led a footwashing liturgy on Maundy Thursday, and repeated for the third time their sharing of a Jewish Passover Seder meal. Shared WIT and CWN Good Friday liturgy included marking the stations of the cross around the perimeter of the Greenham base (*GPV NL* Summer 1987:1).

Womanspirit commentators emphasise the empowerment of women and development of women's spirituality within the movement in general, and at Greenham in particular. Thus Asphodel testifies to a growing "forceful spiritual feminism" *against* the missiles and *for* world peace. She reports that ritual drawn from prominent American Womanspirit leaders, Budapest and Starhawk, from Celtic mythology and mysticism, and from the Kabbalah and European magic was created at Greenham as "good magic" towards removal of the missiles (Long, 1994: 27).

In Christian feminist liturgies and Goddess rituals performed in the public space of Greenham, the two religious networks are visible as religious aspects of the predominantly secular "second-wave" women's movement. The next section moves to a closer analysis of the distinctive shaping of sacred space in feminist liturgy and ritual. The standpoint of the investigation is Christian, with reference being made to Womanspirit in order to clarify points of convergence and divergence between these two feminist spiritualities.

Celebrating Women: Shaping Sacred Space

Christian Feminism and Womanspirit Spirituality Compared

At one level there is a simple dichotomy between the two feminist spiritualities: the emergent theme of Christian feminism as gift to the Church contrasts with the post-Christian stance of Womanspirit, with its shunning of Christian sacred spaces. In *Map of the New Country* Sara Maitland writes of this gift as follows:

> [Christian feminist liturgies] combine creative imagination with an acceptance of and confrontation with the reality of sexual discrimination within the Church. [Such liturgies] can also so strengthen women while offering a route back into the institutional church that we can return with gifts in our hands, empowered by the experience of the desert. The Church needs the creative and innovative power of women's worship, I believe, more than it needs a few more priests – of whatever sex – doing the thing that priests have always done (1983: 111).

But there is much common ground none the less. Both movements agree on the patriarchal nature of religion. Both aim to recover usable women's traditions, harnessing creative imagination and innovative practice, in order to raise up women who have been damaged by patriarchal exclusion and control. However, they look in different places: Christian feminists to women within the Bible and Christian tradition; Womanspirit to a recovery of women-centred traditions of autonomy, nurture and healing. Both create feminist spiritualities, where liturgies and rituals set out to heal "the broken heart of patriarchy", as the Asian American feminist theologian Rita Nakishma Brock puts it (1988:87–8). Finally, both seek a female divine or God in the feminine: for Christian feminists the search is for neglected feminine imagery of the triune God in Bible and Christian tradition; for Womanspirit, the quest is for the Goddess within, whose ancient image can be reconstructed to empower the women of current times.

Innovative feminist reshaping of sacred space is evoked in the Greenham juxtaposition of Christian feminist vigil and Womanspirit "good magic". Womanspirit sought to recover and reconstruct a matriarchal Goddess tradition suppressed beneath the weight of Jewish, then Christian patriarchal monotheism: sacred space was represented in the sacred grove destroyed in the assertion of monotheistic Judaism, and the sacred sites of the old religion, which were later incorporated with Christian sacred space.

Christian feminism is heir to this suppressed feminine tradition, which emerges anew within the broken heart of patriarchy. For Unitarian minister Ann Arthur in her piece 'In the Image of God', exclusive male imagery for God is idolatrous; she traces the Old Testament record of the submerging of goddess religions by patriarchal society and religion, then retrieves neglected female imagery in the Bible, medieval Christianity and the Unitarian tradition (UWPFT, 1985: 3.1–2). Within this freethinking tradition, UWG openness to Womanspirit led one group to create a ritual based on American Womanspirit practices, symbolising the four elements with salt, incense, candle and water, and casting a circle; among the words spoken were:

> Together we take a journey back to that time when Mother Earth was revered as the sacred giver of life, loved and worshipped by all that understood her. Her rhythms were sacred and her abundantly life-giving force was in each woman (*UWG NL* Aug 1982).

The full account of the liturgy synchronises with Asphodel's view that, within Womanspirit, "the Goddess within" gained importance over the female divine as source of empowerment. "In raising Her, we raise ourselves; in raising ourselves, we raise Her" (Long, 1994: 17).

But Christian feminists of other denominational traditions claimed their place within a more orthodox Christianity, so their liturgies looked back to women in the Bible and the tradition, celebrating the "lost coins" found in their search (Loades, 1987). Liturgies might symbolise resistance to patriarchal exclusions – as for example in one of the liturgies celebrated on 29

April 1979, a day of action organised by American Catholics in support of women's ordination, where misogynistic sayings of Augustine, Jerome, Tertullian and Chrysostom were torn in two (Dowell & Hurcombe, 1987: 95–6). But the aim of this resistance is to reopen the space of Christianity to women.

'Oasis and Journey'

Suzanne Fageol, an American priest active in the St. Hilda Community, described it as "both oasis and journey for many Christians" (Fageol, 1989: 25). Her metaphors could be applied more widely. Oasis could take the form of major services shared with the broad constituency of support for women's ordination, such as the celebration in Westminster Abbey of the 40th anniversary of the ordination of Li Tim Oi in wartime Hong Kong. Or oasis was created in countless examples of mutual affirmation in smaller groups, where water, oil or flowers might be used as ritual objects, such as CWN members anointing one another to a royal priesthood (*CWN NL* 7:11), or the symbolising of connections across difference with the tying of ribbon (*CWN NL* 22:5). This affirmation was needed given the "wilderness experience" articulated by Maitland in the quotation above, and more widely among supporters of MOW, or the "alienation" from their church expressed by many Catholic women of the time (McEwan, 1991). Certainly it could be said of both Christian feminist liturgy and Womanspirit ritual that these spiritualities were both sustaining oasis and meaningful journey.

God in the Feminine

The issue of inclusive liturgical language was raised in this context of felt exclusion. Among the women of the movement, Janet Morley emerged as a facilitator of women's liturgy, during her participation across a wide range of Christian feminist groups. Morley also articulated the views of many others, while thoughtfully exploring the theological implications of this liturgical experiment.

For Morley, the rationale for inclusive language was clear: exclusive language has a negative formative effect on men as well as women. The introduction to *Celebrating Women*, co-authored by Morley and Hannah Ward, refers to exclusive language as both

> a symptom of women's . . . exclusion from . . . ministry and decision-making *and* a means of continually recreating . . . such exclusion as "normal", or within the purposes of God. (1986: 2)

Morley sees traditional liturgical language about God as "constructed over against the feminine" with longstanding effects in the exclusion and undervaluing of women; she therefore advocates positive celebration of the feminine and of women as made in the image of God (1984a). Her recommendation is embodied in Christian feminist experimental liturgy, finding expression in Morley's own liturgical language, and in the wider body of collected feminist liturgy.

The discussion of liturgy to this point has focused on liturgy as oasis and journey for the women participants. Where, you might ask, is God in this? If sacred space is a place of divine–human encounter, where is the divine in feminist liturgy? Morley is clear that liturgical experimentation concerns women in their relation to God; this is a core aspect of women's gift to their churches. The link is in the reaffirmation that women, no less than men, are *in imago Dei.* Morley uses Julian's image of Jesus as mother who feeds Christians in the Eucharist to argue the need to distinguish male images of God from God's essence; use of feminine imagery is iconoclastic, exposing masculine essentialism and recognising "the richness of women's lives as a source of metaphor for the divine" (1981).

In her collection of her own liturgical writing, *All Desires Known*, Morley retrieves female imagery so that human experience of women's love may be taken up into imagery for God (1988a: 5). But she is equally concerned that where experience of God is strange, difficult or frightening, that women conceptualise this in feminine terms, intimate with their own experience, rather than distance these as aspects of a 'male' God (1988a: 5). Thus, for Morley, sexuality, desire and darkness suggest language for addressing God (1988b, 1988c). The project of the Christian women's movement can be seen as an attempted rehabilitation of Eve, so that aspects of women's being that have long been subject to patriarchal control and rejection, through exclusion of all feminine imagery for God, may once again be welcome within sacred space, and present in the divine human encounter.

The Legacy of Feminist Liturgical Experiment

What is the legacy of this period of liturgical experiment? There has been a widespread – though by no means universal – turn to inclusive liturgical language, at least when referring to the women and men who make up a congregation or meeting. Often this language is of a gender-neutral kind, where common humanity is emphasised and gender difference rendered invisible. The result can be to create the illusion that gender issues have been resolved: the process is complete. I suggest that something is lost in this attempted neutrality. Inclusive language is largely confined to the human, while male language for the divine remains largely intact. This indicates that the gifts shaped in Christian feminist liturgy and inscribed in Morley's writings have been little valued by the church.

On the positive side, a second 1995 edition of *Celebrating Women*, a third 2006 edition of *All Desires Known* and a second 1996 edition of *Women Included* are all still in print, together with newer texts, such as Nicola Slee's *Praying Like a Woman* (2004). Standing within this tradition, there is a sense in which a Christian woman today can "pray like a woman". Sometimes, where there is some openness to this feminist tradition, there are resonances of women praying as women in the labour of liturgy shared in hallowed Christian sacred spaces. But a resolute maleness of the triune God is defended in much liturgical language.

I make a final closing point, which makes sense of my inclusion of Womanspirit ritual in this paper. The current moment is one of reorientation of the denominational traditions of Western Christendom within a world Christianity, resurgent in the global south. Western feminist theology is ambiguously placed within this reorientation. A strong theme in Asian theology is the urgency of a new approach to interfaith dialogue, while, concurrently, Western churches are adapting their habitus to the multireligious contexts of contemporary Western societies. In East and West, there is a growing spirit of dialogue between the religions.

I suggest that those feminist theologians that explore the female divine are worthy dialogue partners with Christian feminist theologians who seek to take further the work begun in feminist liturgies and theological reflection upon these by Morley and others. Interfaith dialogue can deepen our understanding of the triune God of Christianity. The gifts first offered to the churches during the life of the Christian women's movement may be presented anew. A continued dialogue with postChristian feminist theology might illumine our dim understanding of the Christian God, whose image is found in women as in men.

Fig 6-1
Christian women's groups concerned with the position of women in the churches, 1960–1990

Groups founded pre-1960				
St. Joan's International Alliance	SJIA	(1911)	Origins in Catholic Women's Suffrage Society (CWSS)	The *Catholic Citizen*
Society for the Ministry of Women in the Church	SMWC	1930	Founded on disbandment of the League of the Church Militant	*SMWC NL*
Anglican Group for the Ordination of Women	AGOW	1930	Founded on disbandment of the League of the Church Militant: merged with MOW in 1979	?
Pre-CWIRES groups, 1972–1978				
Christian Parity Group	CPG	1972	Founded by Una Kroll	*CPG NL*

Student Christian Movement of Britain and Ireland Women's Project	SCM WP	1976	Developed from the World Student Christian Federation Women's Project founded at the 1975 WSCF conference in Lillehammer	
Roman Catholic Feminists	RCFs	1977	Founded by Jackie Field (Bibb)	*RCF NL*
Oxford Catholic Women's Group and Oxford Christian Feminists		mid 1970s	The Catholic group grew from Catholic renewal activity; it was one of a number of groups that together formed the loose coalition named the Oxford Christian Women's Group. Jo Garcia founded the Oxford CFs	
New Initiatives in 1978				
CWIRES project (Christian Women's Information and Resources)	CWIRES	1978	Founded by members of London Christian Feminists, Oxford CFs and other groups. Blackfriars, Oxford.	*CWIRES NL*
Ecumenical Feminist Trust	EFT	1978	Soon merged with CWIRES	
Movement for the Ordination of Women	MOW	1978/9	Founded after 1978 vote in Church of England Synod against women's ordination	*MOW NL* then *Chrysalis*

The *Christian Feminist Newsletter*	*CF NL*	1978	Founded by Sheila Robinson as ecumenical version of the *RCF NL*	
CWIRES period phase one: 1978–1983				
Variety of new CF groups formed across the country, eg the East London Christian Feminists and the Plymouth Women's Theology Group		1979–1983	Network of groups based on the *CF NL*	*CF NL*
Feminist Theology Project	FTP	1980–1982	Founded by Judith Jenner : Fixed Term	*Our Stories*
Quaker Women's Group	QWG	1978	Founded at Yearly Meeting	*QWG NL*
Unitarian Women's Group	UWG	1981	Founded at General Assembly	*UWG NL*
CWIRES period phase two: 1983–1990				
Women in Theology	WIT	1983/4	Origin in Women's Training for Ordination Project	*WIT Mailing*
Catholic Women's Network	CWN	1984	Founded at conference held at Strawberry Hill, Called to Full Humanity	*CWN NL*

Notes

1 Women were also active in denominational reforms, such as the Methodist initiative towards inclusive language, which led to agreement on a new version of the Methodist hymnbook – a significant venture for a denomination where hymn-singing has pride of place. The campaign aspect of the movement is beyond the scope of this article.

2 *Women Speaking,* 5(3): 10–11; *MOW NL* 10: 11–16.

3 *MOW NL* 1984(Feb): 1–2.

References

Brock, Rita Nakishma. 1988. *Journeys By Heart: a Christology of Erotic Power.* New York. Crossroad.

Campbell, Liz. 1984. 'Women's Spirituality', in *Lighten Our Darkness* (BBC Radio 4 programme, 7 Jan 1984. Reprinted in 'Christian Believing 2' in *ONE* 3.

Fageol, Suzanne. 1989. 'The St Hilda Community', in *ONE* 3.

Furlong, Monica. 1991a. 'Introduction: a "Non-Sexist" Community', pp. 5–15 in *Women Included: a Book of Services and Prayers.* London. SPCK.

Furlong, Monica (ed.). 1988a. *Mirror to the Church.* London. SPCK.

Dowell, Susan and Linda Hurcombe. [1987] 1981. *Dispossessed Daughters of Eve: Faith and Feminism.* 2nd edn. London. SPCK.

Loades, Ann. 1987. *Searching For Lost Coins: Explorations in Christianity and Feminism.* London. SPCK.

Long, Asphodel P. 1994. 'The Goddess Movement in Britain Today', in *Feminist Theology* 5(Jan): 11–39.

Maitland, Sara. 1983. *Map of the New Country: Women and Christianity.* London. Routledge.

McEwan, Dorothea (ed.). 1991. *Women Experiencing Church: a Document of Alienation.* Leominster. Gracewing.

Morley, Janet. 1981. 'In God's Image?' Draft Chapter for *Women and the Emerging Church.* Unpublished.

Morley, Janet. 1984. '"The Faltering Words of Men": Exclusive Language in the Liturgy', pp. 56–70 in *Feminine in the Church* (ed. Monica Furlong). London. SPCK.

Morley, Janet. 1988a. *All Desires Known.* London. WIT and MOW.

Morley, Janet. 1988b. 'I Desire Her with My Whole Heart', in *The Month* 21(2): 541–4. Reprinted as pp. 158–163 in *Feminist Theology: a Reader* (ed. Ann Loades). London. SPCK. 1990.

Morley, Janet. 1988c. 'Liturgy and Danger', pp. 24–38 in *Mirror to the Church* (ed. Monica Furlong). London. SPCK.

Morley, Janet and Hannah Ward (eds). 1986. *Celebrating Women*. London. WIT and MOW.

Movement for the Ordination of Women. 1984. 'A Wilderness Liturgy'. Unpublished.

Oxford Christian Women's Group(s). c.1982. 'The Women's Mass'. Unpublished.

Pratt, Ianthe (ed.). 1987. *Woman-Created Liturgies*. London. CWRC.

Quaker Women's Group. 1986. *Bringing the Invisible into the Light: Some Quaker Feminists Speak of their Experience*. Ashford. Headley.

Rees, Bridget. 1983. 'Wilderness Liturgy'. Unpublished sermon.

Slee, Nicola. 2004. *Praying Like a Woman*. London. SPCK.

Unitarian Working Party on Feminist Theology. 1985. *Growing Together: the Report of the Unitarian Working Party on Feminist Theology to the Unitarian General Assembly*. Unitarian General Assembly.

Ward, Hannah, Wild, Jennifer & Morley, Janet (eds). 1995. *Celebrating Women*. 2nd edn. London. SPCK.

Chapter Seven

Sacred Space and the Singing Voice

Robin Hartwell

A first instinctive response to any consideration of what is meant by 'space' is to consider space as a matter of vision, something located at a specific geographical location, delimited by a boundary, perhaps with a particular volume. Secondly it might be remembered that such a space will have an aural quality, which might indeed be connected to the physicality of the space. Thirdly one might think of a space as a period of time, and there is an element of the metaphorical in saying that one "makes space for something", meaning that time is set aside. The degree to which it is metaphorical indicates, again, the dominance of the eye, firstly over the ear, and then over the perception of the passage of time.

The prevalence of such a hierarchy which can take on the force of something natural and incontestable has been linked to issues of gender, particularly those which link the voice and the aural to the feminine and look to re-evaluate the significance of the aural in the formation of the human. Mikko Keskinen (perhaps rather wryly) has termed this "gynophonocentrism" and indicates some points in the history of the notion (Keskinen, 2000: 16). Keskinen points to the danger that the idea may result in an essentialist notion of womanhood, even though, within the context of the development of certain discourses (feminism and deconstruction) it provides a useful temporary political corrective.[1] Further, the move to "a post-structuralist condition, where categories, including women, are destabilised" identifies a historical development in which the current point of arrival is, nonetheless, informed by the trajectory of the route taken to get there. The conditions pertaining at a particular place and time may still contain, or indeed be enacting this history. A consideration of the singing voice (and in particular a female voice) in a specific sacred space, can uncover some of the issues that inform our understanding. The thoughts in this essay were provoked by the author working with Jane Poulton, one of the Artists in Residence at the two Liverpool cathedrals. I provided music in relation to a piece called *Heartsounds*. The music is for a solo female voice (accompanied by some tuned percussion) and lasts eight minutes. It was written specifically for the acoustic of the Anglican Cathedral Liverpool, and indeed was designed to be sung from high in the central tower from the Corona Gallery. It was performed twenty-seven times over at period of five weeks at 11.00 a.m. That is, it was designed as being gender specific, place specific, duration specific and time specific. The words were drawn from writings by Elsie Price (Jane Poulton's mother, recently deceased) and Lin Holland (the other artist in residence). The work is specifically a memorial to Elsie Price, but more generally a celebration of motherhood. This essay is an exploration of the context into which this was placed by the artist, Jane Poulton, rather than a discussion of the structure and content of the music.

The notion of a sacred space appeals to something other than a natural phenomenon but suggests a demarcation, culturally defined. The cathedral is a specific instance which can be positioned within more general concepts. Such a place (let us adopt the conventional hierarchy as a starting point) might be marked by a boundary, or series of boundaries. That is, there may be a hall (the body of the church) enclosed by walls, itself part of a larger collection of rooms and spaces (the church as a whole), set in the church grounds (perhaps surrounded by another wall). Chapels, churches and cathedrals arrange space according (largely) to function: a congregation facing the altar, aisles for the movement of people to take communion etc. Additionally, the shape of the space may be symbolic: the cross shape of many churches, the altar at the east end etc. From the standpoint of the aural the core space might be the limits of the audible and the building might be seen to provide this. The space can be considered as a container of the sound, setting an aural boundary, and also sustaining the sound by its interior reflections. The shell of the building will exclude the sound of the external world and, ideally, concentrate the sound of this interior world.

Many social spaces can be identified by the extent of the sound boundary, and are partly constructed and controlled by the aural ambience. Instances include a supermarket with shopping music; a train station with departure announcements; a restaurant for conversation with background music; a party with music for dancing and the obliteration of deep conversation; concert halls and theatres with directional acoustics for the projection of sound from the stage. Sizes and types of spaces can be thought of as constructing aural experiences and related as such to social function. A large reception area is felt unsuitable for an intimate conversation (even though this is possible), while a formal lecture in too small a space overpowers and appears absurd. The modes of social interaction interact with both the visual and the aural qualities of the spaces they take place in.

Liturgical Space and Collective Singing

One might consider two types of religious buildings, the parish church and the cathedral. The church and the cathedral often share the same template but the difference in scale changes the function and the social exchange. In the church the speaking voice is usually clearly audible. Words, liturgical or in sermons, are present with a minimum of distortion, allowing the participants to engage in intellectual understanding and reasoning. The more compact space gives the sound directionality, which creates both a position of authority and a position of reception. The singing voice is similarly directional, though within a standard Anglican liturgy the solo singing voice is something of a rarity, and the most common example of this, intonation by a minister, perhaps relates to the ritual in larger spaces. Intonation separates words from mundane speech, emphasising their ritual function. The voice, which in the spoken form retains the implication that they are the beliefs of the speaker of the text, are becoming transformed into an impersonal voice, which may be thought of as "the voice of the Church" or "the voice of the ritual". In this smaller space, where speech is clear, to intone signals a move to a more impersonal mode.

More common than solo singing in churches, particularly in the Protestant tradition, is collective singing. In part this is an extension of collective speaking, which recreates the congregation as a body of like-minded believers. In collectively spoken prayers and texts the individual voice is still a personal voice, but is co-ordinated with others. In song (hymns and the like) the transformation is more radical; a single entity is created from the multiple voices. In collective speech the meaning is scarcely altered if there are slightly different rhythms or intonation patterns. In song such things are set down and are identifiable as deviations from the musical text: a "many in one". The acoustic for song is required to maintain a balance between two aspects. On the one hand the reverberation must be large enough to allow the sounds to blend, to enable this unity to appear, and on the other it must be sufficiently dry to allow the singer to be able to be aware of their own voice, to enable control of their contribution to the totality. In congregational singing the sound is omnipresent (not coming from a single direction) and the congregation stands within their own sound. The totality of the sound is perforce directional as the majority of those present are facing the altar but the act is designed more to create solidarity within the communion, of externalising the interior to demonstrate a shared understanding and experience rather than as directed towards a spiritual focal point.

The cathedral space creates other relationships. It may be that the size of the interior is intended to produce awe by visual means, but the effect of this space for sound is that an unnaturally (even supernaturally) large space is created, especially in a time before electronic amplification. The building removes the sounds of the external world and also permits the transmission of sound (through echoes and reflections) through a large volume of air. While the church may be a large room, the cathedral acoustic, through the technology of architecture, points to another reality. It is notable that similar acoustics in the natural world (such as caves) are sometimes marked by being regarded as being sacred.[2] The size of a cathedral may visually provoke awe, but sound, invisible and intangible, evokes a sense of mystery. In such spaces the speaking voice loses clarity. Intonation patterns become jumbled in the reflections and the flow of sense becomes difficult to follow in the smudged sound. The indistinct individual voice is relegated in importance and the emphasis is thrown upon the ritual aspects. Within the reflections the exact direction from which the sound comes is obscured and the words become disembodied. Perhaps for reasons of pragmatism many parts of the liturgy are intoned. The single tone increases the unconfused projection of the solo voice (which may in actuality also be louder) and also increases the impersonality of the voice. What is presented is closer to text than a speech act. The implication is less that the voice is that of a believer than that the voice gives that which is to be believed. The characteristics of an individual are weakened to strengthen the authority of the institution. In recent times amplification is often used to overcome the difficulties of hearing speech in such large spaces. One might note that something here is seen as a problem (perhaps that the congregation are observers rather than participants and the remoteness of sermonising). The use of such technology reveals a mismatch between the values inherent in the building and a modern conception of its function, notably in that the rationality of the word is valued more highly than the emotional response to the sound. In Liverpool the (mock) Gothic Anglican cathedral, while evoking notions of religion as nostalgia (the reference to the historical legacy of British cathedrals), Protestant Britishness (in distinction to Liverpool's large Irish Catholic heritage) and Empire (Liverpool's wealth founded on the port), also points to an architectural manifestation of an earlier pre-Reformation religious sensibility. The qualities of the sound invite attention to the hard-to-perceive margin, sensed but intangible. The lack of clarity of the acoustic of the Gothic Cathedral becomes a problem to be solved rather than taken as a construct to be contemplated and preserved.[3]

A cathedral may be less satisfactory than a church for participatory singing, even though this is a common feature of the liturgy. In actuality the common occurrence is for the congregation to be near-silent during a service (more sound in the hymns, but little attempt to join in any collective singing of the psalms and none in choral responses and anthems). The larger acoustic now separates the individual and the collective voice. Within such a large space the reflections of the voice are slow to return, repeating and quiet. The individual has a self-awareness of speaking or singing, with little blending of the personal with the collective. Only the brave use the full voice in such a cathedral congregation as the voice feels isolated and exposed, and the more common response is a self-conscious sotto voce. The time delay usually results in rhythmic dislocation rather than unity, and the collective is more conceptual than actual. Participation is then physical (one is there at that time) and conceptual (one mentally traces the course of the service and the words). The choir takes on the role of the voice of the congregation.

The choir is unamplified. There is an interaction between the music and the specific acoustic defined by the space in which the sound is a composite of two natural entities, voice and building. In many cathedrals the choir is split in two on either side of the chancel, and in some parts of the service the two parts will sing in alternation, antiphonally (typically in the psalms). However, the effect within the building is more confused and the simple spatial alternation is transformed by reflections into more complex differentiations, such as volume and timbre (the particular colour of the sound). The ideal of the choir is that it will obliterate the individual voice and replace this with a collective sound, though a good choir will reproduce the musical flexibility of the individual voice. The words which are sung are not given as expressions of belief of the individual singers but are offered as common, social text (with musically encoded emotion). The acoustic aids this in two ways. Firstly, the multiple reflections in such buildings smoothes out the idiosyncrasies of the individual voices. Secondly, it reduces the directionality of the voices and the singing may appear to come more from reflections in the building than as direct sound. The sound heard is a combination of the voices and its transformation through the architecture. The building is, during the singing of the choir, a space sanctified by the impersonal voice. Or, to reverse the hierarchy of ear and eye, the voice creates a space separated out from the mundane.

The differing functions of the space present some conflicts. In the traditional design of the cathedral the High Altar is at the east end, with the choir split on either side of the chancel, fundamentally at ninety degrees to the altar and the congregation. In recent times this appears to have led to the sense that the action of the officiants is remote from the congregation. One solution to this in Liverpool has been to construct an altar where the transept meets the nave, and move the choir so that it faces the congregation down the nave. While it might be expected that this would increase the audibility of the choir (they are closer and facing the congregation rather than at right angles facing each other in the choir stalls) there is an opinion that the sound disperses backwards and upwards rather than forwards and the sound might project better into the building if the singers were in front of a reflecting wall, such as the traditional choir stalls provide. The conflict is partly between the eye, which wishes to see to feel connected to the liturgy, and the ear. It may also be true that if one can see the source of the sound then it is believed that the sound is clearer. The evocation of tradition in the visual domain brings with it undesirable consequences in the aural domain where taste and sensibility have changed and the search for solutions is a symptom of the cultural shifts in time.

In the Anglican cathedral vocal colour has developed a specific aesthetic, traditionally made by male singers. To make a distinction, the opera house requires a high degree of projection and the operatic singing style is thought to aid this by the use of vibrato. Vibrato can also be associated with personal emotion, particularly of the solo singer. The voice is embodied, and the singer is visibly set on the stage. By contrast the traditional English cathedral sound minimises the amount of vibrato, the choir stand at an angle to the congregation and are dressed uniformly. The less complex timbre is better able to blend and helps the choir, "in the wings", to present a disembodied voice. The reduction in vibrato is especially notable in the timbre sought for the top of the texture, in the treble voices and the falsetto male altos.[4] The code appears to look for a "purity" of tone which reduces the emphasis on the individual body and consequently the sexual being. The top line is typified by pre-pubescent youths (who one imagines as being innocent of sexual knowledge) and the falsetto alto perhaps is a version of the defunct castrato: this voice might be better thought of as renouncing male sexuality rather than indicating a physical perversion. The excluded voice is that of the mature female, either as soprano or contralto. An argument might be made for the better blend (or at least characteristic sound) that male voices give, but the practice sits uneasily in relation to the churches' historical wariness of the female and the body. Indeed, the effort required to understand the rather exotic cultural development of the English cathedral sound as "the norm" and for a rather less tutored voice from a female as the "other" throws light on the distance between this aspect of the Anglican tradition and the culture it inhabits.

The Female Voice and Prenatal Consciousness

But let us suppose there were to be a solo singing voice in the cathedral and this voice were that of a mature female. Let us suppose that the source the voice were to be near invisible, say high in a gallery, how then would this voice appear? It would retain the some of the quality of being disembodied, and would speak with the authority of the impersonal. This much would be similar to the impersonal intoning male voice, but the female voice has a particular resonance created through the connection to the Mother and the maternal. There are reasons to believe that the voice of the Mother connects deeply to human formations, as it is known that a child hears in the womb and arrives in the world already prepared for the sound of the language it will acquire.[5] We have also already heard, before our physical birth, the music of our culture, mixed with the heartbeat of our mothers. Before sight dominates, hearing connects us to the outside world and the mother who carries us. This voice, especially the singing female voice, later reconnects us to a consciousness before birth where one is neither fully separated from the mother, nor identical with her. That such biological facts might connect to religious sensibility is indicated in the tone of this passage from Michael Chion:

> In the beginning, in the uterine darkness, was the voice, the Mother's voice. For the child once born, the mother is more an olfactory and vocal continuum than an image. Her voice originates in all points of space, while her form enters and leaves the visual field. We can imagine the voice of the Mother weaving around the child a network of connections it's tempting to call the *umbilical web*. (Chion, 1999: 61)

The voice in the cathedral returns us to the primal source, the voice of the Mother. Keskinen has usefully traced this notion through a broad range of writings, tracking the recent evaluation of the voice back to Derrida. When Derrida examines Rousseau's *Essay on the Origins of Languages*[6] he meets the phrase "its gentle voice" as a description of the voice of compassion. The relationships are teased out:

> Natural pity, which is illustrated archetypically by the relationship between the mother and child, and generally by the relationship between life and death, commands like a gentle voice. In the metaphor of that soft voice the presence of the mother as well as of Nature is at once brought in. That the soft voice must be the mother's as well as Nature's is clear from the fact that it is, as the metaphor of the voice always clearly indicates in Rousseau, a law

> . . . being natural, and absolutely original, it is also inexorable. That maternal voice is a law. Pity is a voice. (Derrida 1976: 173)

This can be connected to Hélène Cixous writing some twenty years later:

> There never stops reverberating something that, having once passed through us, having imperceptibly and deeply touched us, still has the power to affect us – song, the first music of the voice of love, which every woman keeps alive.[7]

The course of the debate concerning the feminine and the voice are taken by Keskinen as moments in a temporal process, suggesting that in Cixous

> the necessary return to logocentric concepts may not only destabilize patriarchal ideology but also criticize early deconstruction, which tended to overlook the problems of gender (Keskinen 2000: 13).

Given the provisional nature of any historical viewpoint stances may be taken for strategic reasons: "a matter of gaining the female voice, not of regaining an origanary fantasm of symmetrical voices" (Keskinen 2000: 13). And "feminists may have had recourse to voice for pragmatic political reasons" (Keskinen 2000: 12). Within such a discourse the consideration of the position of the female voice connects seemingly disparate areas of psychoanalysis, politics, cinema and American literature. A work such as *Heartsounds*, as a celebration of the female voice, similarly falls within the scope of this discourse but as a performed act rather than as writing.

In the performances in the Anglican cathedral of *Heartsounds* the solo singer was all but invisible in the Corona Gallery high in the central tower some 175 feet about the nave.[8] The gallery had the intriguing phenomena that the sound intensified as it came down, flowing from the centre of theonbuilding through the nave and transepts. The voice remained generally directional, but sounded closer to the ear than the eye. This natural amplification brought forward the presence of the voice and distanced the body. The work would retain many characteristics if performed in any location at any time, but this specific location (in place and time) opened the work to other meanings. By the context of the Anglican cathedral the work gained the connection to the spiritual, specifically Christian ideas of life after death and the notion of a requiem. The piece was also strengthened by the connection to the singing voice, indeed all singing voices, in the cathedral which is culturally reserved for particular times and locations. By being performed at a particular time the work drew on the idea of a sung ritual, such as Matins or Compline. In the reverse direction the soprano voice raised the question of the female voice in the Church, especially in the manner that the voice was integrated into the structure of the building through the resonances of the acoustic and in that, for that space of time, it became part of the fabric of the building. One can find some cultural resonances here: the special place reserved for the Virgin Mary and the relation to the Father and the Son as gendered beings, but also the metaphorical association of the Church with the Womb, or the Church as a maternal, nurturing protector, as Mother Church. The solo female voice in the cathedral creates, delimited by the audibility of the sound, a space both personal and shared, connecting our interior life to the external world. It suggests the way this sacred space is related to the universally experienced space of the womb, filled with sound, before the Fall. The solo singing female voice, at the least iconically, stands for our coming into the world. In is use of words it connects us to our human contexts, in the use of tone and rhythm it connects us to the physicality of the world and its human codification and in the mystery of music, especially in the sensuous unfolding of melody in time, it connects to the mystery of all beginnings and ends.

The meanings which are created by the presence of a solo female voice in a sacred space are indeed historically positioned, situated within debates within the Anglican tradition and to discourses on the feminine. The debate on the voice – who speaks, who sings on behalf of whom, who is heard in the singing – reveals something in historical transition, something unfixed. While it may appear from any single viewpoint that such little eddies in the play of forces at such a particular time and place have only a specific localised configuration, the elements in the configuration are those of the mainstream. The specific instance was not just in place and time, but also within cultural and political practice, so that the moment of performance not only contained a demonstration of these forces but also contributed, in a small way, to the process of historical change.

Notes

1 Keskinen, 2000: 12: "The insistence of women's voice can be a token of strategic essentialism." There follows a warning (2000: 13): "However, what is taken up temporarily, for strategic and political reasons only can easily stagnate as a permanent condition, in which the momentary brackets petrify and form a rigid wall." The metaphor of the wall as a marker of a space is very apt in the context of this essay.

2 A more thorough consideration of the topic of this essay can be found in Blesser, B. and Slater, L.-R., 2006.

3 The Anglican Cathedral Liverpool is a Gothic Revival building designed by Sir Giles Gilbert Scott, built between 1904 and 1978. Even in the visual and physical aspects Sharples notes the building is "shaped as much by aesthetics as function" and further that "practical considerations seem less important than emotional response" (2004: 78). The solution to the impracticalities of the sound is a sophisticated system of amplification with time delays: "Wigwam installs the largest Yamaha DME DSP system in Europe. As well as serving its own congregation as a house of worship, the cathedral plays a major part in civic and community life within the city centre. The cathedral caters for a varied selection of local services, ordinations and diocesan occasions as well as many national events. This requires a sound system that is both flexible and easy to use. The building is well over 10000 square metres in size and has a reverberation time of over 8 seconds so the Wigwam installation team had to design a system to provide clear, intelligent audio whilst being flexible in use and not causing any architectural problems. The basis of the control system is using the latest DSP units by Yamaha and Allen & Heath. The cathedral boasts the largest Yamaha DME system in Europe and since the installation many of Yamaha's top designers and product specialists have visited the building to view the installation." <http://www.wigwamacoustics.co.uk/page>.

4 The timbre is something of a construct rather than an inevitable biological outcome. There have been successful attempts for mature females to imitate the male treble and in other traditions boys often sing with more vibrato. There has been considerable interest (even anxiety) over this question as girls have increasingly admitted to cathedral choirs. Since 2004 Liverpool Cathedral choir has the treble line sung by boys (until their voices break) or girls (usually to the age of sixteen). It is current practice that while both boys and girls sing with the men, they do not normally sing together. For a broader discussion see Welch, G.F. and Howard, D.M. 2002.

5 See Hepper, Scott and Shahidullah (1993): 'Newborn and fetal response to maternal voice'. "The intrauterine environment presents a rich array of sensory stimuli to which the fetus responds. The maternal voice is perhaps the most salient of all auditory stimuli . . . Newborns (2–4 days of age) discriminated, as measured by the number of movements exhibited to the presentation of the stimuli, between their mother's voice and a stranger's voice and between normal speech and 'motherese', in both cases the former being preferred. Fetuses, 36 weeks of gestational age, evidenced no ability to discriminate between their mother's and a stranger's voice played to them via a loudspeaker on the abdomen but did discriminate between their mother's voice when played to them by

a loudspeaker on the abdomen and the mother's voice produced by her speaking."

6 See *Essay on the Origin of Languages, which treats of Melody, and Musical Imitation* in Derrida, 1976: 172. A main concern here is the connection between song, speech and writing.

7 Keskinen, 2000: 10, citing Cixous, 1998.

8 A plan of the Anglican Cathedral Liverpool can be found in Sharples, 2004: 75. He discusses the gallery in the interior of the tower that was "repeatedly redesigned by Scott". Sharples does not speculate on the reasons for the redesigns, which might have been to exaggerate perspective to increase the impression of size. Sharples describes the interior not in aural but in visual terms, including the drama of a temporal walking through the space: "a highly theatrical round arched bridge across the E end . . . delay[s] the moment at which the full height of the central space is revealed" (2004: 79).

References

Blesser, B. and Slater, L.-R. 2006. *Spaces Speak, Are You Listening? Experiencing Aural Architecture.* Cambridge. MIT Press

Chion, M. 1999: *The Voice in Cinema*, trans C. Gorbman. New York. Columbia University Press.

Derrida, J. 1976: *Of Grammatology,* trans G.C. Spivak. Baltimore. John Hopkins University Press.

Cixous, H. 1988: 'Sorties: Out and Out: Attacks/Ways Out/Forays', in H. Cixous and C. Clément, *The Newly Born Woman,* trans. B. Wing. Minneapolis. University of Minnesota Press.

Hepper, Scott and Shahidullah. 1993: 'Newborn and fetal response to maternal voice', *Journal of Reproductive and Infant Psychology,* 11(3): 147–153.

Keskinen, M. 2000: 'Her Mistress's Voice: Gynophonocentrism in Feminist Discourses', *Journal of International Women's Studies,* 2(1). Also at <http://www.bridgew.edu/SOAS/jiws/nov00/a_gynoft.htm> – accessed 27 November 2008.

Sharples, J. 2004: *Liverpool: Pevenser Architectural Guides.* London. Yale University Press.

Welch, G.F. and Howard D.M. 2002: 'Gendered Voice in the Cathedral Choir' in *Psychology of Music*, 30: 102–120. Also at <http://www.ioe.ac.uk/schools/ah/welchhoward%20gendered%20voice.pdf> – accessed 27 November 2008.

'Wigwam acoustics': <http://www.wigwamacoustics.co.uk/page.php?cid=29> – accessed 26 October 2008.

CHAPTER EIGHT

CONSECRATING THE BODY: THE SACRED AND THE PROFANE IN PERFORMANCE ART

RINA ARYA

In this paper I will examine the phenomenology of the sacred and its relationship to the profane within the context of performance art. My main argument concerns two main ideas. The sacred and the profane are conceived of as related, but different, categories that need to be kept apart in order to affirm their qualitative differences. However, following on from the radical "death of God theology" in the 1960s, in the theology of Thomas Altizer and William Hamilton, for example, the polarity that exists between these two experiential states gives way to a meeting of opposites. The sacred is experienced in, and through, what is *most* profane. The second notion following on from this is that after the cultural shift in the West signalled by the "death of God", a sense of the sacred can be expressed in a variety of different secular practices. The post-Christian narrative accommodates this shift of thinking and entails a move beyond the institutions of the Church and their concomitant representations, and opens up a space to rethink the narrative but from *outside of* the traditions and structures of its practice. I situate in this space examples of performance art by Marina Abramović and Gina Pane. They inflict pain on their bodies as a way of questioning notions of subjectivity, objectivity and the experience of embodiment. They also implicate the audience[1] in the doing/making so that the tension and anxiety created through the enactments of certain rituals, such as self-harming serve to wound psychologically the participants. And the effects of wounding encourages a sense of fellow-feeling and solidarity which engenders a sense of sacred "community".

The Sacred and the Profane

In *The Elementary Forms of Religious Life* (1912) Durkheim speaks of the sacred and the profane as being two realms or domains that are qualitatively different (Poggi, 2000: 146). The realm of the profane is that of the ordinary and everyday world whilst the sacred is distinct from this by virtue of being "wholly other", "set apart and forbidden" (Durkheim, 1995: xlvi). The reciprocal relationship between these two realms are mediated by the ritual which Rambo describes as operating as a "bridge" between these two realms (Rambo, 1983: 509). In general, rituals are held in place to protect the sacred from the profane (from desecration) and conversely to protect the profane from the sacred, where the effervescent and contagious state of the sacred may disrupt the banalities of the profane. This separation is observed in daily life – a church is where we may feel the force of the holy (a related term to the sacred) whilst an abattoir is indisputably profane. Similarly, all major religions take life to be sacred, whilst the cessation of life as evidenced in a corpse is unquestionably profane. The thresholds between these two realms may vary from context to context, for example a Christian may not regard a football pitch as being worthy of the experience of the sacred in the same way that they would a church, whilst an ardent football fan may regard their team's pitch as hallowed ground. In secular culture the designation of the sacred and the profane is widely contested. However, what still holds is the dualistic nature of the dynamic. In the Christian narrative, the sacred is experienced in what is not profane and vice versa. However, in the post-Christian narrative, and more specifically in the death of God theologies of the 1960s, the relationship between the sacred and the profane is reworked.

In his *Gospel of Christian Atheism* (1966) Altizer denounced the Barthian God. Altizer turns what Barth suggested was an "infinite qualitative difference"[2] that lies between God and humanity upside down and emphasises instead the kenotic process in his theology. In a radical coincidence of opposites God must become "wholly other" to himself. By extension of this the sacred becomes profane and the profane sacred. Hamilton states that in order to acknowledge the "possibility of a new epiphany of the sacred" we have to not simply accept but affirm and to descend into the depths of the profane (Altizer and Hamilton, 1966: 31). This post-Christian thinking is demonstrated in the context of performance art, where the sacred is experienced through the depths of the profane and in the utter desecration of the body.

In her performances Gina Pane emphasises the banality of the everyday rituals, such as eating and watching television. She "takes life in its most daily aspect" (Pluchart, 1984: 131). And it is through these banal rituals that she traverses the trajectory from the profane to the sacred. The activities she performs in her pieces do not elicit everyday and natural reactions from her participants, but those of fear and repulsion in equal measure. How can one reconcile the banal and repetitive rituals with the feeling evoked in the presence of her activities, the *mysterium tremendum et fascinans*?[3] The participants' responses are explained by the modification of the ordinary ritual, which renders it strange. For example in *Food, Televised News, Fire* (1971) Pane does not simply eat mince and watch television but consumes half a pound of rotten mince whilst watching television in an intentionally uncomfortable position. And in *Warm Milk* (1972) she alternated the actions of cutting herself with a razor blade (first her back and then her face) and playing with a tennis ball. In the second and third segments of *Autoportrait(s)* (1973), which are entitled "Contraction" and "Rejection" respectively, she made tiny incisions with a razor blade in her lip ("Contraction") and then proceeded to swallow milk from a bottle, gargle and spit it out again, with increasing ferocity until the cut in her lip reopened and her blood started to mix with the milk, at which point she ended the performance (O'Dell, 1998: 48). This remove from normality, which is conveyed through the juxtapositions of familiar with the uncanny, renders the activities completely dysfunctional. Her work articulates how the "habitual character" of life conceals all the pernicious sides it carries (Pluchart, 1984: 130). Through the various desecrations outlined in these performances Pane's body is endowed with a sense of the grotesque that blurs the boundaries between normality and abnormality, order and disorder, and functionality and dysfunctionality.

In *Rhythm O* (1974) Abramović stood by a table and offered herself passively to spectators, who were given the option to do what they liked with her body and a range of objects. A text on the wall read "There are seventy two objects on the table that can be used to me as desired – I am the object" (Warr and Jones, 2000: 125). The objects varied from those that could be used as weapons, including a gun, a bullet, a saw, and knives, to others which were seemingly innocuous, such as lipstick, a rose and olive oil but which could nonetheless be used to objectify the body further. In *The Body in Pain,* Scarry identifies an important tendency in the phenomenology of pain, which is "the mental habit of *recognizing* pain *in* the weapon (despite the fact that an inanimate object cannot 'have pain' or any other sentient experience)" (Scarry, 1985: 16). This predilection is demonstrated in *Rhythm O*. Even before an object is lifted from the table, it was assumed that Abramović was going to be wounded by the instruments that lay before her. The performance lasted for six hours and by the end all her clothes had been sliced off her body with razor blades, she had been cut, decorated, crowned with thorns, and had had the loaded gun against her head (Warr and Jones, 2000: 125). Goldberg explains how "this final act caused a fight between her tormentors, bringing the proceeding to an unnerving halt" (Goldberg, 1988: 165). At the outset Abramović transformed herself from being the agent and author of her performance into completely submitting to the participants. Furthermore by renouncing her subjectivity, Abramović had turned herself into a thing, and the array of objects available invited the participants to explore her as a plaything. If we construe the written invitation as a contractual obligation then it is plausible that Abramović constructed her work to function as what Linderman calls a "limit-text", which queries boundaries that are repressed in other texts (O'Dell, 1998: 3). The boundaries that are queried here are that of subjectivity-objectivity and the sacred-profane.

In the series of ritual actions, the participants transgress the physical boundaries of Abramović's body. Likewise, she transgresses the psychological boundary separating subjectivity from objectivity. In an interview with McEvilley she confesses that, "I realized that the subject of my work should be the *limits* of the body. I would use performance to push my mental and physical limits beyond consciousness" (McEvilley, 2000:15). Ironically, by desecrating these boundaries Abramović and the audience can be seen to be consecrating the body. Transgression involves the temporary suspension of the limit but is also, paradoxically, a reinforcement of the limit. Therefore, the limit or boundary is remade or recreated through the action of overstepping. In the performance itself, the acts of transgression serve to demarcate the boundaries. Evidence for this is provided by the prevention of the potentially fatal gunshot to the head. In other words, transgression does not allay the fear and potency of the taboo but actually reinforces it.

Abramović's body is not regarded as banal and everyday but is "set apart" by its being openly violated. By eliminating the social mores and proprieties that are tacitly observed with due regard to the treatment of an "other", Abramović was rendering the object-body extraordinary. Parallels can be drawn with the kenosis of Christ, who divested or laid aside certain divine attributes, such as omniscience, when he took on human form in the Incarnation. However, Christ did not simply take the form of any man but that of the lowliest status of man and "emptied himself, taking the form of a servant" (Philippians 2:6–11).[4] Metaphorically, Abramović can be viewed as abdicating her role as the author of her performance and being transformed into an abject body. In anthropological terms she could be regarded as the sacrificial victim who purges the wrongs of the community. And similarly, an analogy can be constructed with the Christ figure who was a scapegoat for the sins of humanity.

The Wounded Community

> If human beings had kept their own integrity and hadn't sinned, God on one hand and human beings on the other would have persevered in their respective isolation. A night of death wherein Creator and creatures bled together and lacerated each other and on all sides, were [sic] challenged at the extreme limits of shame: that is what was required for their communion (Bataille 2000: 18).

In the above excerpt from *On Nietzsche* (1945), Bataille discusses the significance that wounding has in Christianity and states how communion was achieved through the wound that was created between God and humankind, as instantiated in the Crucifixion. He is emphatic that this sense of community and intimacy "cannot proceed from one full and intact individual to another. It required individuals whose separate existence in themselves is *risked*, placed at the limit of death and nothingness" (Bataille, 2000: 19). In this state one's sense of self is suspended; is in a state of *ek-stasis* and within the context of the Christian tradition, this refers to Christ on the Cross – who, (using Nietzsche's phrase of 1885-6) is "the most sublime of all symbols" (Bataille, 2000: 17). Scarry emphasises the prevalence of wounding in the Judaeo-Christian tradition, where "God's invisible presence is asserted, made visible, in the perceivable alterations He brings about in the human body: in . . . the pains of childbirth, in a plague that descends on a house", to name but a few examples. She adds

> Man can only be created once, but once created, he can be endlessly modified; wounding re-enacts the creation because it re-enacts the power of alteration that has its first profound occurrence in creation. (Scarry, 1985: 183).

I want to extend that idea here to suggest that the selected works of Abramović and Pane conform to a similar model, whereby the wounded body (of the artist) is generative and creates the feeling of community.

In the Christian tradition the body is fragmented in the Crucifixion and then the fragments are resolved in the Resurrection. In the Christian narrative the sacred is experienced in the salving, or making whole of the fragments. In this post-Christian narrative, we remain only with the fragments but it is precisely this condition of fragmentation and wounding that binds the participants together. The body operates as a channel, which shatters the boundaries separating the self from the other, and the identity of the participants is consolidated into a collective whole, into a sacred community. The participants are bound together through the Dionysian excess that results from the performances. In *Rhythm O* the participants experience the carnivalesque as they subject Abramović to a range of activities. In *Warm Milk* and "Contraction" and "Rejection" (in *Autoportrait(s)*) participants are moved to states of emotional and psychological turmoil due to the violation that Pane inflicts on herself. The physical violence is transferred into psychological violence, which causes disarray in the collective body of the participants. The transition and transformation of identity from individualism to the suspension of individualism in lieu of a collective identity can be viewed from the perspective of Gluckman's theories of ritual, which discusses how ritual is a mechanism for constantly recreating and not simply reaffirming the unity of the group (Bell, 1997: 39). Another switch that occurs is the transition from objectivity to subjectivity. In a subversive turn, the artist assumes a submissive role and the participant becomes the author of making. In *Rhythm O* Abramović presents a situation in which the viewer "implicates him/herself in the potentially aggressive act of unveiling and marring her passive body".[5] In *Warm Milk* Pane cuts her face open with a razor blade and, although the participants are in many respects distanced in comparison with the participants in *Rhythm O*, they still feel complicit in the crime of self-harm. This is exacerbated by the deflection of the video camera from Pane to the participants. This enables them to share visually their horror of preceding actions. In both these situations the participants are bound together through their collective actions or sentiments. They are bound by their experience of the sacred horror of the desecration of the body into the status of a thing – Pane's act of cutting her face is metaphoric of her slicing her individuality.

The formation of communal bonds and the collective identity generated in these performances reconfigures the expectations of the spectators as well as the roles that are bestowed upon the audience. At the beginning of the paper I purposely modified "audience" into "participants" to convey the interaction and intersubjectivity that is engendered through the performance itself. The reciprocal relation that exists between "artist" and "participant" perpetuates this sense of community and is created strategically through contractual exchange. In *Rhythm O* Abramović posts a written invitation to the participants explaining what they are required to do. In *Warm Milk* Pane uses the video camera to reflect the shift of attention from her to the participants. The hierarchical divide, separating artist from participant is eliminated in a Brechtian turn to impose an uncomfortable and self-conscious state on the audience in an attempt to reduce the gap between the two (Goldberg, 1988: 162).

In the performances the body operates as the meeting point between opposites, between self and the other, and life and death. And the violence has anthropological and sociological ramifications. The sacrifice of the bodily integrity purges the community of violence thus restoring harmony and equilibrium. In this meeting of opposites our assumptions as viewers and our conditioned responses to the body are quashed. The Cartesian subject of modernism is dislocated as is the gender-oriented axis of perception. By testing the boundaries of the body, whether through the physical actions that we inflict on the artist's bodies or by our psychological perceptions of what is happening, we experience knowledge *through* the senses. In his formulation of the "Theatre of Cruelty", Artaud states that the masses "think with their senses first and foremost" and that an experience of mass theatre should explore "the limits of our nervous sensibility" (Artaud, 2000: 216). Through the exploration of nerve-exposed sensations the body is undone, is taken apart, which is simultaneously a form of embodying. We learn what it feels like to be embodied. The objects are also transformed through action. In *Rhythm O*, Stooss states that during the performance the objects were supposedly transformed into art objects in their own right (Abramović, 1998: 14). In Pane's performances the seemingly innocuous objects become imbued with sinister associations through shifts of context. In *Warm Milk* the bouncing of a tennis ball is the counterpart action to Pane's slicing her face and in *Food, Televised News, Fire*, the action of watching television and eating are transmogrified.

The Real Presence of the Body

In the performances of Abramović and Pane the participants gain through a sense of loss. They gain an understanding of embodiment by experiencing a sense of the disintegration of language that concurs with the vertiginous experiences and the accompanying loss of a sense of self. This tendency mirrors the practice of the mystics, who through their resolute denial of the drives of the body ironically place it at the forefront of their quest. Vergine states that "mysticism is first of all a physical experience: a source of fluids, of bloods, of humors, of various waters that flow, coagulate, and again grow liquid" (Vergine, 2000: 291). The mystics regarded the moment of the loss of self as a moment of self-discovery and this simultaneous shift can be seen within the context of performance art. It is plausible that the artists employed their bodies or the bodies of others and inflicted extreme experiences on these bodies in order to create an alteration of perception. If that is the case then the performances are not about the body at all but rather are about the mind. They probe us to interrogate our preconditioned responses to the dualisms that we set up between subject and object, pain and pleasure, and viewing and participation. Whether their intentions are to provoke intellectual questions is not the central issue, however. Rather, what seems undeniable is their response to a technological society where corporeality has become sanitised and marginalised. Sobchack makes an incisive distinction between the *viewing of* the body and the *feeling in* the body (my italics). Commenting on the effects of globalisation and mass media Sobchack states that:

> To say we've lost touch with our bodies is not to say we've lost sight of them. Indeed, there seems to be an inverse ratio between seeing our bodies and feeling them: the more aware we are of ourselves as the "cultural artifacts", "symbolic fragments" and "made things" that are images, the less we seem to sense the intentional complexity and richness of the corporeal existence that substantiates them (Warr and Jones, 2000: 41).

In the performances we are not permitted to assume a detached stance and simply view the bodies, but we experience them in their sentient states and even initiate these states of wounding. We see behind the "cultural artifacts" and "symbolic fragments", behind the body as representation and experience the re-presentation of the body. In theological terms we see behind the symbol to the "real presence" of the sacrament. This is experienced in the intoxicated states that the performances induce in the participants. In her video installation, *Spirit House* (1997), which bears structural similarities to the Passion, Abramović presents five separate video sequences, called "stations", one of which involves her flagellating herself with a whip. Its pertinence is exacerbated by the first presentation of the installation at Caldas da Rainha, Portugal, in 1997 in a former communal slaughterhouse (Abramović, 1998: 13). By placing what I interpret as Abramović's "Stations of the Cross" in a slaughterhouse she is paralleling the experience of the Crucifixion with the slaughtering of an animal thereby enhancing the brutality of the suffering of Christ. This questions the legitimacy of the killing in the first place – how can such a treatment be sanctioned? The only justification lies in the fulfilment of the Christian narrative, where eternal life follows death and the sacrifice of the Son confirms God's love for humankind. If we remove this teleology then we are left with the bloody murder on the Cross. Moore conveys the reprehensibility of the act in a very direct and immediate manner:

> My own father too was a butcher, and a lover of lamb with mint sauce. As

> a child, the inner geographical boundaries of my world extended from the massive granite bulk of the Redemptorist church squatting at one end of our street to the butcher's shop guarding the other end. Redemption, expiation, sacrifice, slaughter . . There was no city abattoir in Limerick in those days; each butcher did his own slaughtering. I recall the hooks, the knives, the cleavers; the terror in the eyes of the victim; my own fear that was afraid to show; the crude stun-gun slick with grease; the stunned victim collapsing to its knees; the slitting of the throat, the filling of the basins with blood; the skinning and evisceration of the carcass; the wooden barrels overflowing with entrails; the crimson floor littered with hooves.
>
> I also recall a Good Friday sermon by a Redemptorist preacher that recounted at remarkable length the atrocious agony felt by our sensitive Saviour as the spikes were driven through his wrists and feet. Crucifixion, crucifixiation, crucasphyxiation . . . Strange to say, it was this sombre recital, and not the other spectacle, that finally caused me to faint. Helped outside by my father, I vomited gratefully on the steps of the church (Moore, 1996: 4).

Moore's parallel conveys the similarities between the activities that are carried out in the butcher's shop and the action of the Crucifixion of Christ. However the former domain is more defensible than the signification of events being carried out in church because it does not misconstrue its practice. However, in church the "atrocious agony felt by our sensitive Saviour" is used as a pretext for belief in the Christian narrative. The sermon recounts a brutality that is teleological. And it is this chain of events that causes a turbulence of sensation for Moore. Ironically, he moves from the symbolic event to the physical reality – from "crucifixion" to "crucifixiation" to "crucasphyxiation" to delegitimize the signification. The associative wordplay parodies the justification and conveys the accumulated sense of nausea that finally causes Moore to vomit on the steps of the church. In this post-Christian tradition there is no atonement, and we are punished for our ability to anaesthetise the violence at the heart of the Cross. In the vein of the artist Francis Bacon, there is no beyond and so the proximity of our fate to the animals in the butcher's shop cannot be overemphasised. In an interview with Sylvester, Bacon claims, "if I go into a butcher's shop I always think it's surprising that I wasn't there instead of the animal", bringing him to his overwhelming conclusion that "we are meat, we are potential carcasses" (Sylvester, 1987: 46).

Conclusion

In these examples of performance practices we see the effects of the sacred, which shatter individual identity whilst also reinforcing collective identity. The sacred is experienced in and through the transgression and violation of bodily (and other) boundaries. As the sacred is not a substantive, it cannot be described as being inherently violent. However, an expression of the sacred, which is experienced in the transgression of boundaries, results in fragmentation and disarray. The key idea in the crossing of boundaries is the awareness, and simultaneous, fear of danger and death. Abramović and Pane place themselves in situations of varying degrees of risk and (profane) experiences that degrade and desecrate the sacrality of the body. The performance artist Hermann Nitsch declares how the passage to the sacred is reached through the profane: "histrionic means will be harnessed to gain access to the profoundest and holiest symbols through blasphemy and desecration. Blasphemous provocation is tantamount to worship" (Green, 1999: 132). And it is the collective recognition of this that binds the participants together and underscores the sacrality of the body.

The paradox is that although these works do not support the Christian narrative, and the fragmented body of the performer is not salved or made whole as Christ's was in the Resurrection, the collectivity of the group identity is established precisely because of the fragmentation. In Christianity the ritual, such as the Eucharist, is only made possible and credible by the fragmentation of the body. The ritual is a simultaneous acknowledgement of fracture, which is also a celebration of reconstituted wholeness. In the examples of performance practice, the body of the performer enacts the sacrament by binding the participants into a collective whole.

In the space opened up by the "death of God" the sacred is not experienced in transcendence but in the resolute immanence and brute materialism of the body. I suggest that the works demonstrate an a-theology of incarnation. The term "a-theology", coined by Mark C. Taylor, was employed to accommodate such practices, which cannot be described as theological *per se* but which rethink the margins of theological thinking. In the interstitial space between theism and atheism, "we find the possibility of refiguring the polarities and oppositions that structures traditional religious thought" (Taylor, 1992: 4). I am not purporting that the performances discussed are to be viewed solely within the realm of theology but I think it is necessary to take heed of their religious aspects. They enact, perform and instantiate the intertwining of self and other (Jones, 1998: 38) and we experience what it feels like to be embodied, which in Christian terms is deeply incarnational.

They articulate a counter-narrative to the bodies of the powerless created through the institutionalised power of the Church and invite the possibility of narratives of spiritual empowerment.[6] In a reverse of the Augustinian model in *Confessions* (397) where continence is the route to the spiritual life, here we have a move towards the wounded body as the practice of religiosity. The body becomes the holy text and the performance of the text can be described as "an aesthetic liturgy" (Vergine, 2000: 117).

Notes

1 Who will henceforth be referred to as participants.
2 This phrase was used in reference to the *Epistle to the Romans*, which Barth suggested was Kierkegaard's "infinite qualitative difference" between God and humanity. McEnhill and Newlands, 2004: 60.
3 Which is a phrase used by the theologian Rudolf Otto to designate the feeling on encountering the holy and which is to de distinguished from the "profane, non-religious mood of everyday experience". Otto, 1958: 19, 12.
4 See also Isaiah 53:4–12, the Suffering Servant, as another example of kenosis.
5 This description is used with reference to the role of Yoko Ono in *Cut Piece* (see Warr and Jones, 2000: 74) but I have purposely widened its application here.
6 The examples can also be viewed from the perspective of liberation theology.

References

Abramović, M. and Abramović, V. 1998. *Marina Abramović: artist body: performances 1969–1998*. Milano. Charta.

Altizer, T.J.J. and Hamilton, W. 1966. *Radical Theology and the Death of God.* Indianapolis. Bobbs-Merill.

Artaud, A. 1933. 'Theatre and Cruelty', trans. V. Corti, in T. Warr and A. Jones (eds) 2000, *The Artists' Body*. London. Phaidon Press, p. 216.

Bataille, G. 2000 [1945]. *On Nietzsche*, trans. B. Boone. London. Athlone Press.

Bell, C. 1997. *Ritual: Perspectives and Dimensions*. New York. Oxford University Press.

Bell, C. 1998. 'Performance', in M. C. Taylor (ed.), *Critical Terms for Religious Studies*. Chicago and London. University of Chicago Press, pp. 205–224.

Burden, C. 1975. 'Through the Night Softly', in G. Battcock and R. Nickas (eds) 1984, *The Art of Performance: A Critical Anthology*. New York. E. P. Dutton, pp. 222–239.

Colman, A. M. (ed.). 2003. *A Dictionary of Psychology*. New York. Oxford University Press.

Derrida, J. and Vattimo, G. (eds.). 1998. *Religion*. Cambridge. Polity Press.

Durkheim, E. 1995 [1912]. *The Elementary Forms of Religious Life*, trans. K. Fields. New York. Free Press.

Gorsen, P. 1979. 'The Return of Existentialism', in G. Battcock and R. Nickas (eds) 1984, *The Art of Performance: A Critical Anthology*. New York. E.P. Dutton, pp. 135–141.

Goldberg, R. 1988. *Performance Art: From Futurism to the Present Day*. London. Thames and Hudson.

Green, M. (ed). 1999. *Brus, Muel, Nitsch, Schwarzkogler: Writings of the Vienna Actionists*, trans. M. Green. London. Atlas Press.

Howell, A. 2000. *The Analysis of Performance Art: A guide to its theory and practice*. Amsterdam. Harwood Academic Publishers.

Jones, A. 1998. *Body Art/Performing the Subject*. Minneapolis. University of Minnesota Press.

LaFleur, W. R. 1998. 'Body', in M. C. Taylor (ed.), *Critical Terms for Religious Studies*. Chicago and London. University of Chicago Press, pp. 36–54.

McEnhill and Newlands, G. 2004. *Fifty Christian Thinkers*. Abingdon. Routledge.

McEvilley, T. 1983. 'Art in the Dark', in T. Warr and A. Jones (eds) 2000, *The Artist's Body*. London. Phaidon Press, pp. 222–227.

Miles, M. R. 1993. 'Desire and Delight: A New Reading of Augustine's *Confessions*', in M.A. Tilley and S.A. Ross (eds) 1993, *Broken and Whole: Essays on Religion and the Body*. Lanham, Maryland. University Press of America, pp. 3–16.

Montano, L.M. (ed.). 2000. *Performance Artists Talking in the Eighties*. Berkeley and Los Angeles. University of California Press.

Moore, S.D. 1994. *Post Structuralism and the New Testament. Derrida and Foucault at the Foot of the Cross*. Minneapolis. Augsburg Fortress Press.

Moore, S.D. 1996. *God's Gym*. New York. Routledge.

O'Dell, K. 1998. *Contract with the Skin: Masochism, Performance Art and the 1970s*. Minneapolis. University of Minnesota Press.

Otto, R. 1958. *The Idea of the Holy. An Inquiry into the non-rational factor in the idea of the divine and its relation to the rational*, trans. J.W. Harvey. Oxford. Oxford University Press.

Paglia, C. 2001. *Sexual Personae: Art and Decadence from Nerfertiti to Emily Dickinson*. New Haven and London. Yale University Press.

Pluchart, F. 1978. 'Risk as the Practice of Thought', in G. Battcock and Robert Nickas (eds) 1984, *The Art of Performance: A Critical Anthology*. New York. E.P. Dutton, pp. 125–134.

Poggi, G. 2000. *Durkheim*. Oxford and New York. Oxford University Press.

Raitt, J. 1993. 'Christianity, Inc.', in M.A. Tilley and S.A. Ross (eds) 1993, *Broken and Whole: Essays on Religion and the Body*. Lanham, Maryland. University Press of America.

Rambo, L.R. 1983. 'Ritual', in A. Richardson and J. Bowden (eds) 1983. *A New Dictionary of Christian Theology*. London. SCM Press., pp. 509–510.

Scarry, E. 1985. *The Body in Pain*. New York. Oxford University Press.

Shaw, P. 2006. *The Sublime*. Abingdon. Routledge.

Stiles, K. 2000. 'Quicksilver and Revelations' in L.M. Montano (ed.) 2000, *Performance Artists Talking in the Eighties*. Berkeley and Los Angeles. University of California Press, pp. 473–492.

Sylvester, D. 1987. *Interviews with Francis Bacon*. London. Thames and Hudson.

Taylor, M.C. 1992. *Disfiguring. Art, Architecture, Religion*. Chicago. University of Chicago Press.

Vergine, L. 2000. *Body Art and Performance*, trans. H. Martin. Milan. Skira.

Warr, T. and Jones, A. (eds) 2000. *The Artist's Body*. London. Phaidon Press.

CHAPTER NINE

FROM PILGRIMAGE TO TOURISM: A COMPARATIVE ANALYSIS OF KAVADI FESTIVALS IN TAMIL DIASPORAS

RON GEAVES

As pointed out by Picard and Robinson (2006: 1), festivals, both as observer and participatory activity, have become part of the contemporary tourist experience. Especially "out of the ordinary" events have become points of tourist consumption by "outsider" audiences attracted by the exotic. In particular sacred festivals of unfamiliar religions can in certain circumstances attract the attention of such consumers of culture. Amongst the many social, political, demographic and economic realities that can lead to the reinvention or reinvigoration of such festivals, migration is significant. It adapts traditional festivals in new forms and brings them under the gaze of "outsiders" who would otherwise have required to travel long distances and in possibly difficult circumstances. De Bres and Davis (2001: 326–37) have pointed out that such relocation of festivals in part relates to such communities reasserting their identities after experiencing cultural dislocation. However, the shift in geographical and cultural terrain brings with it problems of visibility; the degree to which a migrant community is prepared to reveal such focused displays of identity to outsiders, especially where the festival acts as a strong location of sacrality (Long, Robinson and Picard, 2004: 1–14). Yet when festivals are held outside in a new location of social and cultural life they cannot avoid becoming part of a new dynamic in which they begin to enter the realm of tourism.

Picard and Robinson (2006: 3) bring to our attention that both festivals and tourism are "liminal and playful practices" and as such it is possible that the borders between "outsider" (tourist) and "insider" (participant) can become blurred when the tourist decides that he/she is not content simply to observe but desires to join in the fun. This may cause a number of problems for "religious" insiders around borders that are demarcated as sacred. In addition, where identity is still vulnerable, such participation may not be welcome. Throughout history festivals have been drawn upon to reinforce or celebrate local, regional, and national identities whereby social continuity and cultural homogeneity has been preserved through dominant myths. However, little consideration has been taken of religion in the literature of tourism and festivals. Yet religious beliefs and practices can be significant in the process whereby festivals shift from pilgrimage to tourism.

This chapter explores the transformations which take place in a range of Tamil diasporas focusing on the ubiquitous *kavadi* celebrations, usually appearing in Tai Pusam festivals. The author will argue that explanations of shifts that occur between two apparent polar opposites of tourism and pilgrimage with regard to *kavadi* display need to take account of the religious domain. It will examine several case studies including Britain, Sri Lanka, Scandinavia, Mauritius and South East Asia. These case studies reflect different periods of Tamil migration which include the original migration of Tamils to Sri Lanka over a thousand years ago, the nineteenth century shift of populations as a result of British recruitment of indentured labour known as "plantation Tamils", and finally the twentieth century migrations resulting from the economic demands of post-World War II Britain and increasingly since the 1980s the Tamil exodus from Sri Lanka as a result of civil war.

The South Indian festival of Tai Pusam is observed on the day presided over by the Nakshatra known as Pushya, in the Tamil month of Tai which corresponds with the months of January and February.[1] The day generally falls on the full moon day of the month. The Planet Brihaspati or Guru (Jupiter) is said to be the presiding deity of Pushya and consequently worship offered to the Nakshatra is considered to have special merit, since Brihaspati symbolises wisdom and Hindus consider him to be the preceptor of the gods and one of the most important of the nine planets. Pilgrimage that included bathing in a sacred river is considered to be very meritorious on this day, and people, both men and women, young and old, flock to the nearest one for the purpose. However, in Tamil cultures the festival has become associated with the god Murugan, also known as Subramaniam, the youngest son of Shiva and Parvati, and foremost of the Tamil deities. It celebrates both his birthday and the occasion when Parvati gave Murgan a *vel* (lance) so he could vanquish the evil demon Soorapadman.

Any account of the *kavadi* rituals must begin with Palani in Tamil Nadu. It is here that we find the legendary origins of the rituals and the mortification of the body associated with *kavadi* itself. *Kavadi* is performed as part of a vow made to the deity to avoid calamity or to achieve success. The devotee promises to perform various traditional acts of mortification if the petitionary prayer is fulfilled. The Palani shrine and hill temple complex is situated sixty-four kilometres from Dindugal on the Chennai Dhanuskodi railway at Tiruvavinankudi. It is associated with a number of popular myths of Murugan, but most famously is considered to be the place where Murugan humiliated Brahmâ for possessing too much ego. This victory of a Tamil folk-deity over one of the major Vedic god may well represent symbolically the triumph of the laudik (popular) or non-Âgamic over the Sanskritic and Âgamic (textual or scriptural) traditions and this assertion becomes of central importance to the arguments presented in this article.

The other story concerns the origin of the *kavadi* (a form of yoke) ritual associated with the shrine. It is said that Shiva presented two hills to the sage Agastya who wished to transport them to the South where he lived but could not find a way and left them by the wayside. His demon disciple Idumbara carried the two hills on his shoulders in the form of a *kavadi.* On arrival at Palani he placed the hills on the ground but could not lift them again. He climbed up a hill and saw a youth clad only in a loincloth and carrying a stick who claimed that the hills belonged to him. Idumbara did not accept the authority of the child and fought with him. The demon was killed. The wife of the demon recognized the child as Murugan and requested that her husband be brought back to life. The boon was granted by the god and Idumbara became his devotee and guardian of the temple gate. He requested Murugan to bless any person who came to the temple carrying a *kavadi.*

The legend states that from that day forth carrying the *kavadi* became associated with the worship of Murugan, and to carry one to Palani is a guarantee of receiving the god's blessings. The Palini shrine is open to all castes but Shakti Gupta claims that the carrying of the *kavadi* is most often performed by Pallis and Kallans (Shakti, 1988: 49). This caste dimension will also become significant when the festival is celebrated in diaspora communities.

Palini is linked to ascetics and yogis, and indeed the icon enshrined at the temple is the child ascetic, the image of his cosmic father Shiva, who becomes the spiritual goal of world-renouncers or bhaktas. It is by their activities that new birth is given annually to the god (Clothey, 2005: 86). Traditionally the temple is linked to the famous story of the competition between Skanda (Murugan) and his more well-known brother, Ganesh. The temple is said to stand upon the hill where the god proceeded in his anger, swearing never to marry after being defeated by Ganesh in a race around the world. As a result of this vow he went on to become an ascetic. But part of the resurgence of Murugan temples in Tamil Nadu in the twentieth century has been the opening up of temples to harijans and scheduled castes and the improvement of transport systems that allow non-Brahmin and lower class worshippers access to important pilgrimage centres (Clothey, 2005: 115). The popularity of Palani to such groups ensures the viability of vernacular non-Agamic religion. Palini is also associated with healing and the legends of the shrine are linked to the activities of Shaivite alchemists who are said to have roamed the hills and to have constructed the image of the deity from a combination of rare metals, medicines and immortalizing substances. The reputation for healing is testified by the number of incurably ill and lamed who throng the steps that lead up from the town to the summit of the mountain.

To experience Palani at one of the great occasions of *pada yatra*, as I did at Vaikâci Vicâkam held in May-June, is not only colourful but provokes a sense of danger not usually associated with tourism. Indeed it is relatively safe to say that tourism did not feature in the awareness of the pilgrims other than through the interlinked motivations of *communitas* and holy day. In traditional cultures religious pilgrimage has always contained a dimension of leaving everyday life behind but in this case I was a stranger with a camera attempting to locate myself and understand the activities of a large number of people most of whom appeared to be in trance-like or frenzied states. In addition, I did not have the security of an official invitation from the administration or a gatekeeper guide as I have had when visiting the hilltop temple of Baba Balaknath in Himachal Pradesh, in many ways a similar location. I soon had to stop taking photographs as it became apparent that it caused offense and created a very hostile environment.

Most of the pilgrims were rural people and Clothey states that they mainly come from the districts of Madurai, Coimbatore, Salem and Eastern Kerala (Clothey, 2005: 120). A number of ritual activities were observed in addition to the carrying of *kavadi*. Many of the pilgrims shaved their heads and offered their hair to the god, dressed in the saffron garb of ascetics and pierced their cheeks with miniature versions of the Vel. Clothey suggests that the temporary guise of ascetic or ascetic behaviour is an attempt to identify with the form of the God. However, my own understanding is that it is a temporary identification with the life of the ascetic associated historically with the temple and would suggest that the predominance of the ascetic alchemists in the area had determined both the form of the deity and the sanctity of the place.

Many of the pilgrims arrive in groups either dressed as ascetics or hill tribesmen. They are accompanied by musicians and dance in circles, stopping regularly on the steps as they climb. They carry with them coconuts, grains, money offerings held in mud pots (*hundial*), gold, silver, cut hair and *kavadis* which hold cockerels, goats, and milk. Many carry water pots on their heads or in *kavadi* brought from a local river, a ritual known as *theerthakkavadi*. They walk apparently twenty-five to thirty-five kilometres a day and on the day of arrival spend the night at the foot of the hill and in the morning bathe in the local river. The pilgrim groups sing traditional Tamil folk songs or poems from Tamil devotional literature. The continuous chants are "*Haro-Hara*" and "*Vetrivel Muruganukku Arohara*". The parties of devotees are generally led by a guide who appears to be intoxicated or possessed as the god is approached. Indeed the music and dancing appear to function more as aids to trance than as entertainment.

Often one person carries a *kattiyam* or long wooden staff, another a banner decorated with the peacock and the cockerel on each side of a Vel, and another carries a highly decorated umbrella, but one unusual feature is the presence of masked figures who sometimes dress in bizarre attire who whirl and dance around the pilgrims. These are known as *kamalis* and their function is to entertain the pilgrims and prevent the journey becoming tedious. It is here that we find a concession to the festival's need to entertain. In addition to saffron dress many dress in a verdant green, an apparent symbol of fertility, but also a reminder of Murugan's origins in nature rites.

Kannan (2000: 4) carried out a study in which he investigated the motives of the pilgrims. Although he concluded that the prize of increased bhakti, realization of transitory nature of the world and the enhancement of the feeling that divine power was nearby and intervened in human affairs were significant features of the Palani pilgrimage, his study of one hundred pilgrims revealed far more pragmatic goals.[2] Forty pilgrims desired wealth or agricultural success, eleven wanted to win the lottery, nine wanted to better their health, five wanted to secure employment or promotion and a further five to improve their businesses, three wanted to pay off debts, three to pass examinations, two to win court cases. However, the traditional apotropaic motives of relief from witchcraft; to resolve marriage settlements; and to secure the birth of children, were represented by only five people. One wanted to go abroad. Spiritual advancement or peace of mind were desired by six.

The small study is revealing. Not surprisingly the vast majority demonstrated the traditional needs of village people for success in harvesting their crops. The small number who wanted to achieve spiritual goals indicates the prevalence of pragmatic or kismetic motivations. However, it is revealing to see the changing nature of the pragmatic dimension as it begins to be adapted to the needs of the urban lower middle classes and less to the ancient requirements of fertility and protection from evil spirits. The demons still remain to be killed by the divine presence but the social context of the twentieth-century environment modifies the forms in which the demons appear to the pilgrims and transform their expectations of the gods."

Urban and Rural Shaivism

I have used the terms "Agamic" and "Non-Agamic" and it is now time to elaborate on their significance. Donald Taylor argues that there are two types of Shaivism in Sri Lanka. One belongs to the world of the village where small shrines and temples belong to kin groups and whose priests are not Brahmans. He states that spirit possession is typical of such village shrines and their religious functionaries are skilled in entering trance states. Accompanying such possession by the deity or spirit are various acts of mortification mainly involving body piercing. Many of the temples are dedicated to goddesses who are considered to be capricious and need of propitiation (Taylor, 1994: 195). It is this bundle of religious practices and beliefs that are defined as "Non-Agamic". The other form of Shaivism, Taylor argues, is urban and takes place in large temples housing either Shiva or Murugan, typically with Vellalar (a high caste) patrons and officiated at by Brahman priests trained in the Agamic tradition of ritual Shaiva Siddhanta. The rituals are performed in Sanskrit with other activities such as communal singing in Tamil. The temple activities revolve around an annual calendar of festivals (*turuvala*) in which all castes take part, including in recent years untouchable groups. The Brahmans are qualified through training under a traditional guru and have received initiation that allows them to perform rituals and rites of passage on behalf of others. Unlike the rural forms of Shaivism, there is a literary tradition (*Vedas, Agamas* and the poetry of the mediaeval Shaivite *bhaktas*) but most significantly there is a deep suspicion and skepticism towards spirit possession and mortification is viewed as backward and does not take place (Taylor, 1994: 194).

Taylor concludes that rural or "Non-Agamic" Shaivism has not entered Britain in the Sri Lankan communities. Although he acknowledges that Mauritian Tamils performed *kavadi* at Tai Pucam and Chittrai from the 1980s in the North London Murugan temple founded by Shri Sabapathipillai, the Brahman priests appointed by the temple stayed away and the activities took place under the direction of a *pucari* (non-Brahman religious functionary) from within the Mauritian community. He states that no Sri Lankans attended and the prevailing attitude regarded mortification as not in good taste and considered it rather primitive (Taylor, 1994: 216). Taylor's conclusion is that the typical Vellular patronage pattern had reproduced itself in British Sri Lankan Tamil temples which typify urban "Agamic" temples found in Sri Lanka. He states that no rituals are performed to the goddess involving the mortifications typical of *kavadi* and thus there is no form of village Shaivism in Britain (Taylor, 1994: 220).

However, Taylor's division of rural and urban Shaivism is problematic in the diaspora communities. There are difficulties with such distinctions even in the context of Sri Lanka or South India. One difficulty concerns the role of the ethnographer and the information that informants are willing to divulge. Middle-class professional South Asians, in my experience, are wary of providing material that might be construed as shaming the community or disparaging to treasured religious beliefs. It also true that they often share the same educational background and class status as the academic investigator and are part of a recent historical process to reconstruct Hinduism based on more monotheistic and doctrinal analyses of sacred texts. In such cases, local or vernacular religious traditions can be viewed as superstitions. They may exist among illiterate villagers but are not part of their own domain, that is, educated urban elites. If this is the case then it would be unlikely that diaspora communities where high-class elites, both priestly and merchant, dominate would display the manifestations of "Non-Agamic" religion in public street festivals. Thus antipathy towards the "Non-Agamic" would be reinforced with regard to *kavadi*, because of the "gore" element contained in the traditional mortifications.

So it would appear that the Vellular elites that began the British Tamil temples did not perform *kavadi*-type activity when Donald Taylor was carrying out his research in the 1980s. This may reflect the situation in Scandinavia. Knut Jacobsen's article (2003) on Tamil Hindus in Norway, where the population of Sri Lankans is around 7000, describes the development of Sivasubramanyar Alayam, the first and only temple constructed to date. To some degree, the pattern follows the British one with a gradual shift from renting local halls to purchasing a property. *Kavadi* is noticeable by its absence from Jacobsen's article although he does publish a photograph of a Murugan chariot procession in 2002 when around 2000 people visited the temple. Peter Schalk also notes the absence of *kavadi* in Stockholm where the Sri Lankan community is considerably smaller than in Norway. He suggests that the community in exile prays for the end of suffering (*tunpam*) to Vinayakar (Ganesha as the remover of obstacles) but avoids the "common form of devotion" to make and fulfil a vow. He notes that the performance of such acts is limited in Stockholm, and "extreme forms are rejected" (Schalk, 2003: 386). Schalk's comment would appear to be a stronger assertion of the absence of *kavadi* rituals than Jacobsen who simply fails to make reference to it.

The situation in Denmark would appear to reinforce Taylor's thesis of a "high" and "low" Shaivism in Sri Lanka and the transmigration of the divide into diasora communities. Marianne Fibiger (2003: 345) reports two Tamil temples in Denmark where the Tamil population is around 9000. One temple, the Sree Sithy Vinayakar Temple in Herning, reproduces the forms of ritual Shaiva Siddhanta, observing the classic rules of architecture, and worship carried out by Brahman priests would appear to conform to Taylor's understanding of urban Shaivism, whereas the other temple, the Sree Abirami Amman Temple, located outside the town of Brande in a converted farm, is not run by a committee but is in the sole control of Lalitha Sripalan who is identified as a "shakti medium" (Fibiger, 2003: 350). Abirami is a local goddess from a rural temple in Jaffna and the money was raised to unite the goddess and her "medium" by shipping the image first to Britain. Lalitha performs healing and is able to answer questions when possessed by Abirami. Her reputation has become international amongst the Tamil diaspora and has even attracted a small group of ethnic Danes (Fibiger, 2003: 350–51). The temple is attended by Tamils of a lower fishing caste, some Vellulars but no Brahmans, who are not comfortable with the idea of a non-Brahman woman touching and communicating direct with the gods (Fibiger, 2003: 351). Since moving to the new location in 2000, several thousand Tamils are performing the chariot festival with Abirami. This would appear to reflect Taylor's description of rural Shaivism. Fibiger also reports (2003: 354) that, although a minority is uneasy with the situation, describing it as a "folk cult", the majority of Tamils state that the two temples reflect the situation in Sri Lanka.

Yet despite these divisions, the situation is not as clear-cut as Taylor describes. It is unlikely that rural and urban forms of religion are so demarcated from each other. Urbanisation in Sri Lanka and most parts of India has resulted in millions of rural workers migrating into the cities from where they maintain contact with their extended families remaining in the villages. Certainly South Indian Tamils who belonged to the earlier nineteenth-century migrations to the plantations have had no hesitation in introducing *kavadi* in all its forms to new locations. Subramaniyam (2000: 1) reports that South African Tamils have been performing *kavadi* since their arrival as indentured labourers from 1860 until 1911. He describes the significance of trance states and states that the devotees performed activities such as piercing their tongues and cheeks, hanging lemons on hooks that pierced their complete bodies and suspending pots of water and milk on hooks that pierced the skin, exactly as they did in Tamil Nadu (Subramaniyam, 2000: 3–5). Subramaniyam makes no reference to folk traditions but rather explains the phenomena as the intense *bhakti* (pious devotion) that exists amongst simple people.

Mauritius too exhibits the same phenomenon. One of the oldest and most established Tamil communities, it began in the eighteenth century with the migration of craftsmen and traders during the French colonisation. Later, in the nineteenth century there was mass immigration of indentured labour to supply the sugar plantations. The Mauritian Tamils are proud of their *kavadi* performance and perceive it as part of their identity along with the worship of Murugan. With over one hundred temples established, the Mauritian Tamils strictly observe fasting, abstinence from sex and alcohol prior to *kavadi* and all participants who carry the *palkutam* (yoke) are expected to either tie up their mouths or pierce their tongues. Others sleep on nails or pull chariots with hooks in their flesh. Trance experiences are common and linked to devotion. Khesaven Sornum (2000: 6) writes that "frenzy is possible and indulged unashamedly by the *kavadi* carrier, especially when hearing devotional hymns and concentrating on the Lord".

The East Asian communities of Singapore and Malaysia also display the same patterns of open avowal of *kavadi* as a central part of their religious and cultural identities. Both communities arrived over one hundred and fifty years ago as part of the British colonial presence in South East Asia and recruited as unskilled labour from the ranks of socially deprived lower castes. Both not only perform the rituals enthusiastically and passionately during the festival of Thaipusam but provide websites that describe and illustrate the variations of *kavadi* that participants undergo.[3] However, the history of *kavadi* in both communities has been difficult and passed through a number of stages. These would appear to be related to caste differences and power struggles but also the perceived acceptability of the rituals to the wider community.

Carl Vadivella Belle (2000: 3–4) notes that the Tamil population of Malaysia consists of a small but important sector of Chettiars, a Tamil merchant class renowned for their worship of Murugan and adherence to Agamic forms of Shaivism. This community comprised of influential merchants has built and maintained Murugan temples in both Malaysia and Singapore, importing Brahman *kurukkals* (priests) from India and advising on proper practice. This community perceives *kavadi* as orthodox although they campaigned against the animal sacrifice that once took place. On the other hand, Sri Lankan Jaffna Tamils, drawn overwhelmingly from the Vellular caste, have been committed to an Agamic orthodoxy that has maintained distance from the Indian community and has been traditionally wary of *kavadi*. The original indentured labourers, according to Belle, were responsible for introducing the practices of "Dravidian village Hinduism" to both communities (Belle, 2000: 4).

Belle notes that Malaysian Hinduism has been historically dominated by village traditions worshipping caste and guardian deities and the construction of non-Agamic temples but that the need to create a new Hindu identity appropriate to multi-ethnic Malaysia has been achieved by drawing upon Shaiva Siddhanta and the Agamic tradition as a paradigm for restructuring a form of the religion that does not demarcate "little traditions" and "great traditions". This has been moderated by the lessening of caste divisions in Shaiva Siddhanta and thus influencing the ability of low caste Tamils to accept the Agamic tradition as a common cultural identity able to provide group cohesion (Belle, 2000: 5). At the same time, the practices of *kavadi* associated with "village" Hinduism have been embraced by high-caste and educated Tamils who now participate in the processions. Belle suggests (2000: 6) that it is the worship of Murugan that functions as the "central unifying figure" in the recasting of Malaysian Hinduism.

Gauri Krishnan (2000: 5) notes that during the 1940s and 1950s post-war Hindu reform movements had an impact on the practice of *kavadi* in Singapore. The Tamil Reform Movement (TRA) founded in 1932 campaigned to remove superstitions and outmoded practices or beliefs such as self-immolation in Tai Pucam and Timiti, the sacrifice of animals, and the performance of elaborate rituals or ceremonies. Although the TRA were unsuccessful in their attempts to persuade the British administration to ban the festivals, surveys of the local Tamil language newspaper *Tamil Murasu* demonstrate the negative views towards *kavadi* in the 1950s. However, by 1983 the tone had changed and *kavadi* was no longer regarded as a deviant folk practice but a significant aspect of national identity in which not only wealthy and educated Tamils participated but also Sikhs and Chinese (Krishnan, 2000: 6–7). The pattern is similar to Malaysia but significantly the festivals are promoted by the Singapore Tourism Board as part of Singapore cultural identity. Krishnan also comments (2000: 14) on Murugan's dual role as both a Sanskrit deity drawn from Skanda/Subramaniyam traditions and as a Tamil icon linked to the ancient practices of possession. Although he doesn't comment, it would seem that worship of Murugan is ideally placed to integrate Agamic philosophical and ritual traditions with possession practices.

The British Context

Although Taylor (1994: 217) observes that very few Indian Plantation Tamils are present in any of the British temples, the situation has changed dramatically since his research was carried out in the early 1980s. There are now over twenty Tamil Shaivite temples in London and its suburbs and one purpose built temple in Birmingham. The Birmingham temple dedicated to Ganesh is in addition to the purpose built Murugan temple in East Ham. Although the latter is to some degree separate as it is used by South Indian and South African Tamils who did not want a temple in which Sri Lankan Vellulars are patrons, the others in London have essentially followed the model of organisation developed at the Highgate Murugan temple and in many cases, the founders were originally involved with the Hindu Association of Great Britain.[4] All the temples are either to Murugan, Ganesh or Amman (the goddess) and follow the ritual traditions of Agamic Shaivism. Each employs a number of Brahmans (*kurukkuls*) who are recruited from Sri Lanka and occasionally South India. The Goddess temples are dedicated to Parvatî, the consort of Shiva, and thus fall within the orthodox pantheon of Tamil Shaiva Siddhanta. There are no temples that fall into the category of local goddesses or gods as found in Denmark.

The community is predominantly Sri Lankan Tamil, and they maintain considerable charity work in Sri Lanka, in which support is given to build orphanages, sponsor needy children, and to raise finance for medical treatment for children. All the temples were to donate heavily to disaster funds after the tsunami hit the Sri Lankan coastline in 2004. However, these highly institutionalized temples, dominated by the same Vellular patrons, are since the 1990s at ease with the practice of *kavadi*, and the summer chariot festival at the Ealing Amman temple attracts over 6000 visitors. There is little evidence of Taylor's rural/urban divide or the apparent disquiet concerning "superstitions" that he discovered in the 1980s.

The Tamil presence has been transformed since the civil war erupted in 1983. The small elite Vellular groups are now part of a much more heterogeneous community than the one investigated by Taylor. There are Tamils from Mauritius, Singapore and South Africa as well as Sri Lanka, with a much more diverse range of caste distinctions and educational backgrounds. It is no longer true that "plantation Tamils" are not present in British temples. Both "Ceylon" or Sri Lankan Tamils (sometimes also called Jaffna Tamils) descended from Tamil-speaking immigrants from South India and who came to the island more than one thousand years ago, and the "Indian" Tamils who were brought to the island by the British in the nineteenth century to work on the plantations have been present in the British diaspora since the later 1980s. This diversity brings with it language differences, diverse patterns of worship and different political views. The "Ceylon" Tamils are much more likely to support Sri Lankan separatism whereas Indian or "Plantation" Tamils generally support the government (Jones, 1985: 2). This is a sensitive issue and can be a powerfully divisive one. However, Taylor (1994: 207) makes the point that establishing patterns of worship and temples in which to worship has proved to be a major factor in unifying the Sri Lankan Tamils in Britain and in securing their distinctiveness as an ethnic community.

As in Malaysia and Singapore, the role of *kavadi* rituals functions as a significant celebratory marker of established Tamil communities, that brings together diverse castes and other groups. There would seem to be several reasons for the changes in the British context. The first relates to the diversity of the community, where the old Vellular elites can no longer control expressions of vernacular religion. In addition, their attitudes have been transformed by the globalisation of the Tamil diasporas. Websites, visitors to and from other Tamil communities, the movements of the priests around different temples in the diaspora all tend towards universalisation of worship and ritual practice. Even the Brahman priests have participated in *kavadi*, although I could not find any that would admit to performing mortification. Like Singapore and Malaysia, Britain adopts an official policy of multiculturalism and celebration of religious diversity. The tolerance exhibited helps towards confidence, already increasing with larger numbers migrating and a successful diaspora of worship, education, and commercial enterprises forming an infrastructure that has considerably developed in Britain since the 1980s. The British Tamil Information Directory provides an A–Z of Tamil enterprises consisting of accountants, architects, bookstores, mechanics, doctors, lawyers, repairmen, grocers, restaurants, schools and colleges, tour operators, insurance companies, restaurants, estate agents, computer and IT specialists, fast food outlets and a vast number of other services which is as comprehensive as the national Yellow Pages directory. The diversity of castes now present in the community has considerably strengthened the development of the infrastructure of the communities.

I would argue that it is this confidence that enables communities to introduce forms of worship that fully reflect the diversity of religious practice from the places of origin. However, it should be noted that the British Tamil street festivals remain invisible to the wider population even though performed under their gaze. There is no participation or even audience from outside the Tamil communities. This may reflect the form that multiculturalism takes in the British context, where diaspora communities tend to remain in isolated ghettos or as parallel communities. It may also indicate that the Tamils as relatively new arrivals to Britain are not yet confident or at ease with the idea of promoting the festival as an occasion in which others from outside can participate. In addition, the skills required to contact various agencies that promote and celebrate London's multiculturalism may not yet exist, or may be held in abeyance as Tamil leaders feel hesitant to reveal the mortifications of *kavadi* to the wider British public. To do so will require a shift in perception from pilgrimage to tourism, perhaps as yet one too far to make for a relatively new community keen to maintain the sacred elements of the festival and its rituals.

Tamils have a variety of established "home" centres in both diaspora and Tamil Nadu. These impact on Sri Lankan Tamils. Taylor's "village" and "urban" forms of religion are not so much in opposition to each other but rather fulfil different functions. They co-exist in both urban and rural parts of India and Sri Lanka, and have converged to form an organic whole under the umbrella of Agamic traditions in the diaspora communities but there are vital differences depending on the age of the community, the caste and class divisions, the diversity of the origin of the Tamils and the confidence exuded by the community. Where communities are confident and secure in their environment they are more likely to exhibit non-Agamic elements in the wider public domain, inviting or permitting others to participate in the street festival as in Singapore or Malaysia. Where communities date back to the nineteenth century, the caste make-up will consist of populations more at ease with the non-Agamic; however, this is changing with the arrival of refugee populations since the late twentieth century. The Brahmins and other high-caste groups no longer dominate religious practice and the majority population who are at ease with *kavadi* are less likely to feel the shame that hides the practices from outsiders' eyes. Brahmin priests with experience of employment in temples in Mauritius, Malaysia or Singapore will be less inclined to censor *kavadi* rituals when they are employed in British or European temples. It would seem only a matter of time before British street processions take on the tourist elements that feature in South-East Asia and pilgrimage becomes spectacle. As community isolation and ghettoisation come increasingly under attack from both main political parties, migrant communities such as the Tamils will surely come to realise the integrating benefits of festival participation across communities as in the Notting Hill Gate carnival or in some forms of Mardi Gras. This is likely because the examples of Tai Pucam in Singapore and Malaysia already exist as a precedent. The globalisation of the Tamil diaspora is already having its impact on the acceptability of *kavadi* mortification performances. It must be only a question of time before long-distance tourists who have observed Tai Pucam in India, Mauritius Singapore or Malaysia stumble upon it in London. If such mortifications are, as Bataille suggests (1991 and 1998), temporary permissions for societies to engage in exploration of the "excluded and forbidden" then it is possible that *kavadi* rituals in Tai Pusam will reach out from the ethnic enclave and be embraced by a wider participation in London as they have in South-East Asia. It is certain that in such a process, religious sensitivities will play a dominant role.

Notes

1 A Nakshatra or lunar mansion is one of the twenty-seven or twenty-eight divisions of the sky, identified by the prominent stars in them that the Moon passes through during its monthly cycle, used in Hindu astronomy and astrology. Therefore each represents a division of the Ecliptic similar to the Zodiac (13 degrees 20 minutes each instead of the 30 degrees for each Zodiac sign). Each orbit of the Moon is 27.3 days, so the Moon takes approximately one day to pass through each Nakshatra. The starting point for the Nakshatras is the point on the Ecliptic directly opposite to the star Spica called Chitra in Sanskrit (other slightly definitions exist). It is called Meshadi or the "start of Aries". The Ecliptic is divided into each one of the Nakshatras eastwards starting from this point. (Coleman, 1995: 131.)

2 The popular representatives of religion are likely to be dealing with the pragmatic dimension of religious life and therefore more concerned with seeking miraculous solutions to life crises or channelling the power of the representatives of the divine into healing activities for both physical and psychological ailments than with teaching doctrines which reinforce dharmic codes or means of salvation. Ballard (1996), in providing a useful classification of the manifestations of Punjabi religion, describes these kinds of local traditions as being concerned with the "kismetic". He defines the term as "those ideas, practices and behavioural strategies which are used to explain the otherwise inexplicable, and if possible to turn adversity in its tracks" (Ballard, 1996: 18). Ballard points out that the activities and beliefs of the kismetic dimension of religion are severely under-represented in academic scholarship and that they are also percieved by the practitioners of Hindu, Sikh and Muslim orthodoxies as shameful, misguided and superstitious behaviour of the ignorant rural populations. Roger Ballard's (1996) full classification of Punjabi religion is fourfold: Panthic, Dharmic, Kismetic and Qaumic. These are obviously ideal types and , in practice, there is

considerable overlap. Panthic refers to a type of religious organisation, usually associated with North Indian sant/bhakti traditions, Sufism or where a group of followers organise themselves to promote and follow the teachings of a spiritual master, living or dead. The overriding motive is usually concerned with closer proximity or experience of the Divine through mystical union (Ballard, 1996: 16–17). Dharmic is concerned with a divinely ordained presecribed set of rules that govern the universe and human behaviour (Ballard, 1996: 22–25). Qaumic is used by Ballard to describe the more recent phenomenon where a group of people use a set of religious ideas and activities to close ranks as a community and advance their common social, economic and political interests (Ballard, 1996: 25–28).

3 <http://www.festivalmalaysia.com/thaipusam.html> and <http://glenh.tripod.com/wa_sing_tpsm.htm> – accessed January 2006.

4 For example, Ann David describes the origins of the Sri Kanagathurkkai Amman Temple in Ealing, West London. Mr A. Thevasagayam, the Secretary of the Board of Trustees and one of the founder members of the Ealing Amman temple, explained that he had arrived in the UK from Sri Lanka in 1974 in order to study. He and several of the key members of the temple were regular devotees at the Archway temple, but in discussion with one of the priests there, the issue was raised as to why there was no Amman temple in London, despite there already being temples devoted to the other main deities. A group of Amman devotees began to meet regularly to sing bhajans and to pray to Thurkkai Amman in a community centre in Harrow, North London in 1991. Many Hindus living in Harrow and in Alperton came, and it became necessary to move to a rented hall in Southall, Middlesex, and to hold another weekly meeting on Tuesdays in Wembley. Mr Ratnasingham (founder of the Wimbledon temple) donated a small Amman deity that he had purchased in India especially for this group and an important puja was held for the goddess in January 1993. Up till that point the worship had been conducted with only framed photos of the deities. By this time in 1993, the community had managed to raise £71,000 and began to look for a suitable site for purchase for a temple. An Executive Committee was formed and various locations surveyed. The present site and building, an old and dilapidated chapel in Ealing, was on the market for £500,000 but this was too far beyond their budget. They continued to search for alternative premises. Then, in 1995, the same building and land was put up for auction and they were able to purchase it for £270,000. See David, 2005: 215.

References

Ballard, Roger. 1996. 'Panth, Kismet, Dharm te Qaum: Continuity and Change in Four Dimensions of Punjabi Religion', in Globalisation and the Region: Explanations in Punjabi Identity, eds Pritam Singh and Shinder Thandi. Coventry. University of Coventry.

Bataille, G. 1991. Eroticism (trans. M. Dalwood). San Francisco. City Lights.

Bataille, G. 1998. The Accursed Share Vol 1 – Consumption (trans. Robert Hurley). New York: Zone Books.

Belle, Carl Vadivella. 2000. 'Tai Pucam in Malaysia: An Incipient Hindu Unity'. Paper given at the First International Conference on Skanda-Murukan, held at the Institute of Asian Studies, University of Chennai, India and published at <http://murugan.org/research/index.htm>.

Clothey, Fred. 2005. The Many Faces of Murukan. New Delhi. Munshiram Manoharla.

Coleman, Charles. 1995. Mythology of the Hindus. New Delhi. AES.

David, Ann. 2005. "Performing Faith": Dance, Identity and Religion in Hindu Communities in Leicester and London. PhD thesis. University of Leicester.

De Bres, K., and Davis, J. 2001. 'Celebrating Group and Place Identity: A Case Study of New Regional Festivals', Tourism Geographies 3(3).

Fibiger, Marianne. 2003. 'Sri Lankan Tamil Hindus in Denmark: Internal and External Cultural and Religious Representations', in M. Baumann *et al.* (eds), *Tempel und Tamilen in zweiter Heimat: Hindus aus Sri Lanka im deutschsprachigen und skandinavischen Raum.* Würzburg. Ergon Verlag.

Jacobsen, Knut. 2003. 'Settling in a Cold Climate: The Tamil Hindus in Norway', in Baumann, M. *et al.* (eds), *Tempel und Tamilen in zweiter Heimat: Hindus aus Sri Lanka im deutschsprachigen und skandinavischen Raum.* Würzburg. Ergon Verlag.

Jones, A. K. 1985. *Time for Decision: Sri Lankan Tamils in the West.* Washington, DC. US Committee for Refugees.

Kannan, R. 2000. 'Pada yatra to Palani Murukan Temple – A Folk Tradition', paper given at the First International Conference on Skanda-Murukan, held at the Institute of Asian Studies, University of Chennai, India and published at <http: //murugan.org/research/index.htm>.

Krishnan, Gauri Parimoo. 2000. 'Following Murukan: Tai Pucam in Singapore'. Paper given at the First International Conference on Skanda-Murukan, held at the Institute of Asian Studies, University of Chennai, India and published at <http://murugan.org/research/index.htm>.

Long, P., Robinson, M. & Picard, D. 2004. 'Festivals and Tourism: Links and Developments', in P. Long and M. Robinson (eds), *Festivals and Tourism:*

Marketing, Management and Evaluation. Sunderland. Business Education Publishers.

Picard, David, and Robinson, Mike. 2006. 'Remaking Worlds: Festivals, Tourism and Change' in D. Picard and M. Robinson (eds), *Festivals, Tourism and Social Change.* Clevedon. Channel View Publications.

Shakti, M. Gupta. 1988. *Karrtikeya: The Son of Shiva.* New Delhi. Somaiya Publications.

Schalk, Peter. 2003. 'Tamil Caivas in Stockholm, Sweden', in M. Baumann *et al.* (eds), *Tempel und Tamilen in zweiter Heimat: Hindus aus Sri Lanka im deutschsprachigen und skandinavischen Raum.* Würzburg. Ergon Verlag.

Sornum, Khesaven. 2000. 'The Murukan Cult in Mauritius'. Paper given at the First International Conference on Skanda-Murukan, held at the Institute of Asian Studies, University of Chennai, India and published at <http://murugan.org/research/index.htm>.

Subramaniyam, S. 2000. 'Tamil Language and Murukan Worship in South Africa'. Paper given at the First International Conference on Skanda-Murukan, held at the Institute of Asian Studies, University of Chennai, India and published at <http://murugan.org/research/index.htm>.

Taylor, Donald. 1994. *The Symbolic Construction of the Sri Lankan Hindu Tamil Community in Britain.* PhD thesis. University of London. School of Oriental and African Studies.

CHAPTER TEN

TRIAL, TRIBULATION AND TRIUMPH: THE SACRED SPACE OF THE BULGARIAN ORTHODOX CHURCHES

PEPA GRUNDY

The aim of this paper is to investigate the role of sacred space in Bulgarian Orthodox churches, evaluating its unique transformation through the centuries. I will also reflect on the impact of sacred space on the preservation of faith and Bulgarian national consciousness from glorious beginnings, through foreign domination, misfortune and suffering, to revival and reinstatement. I will show that the sacred space of the Bulgarian Orthodox Churches extends far beyond its constructive elements into a powerful ethnic, ethical, spiritual, cultural, historical and territorial sanctuary, contributing to the development of strong religious and national identity.

I was inspired to start working on this paper after attending a service at the Roman Catholic Cathedral in Liverpool. As an Orthodox Christian observing a Catholic mass, I could not help but notice many differences in the form of worship. The sacred space or "the peculiar arena" (Lewis, 1980: 20) of the forthcoming ritual was odourless, clean, cold, well lit and simplistic, almost minimalistic in terms of layout and number of sacred objects. It was white and crisp, clear and symbolic. Being used to a lavish, colourful, heavily incensed and warm semi-darkness, lit by candles and a multitude of sensory experiences, I discovered that the Catholic decor did not engage my imagination; thus, as an outsider, I did not feel inspired to participate.

Unsurprisingly, I was reminded there of the great medieval theologian Thomas Aquinas who, in his *Summa Theologiae,* establishes the special importance of the place chosen for the liturgy. He comments that liturgy should be held in a consecrated house or a building and gives two reasons for it: to express the fact that the Church is the "house of God", and that this "house of God" extends throughout the world in various buildings made suitable for worship thanks to the sacred liturgical actions and gestures, replicating those of Jesus Christ (cited in Weinandy *et al.*, 2004: 192). Hence the importance of sacred space as a fundamental and unique unity of architecture, lighting, objects, vesture, Scripture and music, and a stage for religious worship, where spiritual experiences of goodness, truth and beauty take place.

Attending mass that morning stirred a range of emotions within me, encouraging me to "contemplate not him who is invisible but rather where he dwells . . . , walking the heights of those holy places to which the mind at least can rise" (Pseudo-Dionysius, cited in Gerhart, 2007: 605).

Reflecting on the liturgy, I thought of our contemporary world, where it is easy to forget about God and where values change or lose their meaning but sacred spaces still exist and still provide solace and sanctuary. Thus, I began to think about the significance of sacred space in religious worship, in the performance of holy rites and rituals and in defining religious beliefs and identities throughout history until today.

This, in turn, raised many questions. The first was about how the traditional concept of sacred space is understood in our contemporary, primarily secular, cultures. And, in the context of Bulgarian Orthodoxy, have the traditional constituents of sacred space changed over time, and do we need sacred spaces today? Do the qualities and features of sacred spaces have an important role to play in the impact of Bulgarian Orthodox Church (BOC) on modern Bulgarian society and the Church's claims to be its moral guide and leader? Are churches and monasteries merely tourist attractions or centres of national identity?

I will start by examining the development of the sacred space of Bulgarian churches, focusing on a church or monastery from each historical period and reflecting on the function of sacred spaces in the preservation of Bulgarian national identity. Consequently, I will suggest that the sacred space of Bulgarian churches is not simply a place of worship but extends far beyond that role, serving as a safe refuge and pylon of faith and hope for many generations.

Trial: Acceptance of Christianity and Summit of Development

Asked once about his personal religious convictions and their relevance to his work at Ronchamp, the Swiss-born architect and designer Le Corbusier responded: "I have not experienced the miracle of faith but I have often known the miracle of ineffable space" (Curtis, 1986: 178–179, cited in Kieckhefer, 2004: 229). Of course one cannot say exactly what Le Corbusier meant by this phrase but if I am to apply his words to a specifically Bulgarian context, it is fair to state at the outset that that the ineffable sacred space of Bulgarian churches has continuously nurtured and helped the survival of Bulgaria's national and religious identity,

The Bulgarian Orthodox Church originates from the first Christian communities and churches, set up in the Balkans as early as the third century of the Chriatian era. Remains of those churches can still be seen today. The high point of development belongs to the ninth and tenth centuries, when an educational movement, uniting Church and State, enveloped Bulgarian language, literature and learning, laying the foundations of the Bulgarian Christian Orthodox culture (BOC official website, 2008: 1). The building of churches and monasteries promoted the development of art with sacred spaces and sites becoming "true spiritual nurseries" (BOC, 2008: 2). This is how Bulgarian national identity and culture came to birth. Even after the fall of Bulgaria under Byzantine domination in 1018, the number of monasteries and churches in Bulgaria not only continued to grow but also greatly influenced Bulgarian national culture and consciousness. One of the finest examples of Christian architecture and art of that time is Bachkovo Monastery. Founded in 1083 by the Byzantine military commander, Grigorii Bakuriani and his brother Abazii, it is still active and has become a popular centre for Bulgarian Orthodox culture, frequently visited by pilgrims, who say they are mesmerised by its unique structural design, its rich theological literature and old manuscripts and its substantial collection of old coins, jewellery and sacred objects. The monastery's most remarkable features, however, are the paintings that are seen everywhere – in the church and ossuary chapel, where the figure of the Bulgarian Tsar, Ivan Alexander, stand out among the eleventh- and fourteenth-century frescoes; in the Old Refectory (1601); in the Assumption of the Blessed Virgin main church (1604); and in the Holy Trinity and St. Nicholas church (1840), which contain some of the first murals painted by the Bulgarian National Revival artist, Zahari Zograph (travel-Bulgaria.com, 2008: 1). This monastery is a fine example of a sacred space of special religious and cultural importance, enriching locals and visitors alike with spiritually intense religious and aesthetic experiences thanks to the beauty and unusual powers of one special resident, the miracle icon of the Virgin Mary (1310).

In addition, Bachkovo Monastery clearly evidences signs of tradition and change in its sacred spaces since the monastery was frequently raided; most of its buildings were burnt and destroyed down the centuries. Repeatedly restored and renovated, it grew larger and more striking every time. These sacred spaces unmistakably illustrate the effect of time and encompass a variety of artistic traditions and cultures.

If you attend a service or simply visit the Assumption of the Blessed

Virgin Church in Bachkovo, you find yourself entering the sacred and mystical world of Bulgarian Orthodoxy. As you walk in, you are struck by the darkness, quietness and white tamyan smoke wrapping around you like a cocoon. Lit candles warm the incensed space as monks in black robes, offset by long, white, untidy beards, converse softly. You notice silver and gold icons affixed to the beautifully carved wooden iconostasis and heavy red curtains covering the main door that leads to the altar. There are two other doors – one is for the deacon, the other leads to the area for liturgical preparation. The iconostasis, the screen with doors and icons set in tiers, which separates the sanctuary from the nave, is central to the internal architectural design of Orthodox churches and entirely conceals the sacrum from the altar, mystifying liturgical preparation and adding to the phenomenon of religious experience even further.

It is dark, profound, soul-penetrating and emotion-stirring, a sacred space,

> where the mysteries of God's Word
> Lie simple, absolute and unchangeable
> In the brilliant darkness of a hidden silence.
> (Pseudo-Dionysius, cited in Gerhart, 2007: 605)

Thus, it is a unique place where traditional Christian Orthodox rituals are performed and is, therefore, sacred by function and by right. But this description would not be complete without remembering one of the most illustrious features of this sacred space – the miracle icon of the Virgin Mary (1310) which is both religiously powerful and aesthetically valuable.

Orthodox icons form a peculiar unity of art and tradition that strives to imprint holy images into the heart of all Orthodox worshippers. Their purpose in a church setting is to reflect the world of the divine and create a miniature copy on earth, to educate the flock about life of Christ and the saints, and to inspire a deep feeling of holy blessing and protection. Orthodox icons are a permanent feature of many homes in modern day Bulgaria. They are placed in the centre of rooms, bringing the sacred within human reach. They give hope and help families to visualise the divine, enhancing human understanding of religion and multiplying the power of prayer.

Thus, Orthodox icons have both a religious value and an aesthetic significance. The icon of Virgin Mary in Bachkovo is a unique example of the art iconography that enhances the power of religious persuasion and opens "a window into heaven" for the souls of the believers. It brings motherly love, compassion and hope to locals and pilgrims. It evokes feelings of heaven coming down to earth, as though a special union is about to happen.

The small church of the Blessed Virgin is really a place where the miracle of ineffable space is intertwined with the miracle of faith. Its influencing presence, along with its cultural and religious value, is an indication that, in modern day Bulgaria, sacred spaces are still redoubtable sanctuaries of Bulgarian spiritual identity, keeping alive a sense of national awareness and Christian orthodoxy.

However, Bachkovo is not only an example of a beautiful sacred space. The monastery is also a symbol of the ever-continuing fight for religious and political independence from Turkish domination. The monastery was the place where Bulgarian Patriarch Evtimii was banished after the fall of the Second Bulgarian Kingdom. After his arrival, the monastery became a centre of national, cultural and ethnic fortification. Although raided and destroyed several time during Turkish rule, its sacred space was rebuilt again and played a decisive role in spreading educational and theological literature in Bulgaria (BOC official website, 2008: 1).

The Clash of Titans: Orthodox Christianity vs. Islam

To what extent, then, do the qualities and features of sacred spaces play a significant role in the state–church relationship in modern Bulgarian society and in the church's own claims that the institution provides moral leadership? To answer this question, our attention needs to focus on the centuries of Ottoman rule in Bulgaria, when the spiritual and cultural development of the Bulgarian nation and its main advocate, the BOC, had taken a huge blow and had encouraged a mass emigration to Europe.

The Christian sanctuaries and the cultural monuments were not spared after the invasion of 1396. Hundreds of churches and monasteries were destroyed and razed to the ground. Many were turned into mosques or Turkish baths. The attempt to desecrate the holy sites of Bulgarian Orthodox Christianity was powerful and effective.

Nevertheless, allegiance to the Christian Orthodox faith lived on in the surviving churches and monasteries, where the flame of Bulgarian national identity and belonging kept burning. The Orthodox clergy were among the first to organise uprisings against the suppressors. Many died as martyrs, inspiring further, and even fiercer, resistance. During the centuries of Ottoman rule, the Bulgarian Christian Orthodox Church made every effort to safeguard its conduct and theological concepts. The religious practices, the liturgical service and the icons were all saved and preserved in the surviving monasteries. But the sacred space of church buildings, chapels and monasteries changed through the influence of Islamic architectural and artistic traditions.

Until the Ottoman invasion of 1396, Bulgarian ecclesiastical art was part of the Byzantine artistic tradition. Icons were painted under the strict canonical rules of the Eastern Orthodox religious practice. After the fall of Bulgaria under Islamic authority, Bulgarian cultural and artistic traditions were suppressed and during the five-century-long occupation naturally acquired common features with the cultural and artistic expression of the ruling Islamic powers. This was reflected in the use of black colour, and through frequent geometric shapes and patterned design in mural church paintings and icons.

Mayfield (2007: 1) claims that some of today's rituals of Bulgarian Orthodoxy even bear resemblance to common Islamic practices. For example, females are told to enter church with their heads covered, while men are expected to shroud their legs and shoulders. Worshippers have to face icons while praying, in much the same way as Muslims would pray facing Mecca.

The influence of Islam in Bulgaria emerged in a variety of ways during the centuries of occupation. For instance, in accordance with Turkish imperial laws, church buildings in conquered Bulgaria had to be humble "without a bell tower or ornaments and not taller than the Islamic buildings in the town or village" (Sarieva, 1995:1). Yet, inside the churches, the sacred space kept most of its distinctive features and through the icons, the iconostasis and the frescoes created an astonishing and holy world which the ruling Muslim authorities were not able to conquer. It was a realm of beautiful icons and paintings, established with "full precision and care, exposed in the holy churches of God, on sacred instruments and vestments, on walls and panels, in houses and by public ways" (Second Council of Nicaea, AD 787). This gave Bulgaria the spiritual inspiration and sense of holy guidance to continue its fight for religious and, later, national independence.

Thus, through trials and tribulations, the Bulgarian Orthodox Church established its position as the intellectual and moral leader in the fight for Bulgarian independence and religious identity. Churches and monasteries were sacred spaces where public national awareness goals were set and reached. Bulgarian confidence grew as did the belief that Christian sacred space offered a form of holy protection, safe refuge and winning strength in the ongoing struggle against the Turks. Moreover, according to Keesing (1976: 386–387), religions reinforce human ability to cope with the fragility of human life, including famine, flood, sickness and death, providing security and meaning in an unpredictable world. This has led to the claim that some sacred spaces in human history are invested with such importance that they completely revolutionise the traditional definition and meaning of "sacred space". With their power and critical role in the collective memory of nations, some are even transformed into sacred subjects of international and intercultural magnitude.

Sacred spaces also provide religious sanctuary. The story of a sacred space that was called upon to provide safe refuge against the attacking Muslim irregulars during the April uprising of 1876 is one of huge importance in the claim that the sacred space of the Bulgarian Orthodox Churches extends far beyond its constructive elements into a powerful ethnic, ethical, spiritual, cultural, historical and territorial sanctuary, contributing to the development of strong religious and national identity.

What follows here is the account of events that have shaped the very core of the collective Bulgarian character and influence religious relations in the country until this day. Bulgarian historian and director of the Museum of History in Batak, Ekaterina Peychinova, explains what happened in the modest St Nedelia church:

> For three days and three nights the people inside the church held together, and the shooting outside did not stop for a minute. The attackers threw beehives and set fire to straw, but the rebels would not give in. Then they began to suffocate and most of the people died of asphyxia. Thirst was the biggest problem for everyone, because there was no water near the church. The mothers used the oil from the icons to moisten the lips of their babies, and when there was no more oil, they used the blood of the dead. An elderly man said they should start digging the earth in search of underground water, but the spring of 1876 had turned a dry one and their attempts failed. (Cited in Ivanova, 2008: 1)

Bulgarian fighters for national freedom, men, women, and children believed that they would be spared if they sought protection in the House of God as every Christian believes that

> in the day of trouble he will keep me safe in his dwelling,
> He will hide me in the shelter of his tabernacle and set me high upon a rock.
> Then my head will be exalted above the enemies who surround me.
> (Psalm 27:5–6)

The protection of the Christian holy place was not enough and the uprising was drowned in blood. The horrific events of that April in 1876 were reported by the American war journalist Januarius Macgahan, who was writing for the *Daily News* of London at that time. What he had discovered in Bulgaria and his urgent calls for help did more than just describe what had happened in the small village of Batak.

His insistent and terrifying accounts introduced the sacred space of St. Nedelia church to the world and testified that in the modest Batak church, the oil from the icons, the blood from the dead, the soil of the church floor, the cries of endless pain and horror, and the last breaths of the dying believers all had come together to expand the power of the sacred space and that Holy Sacrifice that had gone far beyond the events taking place during those three days. The scenery there had ceased to provide decoration because it had taken on the responsibility of expressing the world (Dufrenne, 1973: 181, cited in Torevell, 2007: 167). And what an expression that had been! Tragic and triumphant, the cries of the dying in St. Nedelia church were the last Divine Liturgy ever delivered there. I am reminded of Aidan Kavanagh's words that "the liturgy does the world and does it at its very centre, for it is here that the world's malaise and its cure well up together, inextricably entwined" (Kavanagh, 1982: 46). In this case, the liturgy shook European consciousness to its very core and started an international movement that resulted in Bulgaria winning its religious and political independence.

The church in Batak is now a museum. Nonetheless, it is still a sacred space, although of a somewhat different understanding and quality. It is now a place where objects, which survived the atrocities, tell their horror story to generations of careful listeners. It is a sacred place that still serves the same purpose of providing safe haven for Bulgarian national identity and its sense of belonging. The former church is also a place for pilgrimage, an emotional journey for Bulgarian emigrants and local residents alike. It is a powerful tool in the creation and upholding of national and patriotic pride.

This paper does not, of course, aim to incite ethnic or religious hatred on the grounds of past events. Its goal is merely to assist the reader in understanding just how crucial sacred space is for the self-guarding of Bulgarian cultural and religious identity, and the way in which both Bulgarian Christians and Bulgarian Muslims understand themselves. There have also been more recent developments, as outlined by Petar Kostadinov:

> On April 24th 2007, Bulgarian language media, both press and electronic, reported on a project by the Institute for East European Studies at Free University of Berlin (FUB) called *Batak as a Place of Bulgarian Memory*. The project had to do with a painting of Batak, done by the Polish artist Antoni Piotrowski 16 years after the event. According to initial Bulgarian-language media coverage, Brunnbauer and Baleva claimed that the Batak atrocities were a myth, that the number of victims had been exaggerated, and

> that talk of 500 years of Ottoman rule was actually a fake. "The Batak myth reportedly generates hate between Bulgarians and the Muslim community and harms present-day relations between Bulgaria and Turkey," the media quoted the report as saying. (Kostadinov, 2007: 1)

The response by Bulgarians was overwhelming with a sense of national anger, the threat of civil marches, diplomatic protests, as well as official presidential and government statements. Two days later, the authors expressed their regret that the media coverage had given

> completely incorrect information and that the project did not deny the tragic events that took place in Batak in 1876, but dealt with the depiction of the Batak massacre in pictures, and specifically in a picture by Piotrowski, and with the role of Batak in Bulgaria's collective memory. (Kostadinov, 2007: 1)

What is imperative to consider here is the transformation of the sacred space in Batak into a sacred subject for a whole nation. The level of national rage provoked by this "slightest deflection from the line of cherishing and venerating the memory of the Batak massacre in Bulgaria" (Kostadinov 2007: 1) speaks of the disturbing significance and formative power of the St Nedelia church for creating Bulgarian cultural identity, its sense of national belonging and, especially, its religious and political self-perception. Yet, what is also important here is to account for their critical authority in the formation of Bulgarian national character and Bulgarian Orthodox religious and cultural values. This authority is strengthened by their religious character and should be used to educate and promote tolerance and mutual understanding, not societal division.

Certainly, over the years, there have been those, who have claimed that the Bulgarian Orthodox Church has frequently being an instrument in and at times, an active promoter of nationalism in Bulgarian foreign political aspirations. Moreover, some strongly disagree with the fact that Christian Orthodox Christianity is referred to as "traditional religion" in the Bulgarian constitution (Ch.1, Fundamental Principles, art.13, 2006).

Nevertheless, real-life events of huge national value like the Batak massacre in the St. Nedelia church undoubtedly support BOC claims of moral leadership in Bulgarian society. The role of the Bulgarian Orthodox Church and its sacred sites is vital for the existence of a modern Bulgarian state and, far from being "marked for extinction", as claimed in Ramet (1989: 377), is a vital part of a society that has learned from history and now promotes interreligious and intercultural understanding.

Moreover, the sacredness of spaces and events is an important component of a common national legacy. Sacred spaces, being active places of worship or museums, should be used to unite rather than set apart and certainly not for serving nationalistic goals. Hence, the huge potential of sacred spaces as both centres of faith and public educational spaces that could provide the so needed unbiased common ground for intercultural and interfaith communication.

Restoration and Revival

The gruesome events of 1876 were, in part, a reason for Bulgaria winning its political and religious independence in 1878. A period of revival for BOC had arrived. Sacred spaces that provided solace and sanctuary during the hardest times of Bulgarian history were now actively promoting Bulgarian Christian Orthodox culture, identity and confidence.

In 1945 Bulgaria fell under Russian domination and became the People's Republic of Bulgaria. An astonishing amount of literature, academic and journalistic, was written in a relatively short space of time about the fate of religion, churches, monasteries and the Eastern Orthodox clergy under communism.

So are churches and monasteries just tourist attractions or centres of national identity?

It has to be remembered that communism was deeply anti-religious by nature. No one could deny the leading role that BOC had played in the fight for Bulgarian political independence, and its influence on the people of the newly established republic could not be underestimated. The Bulgarian communist elite understood the influence of sacred sites and spaces only too well. As a consequence, liturgical attendance in churches, while not officially prohibited, was strongly discouraged. In a swift attempt to limit their function as places of worship, all churches and monasteries, which contained samples of beautiful woodcarving, mural paintings, precious icons and theological literature of historical value, became the official property of the Ministry of Education and Culture and national museums. This way they ceased being places of active worship and became tourist attractions. The newly established "museums" were used to propagate "Bulgarshtina" or the supremacy of Bulgarian national spirit, traditions, art and culture around the world, thus serving nationalistic goals. This was the fate of Rila Monastery which became "a popular cultural and touristic object, a hearth for patriotic education of the generations, but no more a place for religious education and spiritual elevation" (Open Society Archives, Rabotnichesko Delo, 1962).

Any religious activity outside churches was deemed illegal. Even Christian baptism received a new identity – it was to be known as a "civil baptism". The sacred space of the Bulgarian Orthodox Church, therefore, became more fluid in its definition and underwent adaptation. But it still unofficially resided in homes and hearts, where it remained untouched as a source of hope. It stayed alive long enough to flourish again freely and find new expression in another wave of restoration of churches and monasteries from 1990 until the present day.

Conclusion

Sacred spaces are special sanctuaries that enhance the power of religious experience and multiply the authority of the transcendental in our human world. With their commanding presence and mystical beauty, Christian sacred spaces are a unique meeting point for heaven and earth, benevolent divine gift, where human souls are reborn in Christ and begin new, exiting spiritual journeys. They are, indeed, places, where *lex orandi, lex credendi* or "the way we pray determines what we believe" (McGrath, 2007: 140–141) but that is not their only function.

As essential and unmistakably familiar features of ancient and modern civilizations, sacred spaces have held an influential position in the formation of societal cultural or political foundations of many empires and democracies, associating those with respectively oppression or freedom. In Bulgarian religious and cultural context, Christian Orthodox sacred spaces and sites have played a vital role in the constant struggle for preservation of national character, with churches and monasteries remaining strongholds of Bulgarian national identity through 200 years of Byzantine political domination and 500 years of Islamic yoke, misfortune and anguish.

As you would expect, the characteristic features of Bulgarian Orthodox sacred spaces have, indeed, changed over time and reflect, to some extent, external influences owing to centuries of detrimental acts aimed at erasing the very memory of Bulgarian national individuality. But even so, consecrated through countless acts of collective worship and selfless individual spiritual devotion, these Bulgarian holy places have conserved their distinctive qualities and features; the sacred space of Bachkovo monastery is a fine example of that.

Having survived atrocities and mistreatment, still an active monastery and a tourist attraction of huge aesthetic worth and significance, the monastery still continues to be regarded as one of the most valuable assets of Christian Orthodox cultural heritage and a safe haven for

Bulgarian national spirit and cultural self-perception.

The need for sacred spaces in modern-day Bulgaria is as important as ever. Centres for religious pilgrimage or sacred places of national imminence, they are precious instruments, which, if used wisely, could play a decisive role in endorsing multicultural understanding and forbearance in Bulgarian society. A modest, stone-built church in the small mountain town of Batak knows all about this, and tells stories of sacrifice, compassion and heroes. At both, secular and spiritual level, the church was counted upon to provide refuge for two thousand freedom fighters in the April uprising of 1876, its sacred objects used nor to deliver nor to participate in religious worship but for worldly goals: to fight the enemies and save the lives of the helpless defenders, as it says in Scripture that ". . . the LORD is my stronghold, refuge and saviour, from violent men I am saved" (2 Samuel 22:3).

The lives of the innocent were not spared that day but the echoes of their never-ending horror brought, in fact, salvation as they were powerful enough to invoke military action that led to the liberation of Bulgaria. The image of the church of St. Nedelia is now imprinted in the collective memory of the Bulgarian nation. It is an example of a sacred space that has expanded beyond its primary function as a forum for religious worship and has taken on the duty of communicating the importance of nurturing public values of tolerance and intercultural dialogue.

Finally, the sacred space of Bulgarian churches and monasteries has been a source of spiritual inspiration for the faithful Orthodox denomination in Bulgaria for many centuries but its role expands beyond that into an influential moral, religious, educational, intellectual and protective sanctuary, fundamental to the development of strong Bulgarian national identity. It is a "statement of faith in stone, metal, wood and glass; the place, where the sacred meets the profane, where heaven touches earth, and where the ordinary space is given extraordinary meaning (Gwynne, 2008: 345).

References

[Bible. 1985] *The Holy Bible: New International Version.* London. Hodder & Stoughton.

Bulgaria. 2006. Constitution of the Republic of Bulgaria <http://www.parliament.bg/?page=const&lng=en> – accessed 23 November 2008.

Bulgarian Orthodox Church. *History of the Bulgarian Orthodox Church* <http://bulch.tripod.com/boc/historyen.htm> – accessed 11 July 2008.

Curtis, W. 1986. *Le Corbusier: Ideas and Forms.* New York: Rizzoli.

Gerhart, M. & Udoh, F. 2007. *The Christianity Reader.* Chicago. University of Chicago Press.

Green, Alfred G. *Icons and iconography.* <http://aggreen.net/iconography/icons.html> – accessed 8 August 2008.

Gwynne, P. 2008. *World Religions in Practice.* Oxford. Blackwell.

Ivanova, M. 2008. *St. Nedelya Church in Batak.* Available at <http://www.pravoslavieto.com> – accessed 12 April 2008.

Kavanagh, A. 1982. *Elements of Rite.* Collegeville, Minnesota. Pueblo Publishing.

Kostadinov, P. 2007. *Reading Room: The Batak Massacre: A Sacred Subject.* Available at <http://www.sofiaecho.com/article/reading-room-the-batak-massacre-a-sacred-subject/id_22279/catid_29ER YUGOSLAVIA> – accessed 27 August 2008.

McGrath, A. 2007. *Christian Theology: An Introduction.* 4th edn. Oxford. Blackwell.

Mayfield, J. 2007. *Inside Bulgaria, the 1st Slavic Nation and the Land of the Thracian Masters of Gold.* Available at <http://www.euroheritage.net/insidebulgaria.shtml> – accessed 4 September 2008.

Mesa Community College. *The Nature of the Sacred.* <http://www.mc.maricopa.edu/dept/d10/asb/religion/sacred.html> accessed 27 August 2008.

Open Society Archives. *The Bulgarian Orthodox Church at Present.* Available at <http://www.osaarchivum.org/files/holdings/300/8/3/text/6-1-68.shtml> – accessed 25 May 2008.

Ramet, P. & Ramet, S. 1989. 'Religion and Nationalism in Soviet and East European Politics' in Raikin, S., *Nationalism and the Bulgarian Orthodox Church.* Durham, NC. Duke University Press.

Sarieva, I. 1995. *Some Problems of the Religious History of Bulgaria and Fomer Yugoslavia.* Available at <http://www.georgefox.edu> – accessed 1 September 2008.

St. George Rotunda (Bulgarian Travel Guide) <http://www.travel-bulgaria.com/content/st_george_church.shtml> – accessed 27 August 2008.

Thiessen, G. 2004. *Theological Aesthetics: A Reader.* London. SCM Press.

Torevell, D. 2007. *Liturgy and the Beauty of the Unknown.* Aldershot. Ashgate.

Walker, D. 1988. *Januarius MacGahan: The Life and Campaigns of an American War Correspondent.* Ohio. Ohio University Press.

Weinandy, T., Keating, D. and Yocum, J. 2004. *Aquinas on Doctrine: A Critical Introduction.* London. Continuum.

Zurkus, J. 2002. *Islamic Art: Exploring the Visual Arts of the Middle East.* Available at <http://www.yale.edu/ynhti/curriculum/units/2002/2/02/02/03.x.html> – accessed 14 September 2008.

CHAPTER ELEVEN

THE POLITICS AND POETICS OF SACRED RUINS

CAROLINE BENNETT

In his most famous sonnet "Ozymandias" written in 1818, Shelley captures the transient nature of civilisations and the irrelevance of human power and effort in the face of eternity. The great king's statue lies fallen in ruins in the midst of a waste land; its arrogant inscription, "Look on my works, ye Mighty, and despair", is a poetic testament to hubris. Ozymandias is the Greek name for the powerful Egyptian king Rameses II who reigned in thirteenth century BCE. Despite its historical specificity, it powerfully encapsulates the "ashes to ashes" nature of the human condition: "for dust thou art, and unto dust shalt thou return" (Genesis 3:19, KJV), which is used in the Anglican burial service. In Shelley's sonnet both king and civilisation have disappeared, and only fragments of this monument survive inspiring a poem three millennia later. The significance of this poem is not only that it is a reflection on mortality, but that Shelley sees that ruins have a politics and a poetics, that they are imbued with aesthetics and laden with meanings.

Unquestionably, the significance and meanings of ruins were seized upon long before the Romantic era. By tracing the depictions of ruins in paintings of Jesus' nativity, for example, we can see that they can be read as gauges of the attitudes towards Christ in the periods in which they were created. For example, works such as Fra Diamante's "The Nativity" (1465–1470) show backgrounds of dilapidated stable buildings in order to reflect the humble origins of Jesus. Later Renaissance paintings, such as the theatrical "L'Adoration des Bergers" attributed to Jean de Gourmont (*c.* 1525) depict the high-flown ruins typical of classical antiquity as a way of establishing the grandeur and power of the birth of Christ as well as reflecting the Renaissance fondness for ancient civilizations. So it is evident that, whether real or depicted in art, ruins are texts which provide both mimetic and diegetic narratives: they show the story and they tell the story. Although the notion of *reading* a building or ruin has a typically postmodern ring, William Durand (2007) as early as 1286 noted that churches could be "read" when he explained the theological significance of church architecture. The act of critically reading ruins informs us not only about the period of their origins but about the time of their reception. Ruins are analysed and interpreted by archaeologists and historians, but the way they are acted upon or *not* acted upon is a cultural investigation. In a largely favourable review of Robert Ginsberg's *The Aesthetics of Ruins* (2004), Patricia Andrew notes the lack of attention given to their construction and their existence in the present (Andrew, 2006: 49), and it is this issue that is addressed here with particular reference to sacred ruins: the meanings that inhere in ruins and in various types of reconstruction. It is my thesis that sacred ruins are viewed in different ways, depending on the circumstances of their devastation. Ruins which come about through the ravages of ages have a picturesque quality as well as a provision of access to the past, both of which are highly valued. Examples of this type would be ancient Roman or Greek ruins such as the Coliseum and the Parthenon, although many of lesser significance could be included. As a consequence of their antiquity, their rebuilding is rarely an issue. However, when the ruin is brought about through different types of recent conflict, then specific outcomes are likely. After some discussion of the complexities of sacredness in relation to buildings and ruins, this chapter examines three different sacred spaces to see what factors have determined their courses. These are, first, the recently destroyed Bamiyan Buddha statues of Afghanistan; second, the Cathedral of Christ the Saviour in Moscow, destroyed by Stalin and replaced at the end of the twentieth century; and third, Coventry Cathedral which was bombed during World War II and rebuilt shortly afterwards in a ground-breaking style.

Complications arise because secular ruins in the West are not infrequently regarded as "sacred" artefacts. Increasingly, we come across adaptive uses of redundant sacred spaces such as those which have evolved into art galleries or restaurants. Their attractiveness may lie in the fact that these retain, to borrow a phrase from Walter Benjamin's *The Work of Art in the Age of Mechanical Reproduction* (1936: 7), the *aura* of the original. Although Benjamin referred to art works, his concept can equally well apply to ruins as cultural objects. We lament this passing as we move through this age of mechanical reproduction. It is this loss of the mystical and any sense of connectedness with origins which Weber saw as a progressive "disenchantment" of the world. It is the ceding of mystery. Charles Baudelaire in *The Painter of Modern Life* (1859) presciently identified the growing tendencies of modernity towards "the transient, the fleeting, the contingent" (1986: 130). As societies shift into the modern age this aura of the original artefact is lost owing to the mass production capabilities of industrialisation and increasing emphasis is placed upon commoditisation. Mass production is a double-edged sword: whilst the democratising effects of large-scale reproduction can be celebrated, the aura of the original is lost. Perhaps a reaction against this is found in the increasing value placed on old architectural structures. This does accord with Baudelaire's view that the artist must "distil the eternal from the transitory" (quoted in Jervis, 1998: 5). So it is that certain ruins are presented, sanctioned, sanctified, and become sacred theatrical spaces in which visitors are actors in a regulated performance. Viewed as a palimpsest, namely a manuscript written over a partly erased older manuscript in such a way that the old words can be read beneath the new, ruins bring the past into a fragile contiguity with the present, and this provides the viewer with the aura of the original.

A sacred place has generally been understood to be either a place where God dwells or a place where the divine is revealed. It may be a place in which hierophany (a perception of the sacred) is experienced. Or, in Rudolf Otto's terminology, the "numinous" refers to the mystical, unmediated experience of the sacred. In antiquity, as Mircea Eliade establishes in *The Myth of the Eternal Return* (1974), there was no secular–profane dichotomy as "the archaic world knows nothing of 'profane' activities: every act which has a definite meaning – hunting, fishing agriculture; games, conflicts, sexuality –in some way participates in the sacred" (Eliade, 1974: 27–28). It is this sense of the sacred that nobles ineffectively tried to recreate when they placed ruins in the grounds of their stately homes in the nineteenth century. Sophie Thomas relates the tale of the removal of some of the Roman ruins in 1818 from Leptis Magna in Libya, and their reconfiguration in the grounds of Windsor Great Park several years later. Lord Elgin's controversial removal of the marbles from the Parthenon is the most famous example. In some cases these reconstructions were no more than follies. The Libyan ruins were rearranged into a fanciful creation called the Temple of Augustus "bearing no direct relation to their original disposition at Leptis" (Thomas, 2003: 177). Re-formed ruins became features onto which Georgian and Victorian nobility projected their subconscious desires: to be seen to be part of antiquity gave them greater ancestral anchorage and thereby higher standing in a culture that venerated hereditary status.

The ruins in Windsor Great Park are palimpsests or spectral presences which have the aura of the original because they *are* original, but as they were dislocated from both their situatedness and their meaning, they have merely been given a pseudo-role as a part of domesticated antiquity in the English royal gardens. Nonetheless, their aura of originality gives them their desirability. A variety of dubious justifications for the removal of ruins has been posited. It had often been stated by richer nations that others did not treasure their ruins as they should. In *The Innocents Abroad*, Mark

Twain reported that mummies were used for fuel in the steam engines of the Egyptian railways (Twain, 1869: 481). Whilst there is some evidence this may be a joke or myth, the fact remains that mummies were freely available and not treated as valuable objects at that time.

Culturally prized artificial remains are ruins; non-valued remains merely constitute dereliction. One is beautiful, the other is an eyesore. One is almost always distanced by time; the other presses its living-memory sadness into our consciousness. One is culturally sanctioned; the other is not. No one asserts that Fountains Abbey disfigures the rural English landscape, whereas the debris of the twin towers in New York certainly provided a scene of shocking devastation. As with these two sites, decisions are made constantly about what should be done with ruins: whether they should be preserved, salvaged, restored, or left alone. In some cases practical considerations of health and safety may impinge on these assessments. Obviously when ruins are rebuilt their meaning is affected because there is a loss of the aura of the original. The late twentieth century saw a rapidly escalating trend towards adaptive uses of buildings, and it is commonplace in Britain to find churches enjoying an architectural second life turned into restaurants, accommodation, art galleries or shops. Some may find this sacrilegious but many are satisfied that beautiful buildings have survived demolition. An example is the Alma de Cuba restaurant in Liverpool, which was once the oldest Catholic Church in the city, St. Peter's. Built in 1788, it fell into disuse in 1978. Much of the interior has been stripped out but the exoskeleton and the stained glass with its depictions of the Stations of the Cross has been preserved, and the venue continues to convey a strong impression of a Catholic church. There is no attempt to hide the religious origin of the building – quite the reverse: it is made into a feature. In fact the altar remains and a gospel choir performs on Sundays. It is a glamorous place of entertainment. Perhaps this signifies a loss of the sacred and a modern fondness for the paraphernalia and architecture of the sacred; the form persists without the function. The formerly sacred spaces are commodified; the sacredness *appears* to endure as it has become inextricably associated with architectures and forms, but it is in effect merely the reification of the aesthetics of sacredness. The subjectivity so crucial in the experience of sacredness is turned into objectivity. To see this phenomenon in a positive light would be to say that the shared experience of the building becomes a collective encounter with re-enchantment; in a more negative light we could say the sacred architecture has become fetishised.

There are three ways in which sacredness is experienced. The first and most profound is an interior faith perspective; this is a spiritual or believer's perspective. The second is as a respecter of another's sacredness so, for example, believers of many faiths will recognise that Varanasi is sacred to Hindus and Buddhists or that the Western Wall is sacred for Jews and so on. This is a pluralistic and concordant perspective. It works from within either a theological framework or a cultural framework which entails respect for other religions. It may also apply to people of one era appreciating the faith of a bygone era, in the way that twenty-first century Christians may be aware of the polytheism of the Ancient Greeks. The third way is a secular sacredness, if such an apparent paradox can be contemplated. It is the type of "sacredness lite" that is taken on by places, artefacts or people because of their current esteem, the cultural meanings that attach, without any necessarily truly religious significance. It is the osmosis of sacredness into secular fields, the gradual and often unconscious absorption of ideas through propinquity and nostalgia. It is a lament for lost enchantment.

This slippage of the secular into the sacred brings into question the dichotomy proposed by theorists Rudolf Otto and Mircea Eliade, and suggests that their sacred–secular polarity is not universally understood at the present time. Timothy Insoll discusses several studies of non-Western cultures which explore the lack of an easily identifiable destinction between the sacred and secular space in *Archaeology, Ritual, Religion* (2004). It is therefore reasonable to suggest that there is no unified understanding of the sacred any more in the postmodern West and, as Conrad Ostwald notes in *Secular Steeples* (2003), rather than a polarisation there is much more of a *continuum* between sacred and secular (Ostwald, 2003: 98). He discusses the "permeable boundaries between the sacred and the secular, and the transfer of religiosity to other cultural forms" (20). This suggests there are multifarious versions of the sacred. In *God and Enchantment of Place,* David Brown argues that there is a "reinvigorated sense of the sacramental" (Brown, 2004: 5). He argues that places and architecture can produce feelings of the sacramental in unchurched Christians which are not inferior to those felt by praying Christians in church (Brown, 2004: 408). This connects with Baudrillard's conjecture (1994), that previously meaningful boundaries have lost power. So, in modern societies differentiation reigned supreme, but in postmodern societies these boundaries collapse or "implode".

The heritage industry is one of those booming areas of the secular-sacred. Arguably, it is in effect a category of pseudo-sacredness. In the West spiritual explanations of the world are eroding, but his fact does not preclude a desire for the numinous, even if it is without the religious convictions or creeds that are its adjuncts. A glance at the National Trust's *Annual*

Report 2007/08 reveals it has 3.56 million members and 52,000 volunteers. In that year over 12 million people visited properties and 50 million visited open air sites. Its investment portfolio is £916 million. This shows what a successful enterprise heritage has become, and how highly the public rates it and the opportunities offered. Although many of the National Trust sites are clearly not religious, the veneration of the old buildings is not dissimilar to the worship once widely participated on Sunday mornings in church. The public spends its Sundays venerating these sites instead.

Ideological Conflict: the sacred ruins of the Bamiyan Buddhas of Afghanistan

This discussion considers the Bamiyan statues, their recent destruction and the feasibility and import of their rebuilding. The two statues were giant standing Buddhas, Vairocana and Sakyamuni, measuring 55 and 37 metres high respectively, the largest standing Buddhist statues in the world. They were carved into massive cusped niches in the red sandstone of the mountains of the Hindu Kush in what is now central Afghanistan. The base structure carved from the rock was then added to with stucco so that details could be sculpted, embellished and painted onto the substructure (Rizvi, 2005: 17). The valley lay at the heart of what was the Silk Route, the principal flow of trade between the Roman Empire and India and China. It was a transcontinental travellers' convergence of cultures and religions with a complex history. In addition to the statues, ancient frescoes were painted on the walls of a system of hundreds of caves and passages that weaves around in the rock behind the statues. The caves once contained Buddhist monasteries and this whole site was a place of pilgrimage. Many of the frescoes are now ruined or in very poor repair, and some of Bamiyan's most destitute people now inhabit the caves. It is thought the Buddha statues were created around the sixth century when the area was part of the Kingdom of Kushan. As Buddhists have not lived in the valley since the tenth century, these were not considered sacred by the local Hazara people, who are Shia Muslims. Until their destruction, the local Afghans had taken a pluralistic and concordant perspective of these statues: they could see their religious significance to others in the past and in Buddhist cultures, but they revered the statues as part of their cultural landscape.

Even prior to their annihilation the Buddhas were not in good condition for numerous reasons. They had been subject to attacks by an eleventh-century Islamic king; in 1747 their faces had been removed on the orders of the

Persian King, Nadir Shah Afshar; they had been looted and vandalised in recent decades. Finally, in 1998 the Taliban seized the area causing havoc and executed many local people who had fiercely resisted them. In February 2001 their leader, Mullah Omar, declaring the statues to be idols and gods of the infidels, ordered their destruction in a campaign which saw the demise of many other pre-Islamic artefacts across the country. Despite protests from the United Nations and several Muslim countries, the two statues were obliterated in a series of explosions in March 2001. Unsurprisingly, the Afghans of the region were fond of the statues and proud of them. The resemblance of figures painted in the caves to the local Hazara people is frequently noted. The influence of Greek antiquity on the Eastern statues has been observed (Rowland, 1962: 20) but not always appreciated, as the first British account of the Bamiyan Buddhas in 1934 reveals. It was written by travel writer Robert Byron, who slated the statues, saying they had no artistic value. Given that this was a man who was full of the prejudices of his time, and who did not rate the Taj Mahal highly, it does not merit serious scrutiny.

A lively debate has arisen about the possible reconstruction or reincarnation of the statues. One challenging question is whether this is a reasonable project to undertake given that the population of Bamiyan is mostly in poverty and the rebuilding of the statues is estimated as costing US $50m. Some argue the remaining recesses should be left empty signifying gaping wounds which bear testimony to human destructiveness. Other projects have been broached, including leaving the niches physically empty but projecting laser images of the statues into them. The reasons stated for rebuilding give an insight into the valuation of the statues. Economic value is cited by Afghanistan's first female governor, Habiba Sarabi, who recognises the interrelatedness of factors: the local economy would bring monetary rewards from increased tourism that the reconstructed statues would bring. Local self-esteem would benefit from the "undoing" of the actions of the Taliban in a form of cultural healing and restitution. Unquestionably, the statues can never truly be rebuilt, only superficial copies of them can be made. This is because they were hewn out of the rock and, as Florence M. Hetzler wrote, this was a part of their uniqueness: "the art is carved out of the land and is part of it" (1988: 53). Any reconstruction would be semantically different, no matter how convincing the replication.

Newsweek's 2001 reporting of the story included a government minister, Mirheydar Motaher, quoted as saying "it felt like Afghanistan lost a child", adding that the Buddhas "must be rebuilt for their historical, not religious, value". Other Afghans hold similar views. A local man states that the Taliban thought people worshipped the Buddhas: "But it wasn't a holy site, it was a historic site" (*Newsweek*, 2001). This sits uncomfortably with the knowledge that the nations keenest to contribute money and expertise to rebuilding are those with large Buddhist populations, suggesting that some do have a religious interest in the statues.

Questions have been raised by critics who think the site has become *more* significant since the demolition of the statues. The rapid dissemination to viewing millions of a very visual act of destruction was ensured by television and internet technologies. Previously the statues were largely unknown except to archaeologists partly because Afghanistan has been off the tourist routes for three decades. It is hoped that new historic discoveries can be made in this region. Indeed, as recently as September 2008 Reuters reported that archaeologists at Bamiyan have unearthed a third-century 62-foot reclining Buddha statue located near the demolished statues. It is badly damaged but it gives hope to archaeologists also seeking a 300m long statue reported by a Chinese pilgrim, Xuanzang, who travelled through in AD 632. Another silver lining is that iconic Buddhist art works, now thought to be the oldest oil paintings in the world, have been discovered in numerous caves at Bamiyan since the destruction of the statues.

As the twin towers of New York proved to be potent symbols of American capitalist domination to the terrorists who destroyed them and their occupants, so the Bamiyan statues were also twin icons destroyed by terrorists. As they were symbols of a religion that had disappeared locally, so the professed reason for their destruction does not stand up to examination, especially since the statues had survived a millennium of Muslim dominance in the area. The Taliban government declared that the Buddhas were "idols", and claimed that since idols are not permitted in Islam they were destroyed. If this thinking were consistent with accepted Islamic teaching then all of Egypt's pre-Islamic monuments, for example, would have been destroyed. However, the reasoning is disingenuous and it seems likely that Taliban leaders used the destruction of the statues as a stick with which they could beat all opponents, a means of punishing local people who opposed them, and a gesture aimed to outrage the watching world. It was a symbolic destruction of an ancient sacred monument and a brute assertion of power.

A number of issues arises when considering the reconstruction enterprise. It is arguably the case that the remaining outlined niches testify to absence even more powerfully than if the whole cliff face had been demolished. Statues carved into the fabric of the landscape have a duality as part of nature and part of culture. They reveal embodiment and disembodiment at once; their essence has gone and cannot be regained. Unesco's position is that reconstruction using original fragments should be undertaken and it has rejected proposals for a concrete substructure. However, as only 200 tonnes of gravel and dust has been salvaged and few large segments survive, the reconstruction is a mammoth, and perhaps impossible, undertaking. The statues will be considered replicas if they are made of more than 50% new material; otherwise they are considered to be reconstructions. Parallels can be drawn here with Baudrillard's (1994: 9) dismissive comments on the simulacrum of the Lascaux caves, in Southern France, a site of some fine Palaeolithic paintings. These replica caves were created in order to preserve the originals from destruction. The copies, known as Lascaux II, were opened to the public in 1983 and are described as a facsimile of the caves (from Latin *fac simile,* "make like"). Conceivably, the replica Buddhas would have this *faux* quality too, rather than the aura of the original.

Ideological Replication: sacred ruins and Moscow's Cathedral of Christ the Saviour

Religious buildings that are deliberately and violently destroyed for ideological or iconoclastic reasons tend to be rebuilt to resemble what they were previously. A prime example of this appears in Moscow in the Cathedral of Christ the Saviour, Russia's largest church. In 1812 Tsar Alexander I commissioned the construction of the cathedral to mark Russia's victory over Napoleon, and to thank God for saving the country from "ruination" (Gentes, 1998). He ordered the destruction of the Alekseevskii Monastery to make way for the new cathedral (Sidorov, 2000: 548). The nuns were so strongly opposed to the plan that, according to urban myth, the abbess cursed the site. Nicholas's decision to raze the monastery set a precedent for Stalin (Gentes, 1998: 69). Even so, the grandiose Cathedral was consecrated in 1883. In 1931, in the Soviet Union's Stalinist era, it was ruthlessly demolished, as were many Russian churches. Stalin's intention was to replace it with a monolith, a grand palace sometimes called the Palace of Soviets, which was to have been the highest building ever created at the time, with Lenin triumphantly standing at its pinnacle (Gentes, 1998: 84). This bizarre conception was never made reality partly because of World War II and also because of problems with the stability of the foundations which were slipping towards the Moscow River.

As with the Bamiyan statues, the destruction of the cathedral was a calculated act of symbolic violence. The new replacement building was completed rapidly; it was started in 1991, after the dissolution of the Soviet

Union, and was consecrated in 2000. It is not only in the same style as the old cathedral; it is almost a replica. On the Russian Orthodox Church's English website it is referred to as a "reconstruction", not a new church. It is a hugely impressive and opulent cathedral, but has been the subject of a good deal of criticism. In religious buildings there is always tension between self-aggrandising and glorifying God. It was proposed at a time of huge economic upheaval when a quarter of the population of Russia was living in poverty. Maria Tumarkin's *Traumascapes* (2005) recounts the tale of the new cathedral. In 1991, the same year that the red flag was lowered from the Kremlin, President Boris Yeltsin ordered that an exact replica be constructed on the same site but it was not universally seen as a phoenix-like symbol of the rebirth of spirituality and renewal. Some saw the proposal as "a monstrosity on the same scale as its destruction – an expression of megalomania, not of far-sighted reparation" (Tumarkin, 2005: 16). The methods used to raise funds were secret and "dubious"; some felt it was a "second Kremlin" (Tumarkin, 2005: 17). It stands as testimony that the past can neither simply be erased nor reconstructed. For her, it gives the impression of an opulent palace rather than a place of prayer. Indeed the cathedral's English website <http://www.xxc.ru/english/index.htm> contains many beautiful photographs of the church in its various stages of construction, but tells us nothing about Christianity or faith; it is all about the building.

To reconstruct a building as closely as one that previously existed and was deliberately razed is a political decision, reflecting the pride of politicians in manifesting their desire to erase the communist era by the recreation of a nineteenth-century church which was also in 1818 a political building, given that it was built to commemorate Russia's recent victory over Napoleon. The building would appear to be significant to Russia, as a symbol of a powerful and proud nation which endured a traumatic twentieth century. If, as Foucault's *The Order of Things* demonstrates, only historical difference can highlight the presuppositions of an age, then there must be a suggestion that Russia is reproducing the power relations of the nineteenth century when it was ruled by tsars who were autocratic emperors following rules of patrilineal descent. In what sense is it a discontinuity, and in what sense is it continuity? Is it part of Russia's heritage, or Russia's heritage industry? It is clear that the new cathedral represents more of a nineteenth-century sense of Russianness rather than a contemporary one. Its presence poses the question of what a twenty-first century sense of Russian identity and Christian sacredness can be – about the nature of Russia's own cultural imaginary. Arguably, the building is de-spiritualised and de-historicised. It symbolises a denial of historical process not an acknowledgement of it. It raises questions about what kind of cultural competence is required to read the cathedral. To understand its meaning, one needs to know its history and the history of its predecessor. In Pierre Bourdieu's terms, it represents the *petrification* of history and cultural process. The political discourse about why it was rebuilt is taken as read. It is doxa: there is no need to explain. There is an apparent co-extensiveness of signs and thought. If we read the cathedral as a text we can see that it has other texts interwoven with the first. Its function is that it is more than a place of worship: it is part of a developing sense of continuity between the present and the past. It cannot be claimed to be an exact replica given that it incorporates the latest technology and was built using modern construction methods and materials; it has air-conditioning, elevators and underground parking. David Remnick in *Resurrection: The Struggle for a New Russia* (1998: 174) suggests that, despite many obstacles, it may mark the rebirth of a nation. Controversially, the Tsar Nicholas II and his family were canonised as "passion bearers" of the Russian Orthodox Church. In Orthodox Christianity a passion bearer is a person who faces death with Christ-like humility. Monuments to Tsar Alexander II and Nicholas II have recently been erected nearby.

The Orthodox religion in the imperial age was officially sanctioned and its senior members were close to powerful monarchs; this has been a feature of Orthodox Christianity. Sidorov writes that pre-revolutionary Russia was "Orthodoxy, Autocracy, Nationality" and that "[t]o convert to Orthodoxy meant to become Russian" (2000: 550). This was, of course, one of the reasons for its persecution and for the communists' hatred of religion; without doubt they saw it as ideologically void, but they also considered the church to be in an unhealthy collusion with the autocratic royals. Following the death throes of communism there is an uneasy relationship between Orthodox Christianity and post-communist Russia. The authorities' privileging of the Russian Orthodox Church has led to resentment from smaller Protestant churches. A law passed in 1997 required churches to have existed in Russia for fifteen years before being permitted to register. The avowed aim was to prevent incursions from Western proselytisers who it was feared would take advantage of the weakened state of the Russian Orthodox Church. This association with restrictive practices harms the organisation which was hated initially by the Bolsheviks, not purely out of ideological opposition, but for the pragmatic reason that it supported and was in turn assisted by reactionary and repressive royalty. It is feasible to propose that the replica cathedral represents an abreaction: a release of tension by recalling trauma. Russia is releasing unconscious psychological tension by reliving the past. Given that the cathedral has been replicated, in its presence it implies its absence.

New Incarnations: sacred ruins and ideological renegotiations at Coventry Cathedral

During World War II many churches across Europe and beyond were destroyed by bombing but not all were rebuilt. Many historically insignificant churches survived demolition but have not been used for worship for 60 years. Coventry Cathedral, also known as St. Michael's, provides an interesting illustration of the synchronous preservation of ruins and reconstruction. Initially, after the end of the war, there was strong local feeling that a replica of the previous cathedral should be built (Campbell, 1992: 210). Some held a strong conviction that the existing ruins should remain as a war memorial; indeed they had already served this purpose since 1945. Others became irritated at what they saw as a sentimental attachment to rubble (Campbell, 1992: 212). Debates took place in *The Times* (Campbell, 1992: 208) about the relative merits of different designs: revivalism versus a new kind of architecture. The new design was chosen by means of an open competition overseen by a Reconstruction Committee. There were conflicting views about the kind of cathedral that should be built. Although the brief claimed to be open, in practice restrictions and compromises soon developed that meant that it was difficult to resolve these religious, historical and architectural tensions and accommodate them into an aesthetic and functioning sacred space. Campbell details the lengthy and almost absurd process that followed in selecting a winning entry. The entry of Basil Spence was chosen and became a reality. An element of congruity was brought about by the use of the same type of stone, but the architecture is a text that is very much of the twentieth century. A sense of connectedness with origins, and with the natural world, is established in the form of the font, which is a boulder from Bethlehem.

As we have seen, religious buildings that have been destroyed because of an attempt to suppress Christian ideology are more likely to be to be reconstructed as replicas; those that are destroyed as collateral by a foreign aggressor during a war, such as World War II, were *not* reconstructed in the same style. The new Coventry Cathedral is a construction with no pretensions to be anything other than modern, whilst the ruins of the former cathedral lie nearby. It had been a beautiful medieval sandstone building with a carved oak roof, and stained glass windows. After the bombing raids only the spire remained and the rest was ruins. It was decided that it should be left to symbolise destruction and remembrance. Following the bombing, a clergyman made a cross out of three giant nails found in the rubble which became a significant part of the altar in the new building.

The new cathedral followed an innovative design. It is both a popular and critical success because there is a diachronous connection with the old cathedral, in that the ruins remain, but there is a sense of progression and renewal in the new form. Worshippers and visitors can read the two side by side and understand their story. Whilst it is not unique in leaving its ruins as a memorial, it is one of the most successful examples. It has ambitious plans for Golden Jubilee celebrations in 2012 that focus on its reconciliation ministry, a key part of the dynamic identity of the cathedral. The Community of the Cross of Nails, based at the cathedral, is a network of 150 organisations from 60 countries who have committed themselves to a shared ministry of reconciliation.

Conclusion

The different ways in which the sacred is viewed in contemporary society effectively opens up new negotiations about the rebuilding of ruins. Whilst the Bamiyan Buddhas are irreparable and irreplaceable as sacred ruins, they could feasibly be replicated so as to give a Baudrillarian simulacrum of the originals. Coventry Cathedral presents a sense of Renaissance, of renewed hope and reconciliation. Even the manner of its planning and design took on board extensive consultation and open, fair competition. The Moscow Cathedral presents a vision of the restoration of an old order, or at least a lack of clarity in a vision of a new Russia. Of course, as the Church of England did not suffer the execution of 95,000 of its priests and bishops as the Russian Orthodox Church did, this may account for its ability to move forwards. The Anglican Church was able to live and breathe, and its *faith* as such was not under attack by the Nazis, as the Stalinists assaulted the Russian Orthodox Church wholesale.

The pain and loss endured by the destruction of sacred spaces and monuments serves as an acknowledgement that humankind's desire for enchantment is hard-wired. Whether it is heritage that vanishes, or the sacredness of the space, it is significant for religions and for the sense of identity of the people who see them as part of their cultural landscape.

Fig. 11-1.
One of the Bamiyan Buddhas as it was before 2001.

Fig. 11-2. Cliff face where the Bamiyan stood until it was blown up by Taliban militants in 2001.

Fig. 11-3. Coventry Cathedral, old and new buildings.

Fig. 11-4. The rebuilt Cathedral of Christ the Saviour, Moscow.

References

Andrew, P. 2006. "The Aesthetics of Ruins: Review", *BPL/AHH: The Art Book*, 13(2): 47–49.

Baudelaire, C. 1986. *The Painters of Modern Life and Other Essays*. New York and London. Da Capo.

Baudrillard, J. 1994. *Simulacra and Simulation*. Translated by S. Faria Glaser. Ann Arbor. University of Michigan.

Benjamin, W. (1936) 2008. *The Work of Art in the Age of Mechanical Reproduction*. Translated by J.A. Underwood. London. Penguin.

Brown, D. 2004. *God and Enchantment of Place: Reclaiming Human Experience*. New York. Oxford University Press.

Campbell, L. 1992. "Towards a New Cathedral: The Competition for Coventry Cathedral 1950–51", *Architectural History*, 35: 208–234 <http://www.jstor.org/stable/1568577> – accessed 11 September 2008.

Dehghanpisheh, B. 2001. 'The New Afghan Government Hopes To Restore The Archaeological Treasures Destroyed By The Taliban', *Newsweek <http://www.newsweek.com/id/75224>*.

Durand, W. 2007. *Rationale Divinorum Officiorum of of Mende: A New Translation of the Prologue and Book One* (Records of Western Civilization Series). Translated and edited by Timothy M. Thibodeau. New York and Chichester. Columbia University Press.

Eliade, M. 1974. *The Myth of the Eternal Return: or, Cosmos and History*. Translated by W.R. Trask. New York. Princeton University Press. (First published in French in 1954.)

Gentes, A. 1998. 'The Life, Death and Resurrection of the Cathedral of Christ the Saviour, Moscow', *History Workshop Journal*, 46 (Autumn): 63–95.

Hetzler, F.M. 1988. 'Causality: Ruin Time and Ruins', *Leonardo*, 21(1): 51–55.

Ginsberg, R. 2004. *The Aesthetics of Ruins*. New York and Amsterdam. Rodopi.

Insoll, T. 2004. *Archaeology, Ritual, Religion* (Themes in Archaeology). London and New York. Taylor & Francis.

Jervis, J. 1998. *Exploring the Modern: Patterns of Western Culture and Civilization*. Oxford. Blackwell.

National Trust. *Annual Report 2007/8*. <http://www.nationaltrust.org.uk>.

Ostwalt, C. 2003. *Secular Steeples: Popular Culture and the Religious Imagination*. Harrisburg, London and New York. Trinity Press Continuum.

Remnick, D. 1998. *Resurrection: The Struggle for a New Russia*. Vintage Books.

Rizvi, S. 2005. 'Reimaging Bamiyan's Lost Buddhas: The Art of Xie Chengshui', *Eastern Art Report*, 49(1): 17–22 <http://www.eapgroup.com/articles/ear49_xiechengshui.pdf> – accessed 11 November 2008.

Rowland, B. 1962. 'Religious Art East and West', *History of Religions*, 2 (1): 11–32.

Sidorov, D. 2000. 'National Monumentalization and the Politics of Scale: The Resurrections of the Cathedral of Christ the Savior in Moscow', *Annals of the Association of American Geographers* 90(3): 548–572.

Thomas, S. 2003. 'Assembling History: Fragments and Ruins', *European Romantic Review,* 14(2): 177–186.

Twain, M. 2003. *The Innocents Abroad.* London and New York. Penguin.

Tumarkin, M. 2005. *Traumascapes*: *The Power and Fate of Places Transformed by Tragedy*. Carlton. Melbourne University Press.

Weber, M. 1946/1958. *From Max Weber*. Translated and edited by H.H. Gerth and C. Wright Mills. New York. Galaxy.

Chapter Twelve

Tracing Bodies: Jane Urquhart's *A Map of Glass* and Sacramental Geography

Mark Godin

As much as sacred space is inscribed by places of worship – churches, synagogues, mosques, temples – or specific holy sites – lands or cities, shrines, burial grounds, memorials – the idea of sacred space may also refer to a particular way of looking at and inhabiting the world. Sacred space then construes a relationship to natural or built landscape that is anchored in theological concerns, broadly understood, meaning theology from various faith traditions. In order to investigate this, however, this essay looks at one particular faith tradition and particular liturgical constructions which help to generate that relationship; that is, I look at Christianity and that faith's sacramental life, drawing specific examples from the Reformed, Presbyterian tradition, but hoping that conclusions may be applied to other traditions as well. At least, I explore the possibilities that are extant for understanding that relationship imaginatively, for hinting at what the claim might mean, with the help of another text, the novel *A Map of Glass*, by Jane Urquhart. This novel offers a writer's image of mapping the world of its characters, tracing bodies in their relationship with one another. Theologically, I believe that this image of mapping suggests a key to understanding what happens for Christians who participate in sacraments.[1]

The geographers Denis Wood and John Fels write:

> And this, essentially, is what maps give us, *reality*, a reality that exceeds our vision, our reach, the span of our days, a reality we achieve no other way. We are always mapping the invisible or the unattainable or the erasable, the future or the past, the whatever-is-not-here-present-to-our-senses-now and, through the gift that the map gives us, transmuting it into everything it is not . . . *into the real* (Wood, 1993: 4).

This is the power that maps have: with them, we mark out the emplacement and displacement of the people and objects that connect stories, bodies, landscapes and memory. The maps we make go beyond city plans and road atlases, to record and project a multitude of complicated relationships; so it is no wonder that, when a theologian believes that the way people worship God gives them a place and direction in the world, the same theologian might also think of that worship as a kind of map. Gordon Lathrop, for instance, has connected Christian liturgy to the 'known places [which] enable us to have an experienced map of space [and] make possible our explorations into unexperienced space' (1993: 105). Yet, when he went on to write a book called *Holy Ground*, he pulled back from the word "geography", writing "A Liturgical Cosmology" instead. To speak of liturgy as a map or geography is only metaphorical, he writes, because "worship is . . . no essay on the interdependence of landmass, living creatures, and weather" and "liturgy is not writing and study, not any kind of 'graphy'" (Lathrop, 2003: 56, 57). Fair enough; but in this paper I will argue that the image needs to be pressed further, that with liturgy, specifically sacraments, writing does happen. Participants write on each other and are written upon. We will see this with the help of that other map, *A Map of Glass*.

Lathrop's hesitancy with geography perhaps stems from the fact that maps are unstable texts. The bodies in the world which we map – human and otherwise – are fluid. Maps are also symbolic texts; their marks and images point us elsewhere, to the world. Yet they also define the world we know. Mapping is a hermeneutical exercise; that is, when we are mapping, we are engaged in interpreting both the world and the signs and symbols used on maps. Where people are is worked out through tracing bodies in relation to one another. Bodies are touched into understanding, but that touch also marks what it touches – traces are inscribed, and every writing on and of the body is a writing over.

I should say a word about Urquhart's novel, which has an extremely complex plot and cast of characters. The book wraps around Sylvia, the lover of a man who dies from Alzheimer's disease, and her need to tell the story of her affair to Jerome, the artist who found her lover's body. Yet the story Sylvia tells is also the story of her life, her lover's family, and all of their connections to landscape. The reader learns that Sylvia's lover, Andrew, was an historical geographer, spending his life at tasks such as "mapping the scant foundations of houses abandoned by vanished settlers" (Urquhart, 2005: 28). The poetry of geographical names intertwines with the story of Sylvia's lost love, unfolding among the flashbacks, giving form to the memories. The structure of the book itself becomes a kind of map. Although the first and the last part of the novel narrate Sylvia and Jerome's meetings, the middle part takes the form of Andrew's story of four generations of his family, written in notebooks Sylvia lends to Jerome. This story-within-the-story constitutes a well of memory which draws upon landscape for its imagery. The relationships of characters are viewed in proximity to place.[2]

I also should clarify references to sacraments, which, for the purpose of this paper, is restricted to baptism and Eucharist.[3] Baptism initiates a person into a Christian community. The Eucharist is a sharing of bread and wine among the community to make real the presence of Christ as God's generous love. Of course, any such definitions are reductionist. Sacraments are symbolic acts using physical, earthly items – water, bread, wine – which take on meaning only in contact with people in the context of prescribed language and action, and that meaning is polyvalent. As with *A Map of Glass*, sacraments draw from a well of memory, referring participants to stories narrated in sacred texts. The actions of baptising with the sign of water or breaking bread, sharing wine, also are surrounded by prayer. Both sacraments have prayer with two main parts: *anamnesis*, the work of remembrance; and *epiclesis*, calling upon God's Holy Spirit. The remembrance chiefly thanks God for what God does and contextualises the action, referring to the story of the people gathered to pray. The call upon the Holy Spirit asks God to make the events real, to unite people not only with God but with one another – to draw a map of relationships, one might say. Yet this sacramental map is drawn by the relationships involved as much as it is a sketch of them.[4]

Tactile Maps

In *A Map of Glass*, Sylvia's story is complicated because she might have an autism spectrum disorder. She finds human interaction difficult, though she has an eye for the detail of things. This allows her to befriend Julia, a blind woman for whom she makes tactile maps of the county in which they live:

> "She's blind," Sylvia explained [to Jerome], "but touching a map is one of the ways she is able to see. I didn't think I could do it at first, didn't think I could translate landscape into texture on a board. But then I know the County so well; I suppose that made it easier" (Urquhart, 2005: 123–124).

Sylvia represents what she knows and loves of her home geography with a variety of materials – everything from fabric to wood – which symbolise varieties of terrain. The symbolism must be very exact – to mean not just "water" but water that can be rough, not just a beach but one "filled with small, smooth stones" (Urquhart, 2005: 68 and 146). This is because Julia "not only wanted to know how to get to a place . . . she wanted to be able to see what was in the vicinity" (Urquhart, 2005: 69). Using her imagination, Julia could experience the world through touch.

When Sylvia tells her friend that "she knew a man whose profession allowed him to explore not only geological phenomena but also the traces of human activity that were left behind on the textured surface of the earth", Julia comments that "the whole world is a kind of Braille" (Urquhart, 2005: 68). Note that Julia's association of exploration with a reading and writing system springs specifically from the leaving behind of human traces: it is not only that human beings can read the earth's story from the stones, but that we also write our own story in the dust. Of Andrew, Sylvia says that

> "He claimed that everywhere he went he found evidence of the behaviour of his forebears: rail fences, limestone foundations, lilac bushes blooming on otherwise abandoned farmsteads, an arcade of trees leading to a house that is no longer there." (Urquhart, 2005: 96–97).

These are "remnants" and the "sad refuse" of lives lived, but still they do remain; they have been written upon the world and so provide a kind of material memory (Urquhart, 2005: 97).

The image of tactile maps extends far beyond maps produced on boards or paper; the characters of the novel become tactile maps for one another in their relationships. Sylvia talks about how her affair with Andrew "opened the door of the world for her", letting her experience what she had never known before (Urquhart, 2005: 117). Replete with her memories of intimacies, Sylvia implies that touch and caress draw the boundaries that remap and thus remake her existence. Bodies connect to landscape and make it known in passage after passage; for example, Sylvia speaks of

> the sense that while we held each other we were, in turn, being held by the rocks and trees we could see from the windows and the creeks and springs we could sometimes hear running through the valley. (Urquhart, 2005: 339).

The touching of flesh depicts a web of various levels of intimacy, but also writes relationships upon one's memory. The exception appears in Sylvia's relationship with her husband, Malcolm, who – the narrator often and expressly tells the reader – never touches his wife's body, even when helping her with the clasp of a necklace (Urquhart, 2005: 314). One suspects that Malcolm, a doctor, thinks of Sylvia more as patient than wife; he has rejected her tactile map and can never be truly alive with her.[5]

For Sylvia, living extends out from her memory; her tactile map is composed of all the details she remembers of her clandestine meetings with Andrew. Rather than getting insight into the earth from this map, she scours the earth for its record of her love. She holds onto a geography textbook not so much for what it might tell her about reading the landscape but because of "the incised lines that would indicate that Andrew had marked a particular passage with his thumbnail", so that she could feel "this practically invisible, frail trace of him on the printed text" (Urquhart, 2005: 92). When he finally disappears, missing their last rendezvous, she takes his journals and notebooks away with her because "the ink on the page" was "the last trace of his moving hand" (Urquhart, 2005: 347). Such texts become aids for fixing in Sylvia's memory Andrew's hands moving over another surface, over her skin, writing on her heart.

One may see that sacraments, too, make a tactile map. Contact with physical elements set in a context of narrative and theological meaning shapes people, provides a way to see the world. In baptism, the sign of water functions "to claim us as . . . members of the household of God" and "call us into a new life of growth and service" (PCC, 1991: 121). The baptised one thus is directed to see the world through the lens of the crucifixion and resurrection of Christ, to be oriented towards a hope that what has been submerged may be revealed and what has been broken may be mended. In the Eucharist, one might pray "that all who eat and drink at this table may be one body and one holy people", that "we may be united to Christ and to each other" (PCC, 1991: 90 and 92). Partaking bread and wine from the hands of another engrain in a person the centrality of sharing. Both the changing of perspective in the one sacrament and that sharing in the other recall particular stories, however: Jesus being baptised; Jesus sharing bread. In turn, each of these stories link to other stories, including the stories of participants.

At a very basic level, the physical elements mediate between persons. One person applies the sign of water to another; one person shares a portion of bread, a cup of wine, with another. These actions map physical memory through the meeting of bodies. The memory out of which you live is then not composed only of the stories of sacred tradition but also of and with the people among whom you worship God, and in turn among all the people with whom you live. In a Eucharistic prayer, for instance, one might give thanks to God for sending the Holy Spirit "that we might live no longer for ourselves, but for him who died and rose for us" – and, if for him, then for all others (PCC, 1991: 99). The *anamnesis* situates the participant within the community's story as it is remembered; the *epiclesis* calls on God's Spirit so that this might become a true "re-membering" – a re-embodying of the presence of Christ in the story, a continuing of that story in community.

Participation in sacraments not only locates a person in a sacred geography of time and space, but also projects forward from where a person is.

At this point, we can see that both the literary relationships of the novel and the liturgical relationships generated in sacraments trace out the space in which people move in their habits of touching. The body comes to know and be familiar with another body not statically but in the way they move towards and away from each other. Our tactile maps are formed by habit and routine, something noted geographically and sociologically by Kevin Hetherington, who writes in an article on space and touch, "Whereas we enter our houses through the front door, we enter our homes through our slippers" (Hetherington, 2003: 1939). Our experiences of a space are constructed from the feelings that accumulate with our presence in that space. We locate ourselves by touch. Yes, that touch is fragmentary – as Hetherington notes, it is "local, specific, incomplete, multiple, personal, erroneous perhaps" – but deep connection comes from piecing together an interpretation of the world from the fragments with which we are presented (Hetherington, 2003: 1942). Although his article uses as examples the space created by the visually impaired navigating museum exhibits through touch and the devotional space generated by human contact with religious relics, this creation of an understanding of particular spaces does not occur only with things. As we see with *A Map of Glass* and with sacraments, more than a one-sided gathering of data we also draw maps of human connection from the collection of our experiences with one another, the contact of bodies which each have their own perspectives.

Bodies and Fracture

In the novel, Sylvia strives to learn as much as she can about her lover's last journey: she examines maps to imagine what happened to him and "add some information to the long, sad message of Andrew's silence" (Urquhart, 2005: 348). She seeks to follow Andrew himself, who once said to her that "there was always a mark left on a landscape by anyone who entered it" (Urquhart, 2005: 326). However, Sylvia discovers that reading this is not that easy; the man who spent his life recording a vanishing past did not leave much of a trace of his own – certainly no trace of their affair, unknown to anyone but them (Urquhart, 2005: 326, 328, and 346). "Landscapes are unreliable", Sylvia muses; they "are subject to change" (Urquhart, 2005: 146). She learns one dark undercurrent of the exercise of mapmaking: while you are trying to represent the landscape as accurately as possible, it continues shifting, however minutely, so that you are always only documenting a past.[6] In a way, a map is the result of a violent attempt to arrest the earth, but it remains a kind of phantom. At one point, Sylvia places maps alongside "objects" and "vanished children" in "the family of the dead" (Urquhart, 2005: 76). And though she had once found solace only in this past's family, after experiencing love and loss Sylvia admits:

> I have not been close to many people . . . but I know that once they leave us they become insubstantial, and no matter how we try we cannot hold them, we cannot reconstruct. The dead don't answer when we call them. The dead are not our friends. (Urquhart, 2005: 368)

The tactile maps – the bodies that we experience – are only fragments, never a possession of all the world.

The fragmentary nature of maps in the book is also reflected in another map, Robert Smithson's artwork, *The Map of Glass*.[7] In 1969, Smithson created this piece by heaping broken glass in a field, then waiting for bright sunlight before photographing. In Urquhart's novel, the sight of great slabs of ice during the spring breakup reminds the artist Jerome of Smithson's work. He recalls being attracted by "the brilliance and the feeling of danger in the piece: the shattering of experience and the sense of being cut, injured" (Urquhart, 2005: 18). He has the impression that ice piled on the shore is something of an artistic gift – until he finds Andrew encased in it. Much later, while talking to Sylvia, Jerome makes the connection again, pondering the possible reference of Smithson's title: "I've never known if he meant a map of the properties of glass, or if he was referring to a glass map, which would then be, of course, breakable" (Urquhart, 2005: 337). Perhaps, for Urquhart, the reference is to both: the properties might refer to the way that glass allows one to see through it but also reflects light, so that the novel shows how the maps we make provide a lens for seeing the world and a mirror for seeing ourselves; yet a map made of breakable glass implies that the maps we construct (tactile and otherwise) are fragile. They are as insubstantial as the dead and as ungraspable as memory.

The other side of tactile maps is exactly how one's imprint is inscribed on another person. Fingers and skin do not simply receive information passively; they also cut. Listen from the book. Touch "causes fracture" (Urquhart, 2005: 87). Sylvia thinks of "the risks two people took simply by being alone together in the same room. Murder, love, collision, caress, were they not all part of the same family?" (Urquhart, 2005: 336). She herself had moved away from familiar things toward "tension and deceit and the growing knowledge of inevitable bereavement" and she did not know why (Urquhart, 2005: 332). Jerome dreams of Smithson's *Map of Glass* reflecting broken, shattered fragments of his father in its shards (Urquhart, 2005: 145). The "approach of someone significant in your life, a friend, a lover, an enemy" becomes like "lightning" (Urquhart, 2005: 366). Sylvia has "scraped [her] memory like a glacier through [her] mind" trying to remember every detail, trying to remember the "when" of every storytelling time with her dead lover (Urquhart, 2005: 368). She recalls that long before she lost him, she was walking through "the territory of aftermath", leading finally to an embrace already bereaved (Urquhart, 2005: 341). "That", she says,

> was when I knew that emotionally he had fully entered me, and that from then on his grief would be my grief, his story my story, his enormous waves of feeling, my feeling. I had felt almost nothing until him, and now I would continue to carry all of the rage and terror and anguish that he would leave behind, that he would forget (Urquhart, 2005: 343–344).

Her lover had been mapped upon her, not just in joy and the memories of pleasure but in the acuteness of loss and absence. She cannot shake grief's piercing of her body and her heart.

While the novel makes this explicit, the jagged-edged, fragmentary nature of sacramental maps is a little less easy to see. Yet, they too are maps of glass, holding their own peril. Some of this lies in the stories that they remember. Along with the idea of a washing away of sins, baptism carries the concept of being baptised into the death of Jesus. The telling of the story behind the Eucharist often begins with "On the night that he was betrayed".[8] Embedded in the story is failure, not only the treachery of Judas but also the failure of all the disciples to keep watch, to stay with Jesus, to accompany him. The main action of the Eucharist, indeed, is that breaking of bread called the Fraction: a tearing of one loaf into pieces so that it may be shared with many. The map that is made is itself a map of fragments, a fragile web of islands of memory standing close to death, with most of the territory unexplored.

While sacraments have locative and liberative functions for the community, *A Map of Glass* reminds us that living in this space is not easy. To be located somewhere by the weight of history's burden may also mean being stuck; to be liberated can mean exile. Sacraments also may be a "territory of aftermath", with maps marking out absence, the places and people that used to be, that are elsewhere, not here. Relationships themselves are dangerous, demanding of us that nearness to others which renders us vulnerable.

Maps of Glass, Maps of Flesh

Yet, for all of this, *A Map of Glass* also reminds us that glass maps in the territory of aftermath may reflect tenderness along with all that has been broken. Near the end of the novel Sylvia ponders what matters about her traceless love, and she comes up with this: "What matters is that we ever met at all, the miracle of the life I never could have lived without the idea of him, and the arm of that idea resting on my shoulder" (Urquhart, 2005: 369). While the writing that her lover traced on the world seems all but erased, reading the novel shows that the traces of his life remain mapped in Sylvia; she incorporates him into the roots and branches of her life, and this allows her to flourish in ways that had been impossible for her before. Though they are fragile and full of potential sorrow, these maps of glass – of novel and sacraments – provide more than an orientation for living in the world. Their tensions give them life.

Even as Sylvia carries the story of her lover with her, so does the reader pick up the map. Gingerly perhaps, cautious of the sharp edges, the reader picks up the fragments of stories, memories, places, seeking to join in tracing the almost imperceptible marks made by contact between bodies. And, all the while, those marks are being traced upon the reader, until the story of Sylvia and her love and the stories they have touched become mapped on the reader, too. But remember, landscapes are unreliable. They change. They fade. Still, this is what allows them to hold the traces of our touch, to be able to tell stories: to cry out to be mapped.

When Lathrop connects Christian liturgy, including sacraments, to maps, he is right. When he says that liturgy is like a map of "a few known centres" from which we live in the "surrounding wilderness", he is again right (Lathrop, 2003: 220). However, the wilderness is in the map itself, in the interpretation of the one who engages in it, in the exercise of weaving the symbolic fabric from what is known amid passion and peril. Sacraments are a "graphy", a writing, a tracing out of bodies that makes maps of flesh. These maps draw the landscape of memory, not just to tell us where we are, but to lead us, trembling and vulnerable, into the proximity of others – to trace the shape of our life in the world.

Notes

1 I am being quite precise when I talk about "a writer's image of mapping". As far as I know, Jane Urquhart is not a trained geographer, and neither am I. While I touch tangentially upon mapping as the discipline of geography might understand it, this is to throw light upon a literary use. This image of mapping is not necessarily the same as what geographers and cartographers actually do when they map.

2 For the purposes of size and manageability, this chapter focuses on Sylvia's story, rather than the middle section concerning Andrew's family; however, the themes of mapping and landscape are also in that middle section, specifically in the connection of the generations to the family island.

3 Different Christian traditions recognise different numbers of sacraments; for examples, the Roman Catholic Church has seven sacraments, and most Protestant churches have two. I am referring only to baptism and the Eucharist not only because these are the two sacraments recognised as such in the Presbyterian, Reformed tradition, but also they are the two sacraments which most Christian traditions hold in common – though, that said, what different traditions understand or believe concerning them varies widely. Some churches primarily baptise infants, while others will baptise only those old enough to make decisions for themselves. Where the Eucharist is concerned, groups have traditionally defined the sacrament along the lines of their own interpretations of Christological doctrine; that is, the point of difference has been on just exactly how Christ is present. The Eucharist in Roman Catholic theology is closely linked to the doctrine of transubstantiation, the belief that the bread and wine becomes in substance the body of Jesus Christ, who is really present for those who partake, while the outward form remains the same. On the opposite scale, some Protestant groups declare that the Eucharist is only a memorial of what Christ has done. Reformed theology stands somewhat in the middle, declaring that Christ is really present through the action of the Holy Spirit as people participate in the sacrament. This is to say that the theological understanding of sacraments is by no means the same for everyone, but that aside, I have tried in this paper to give a definition based on what actions are shared, hoping that this will facilitate readings of mapping and touch that can apply more widely.

4 Just as there are many different theologies of sacraments in Christianity, there are also many different patterns of how particular denominations or churches actually do them. For more information on the history and complex breadth of sacramental theology and practice see Osborne (2002) and Sattler (2005). Look also at denominational liturgical resources such as the Missal of the Roman Catholic Church, the various versions of the *Book of Common Prayer* used in

churches of the Anglican tradition, the *Book of Common Order* of the Church of Scotland, and the *Book of Common Worship* of The Presbyterian Church in Canada.

5 This ignoring of the body-as-map does not extend as far as the medical profession itself. Indeed, in one instance, Sylvia thinks of the textbooks in her husband's study, and shoe goes "to sleep comforted by the thought that someone, anyone, had taken the trouble to attend to a tragic alteration of the body, as if they had wanted to draw a map of its regions, then explore its territories" (p. 317). The key to this lies in both the "alteration" and the "explore". Just as Andrew's historical geography records what a place's inhabitants have done to the land, these are maps which chart changes to the body; yet, the comforting part seems to be the idea of exploration, of the mapmaker approaching with interest to see what is there.

6 See Wood (1993) for one discussion of what maps do.

7 Some photographs of the work are available for consulting online at Robert Smithson, 'Photoworks', <http://www.robertshmithon.com/photoworks/hc_atlantis_300.htm> – accessed 6 June 2008.

8 The words come from the earliest description of the tradition, 1 Corinthians 11: 23.

References

Hetherington, K. 2003. 'Spacial textures: place, touch and praesentia', *Environment and Planning A*, 35: 1933–1944.

Lathrop, G.W. 1993. *Holy Things: A Liturgical Theology.* Minneapolis. Fortress Press.

Lathrop, G.W. 2003. *Holy Ground: A Liturgical Cosmology.* Minneapolis. Fortress Press.

Osborne, K.B. 2002. 'Sacrament', in Paul Bradshaw (ed.), *The New SCM Dictionary of Liturgy and Worship*. London. SCM Press.

Presbyterian Church in Canada [PCC]. 1991. *Book of Common Worship.*

Sattler, D. 2005. 'Sacrament', in Erwin Fahlbusch *et al.* (eds.), *The Encyclopedia of Christianity*, trans. and Eng. lang. ed. Geoffrey W. Bromiley. 5 vols. Grand Rapids, MI. Eerdmans. / Leiden. Brill.

Urquhart, J. 2005. *A Map of Glass.* London. Bloomsbury.

Wood, D., and Fels, J. 1993. *The Power of Maps.* London. Routledge.

Chapter Thirteen

Wandering in the Wilderness: The Search for Sacred Space in Jack Kerouac's *The Dharma Bums*

Steve Brie

In 1957, the year that his seminal semi-autobiographical Beat treatise *On the Road* was published,[1] Jack Kerouac began work on a novel which, despite attracting less critical attention, is arguably a text of far greater intellectual substance than its more populist predecessor; the novel was *The Dharma Bums*.[2] Published in 1958, *The Dharma Bums* builds on a number of spiritual themes which Kerouac tentatively explored in *On the Road.* Although there are at least twenty-three references to God or to Jesus in *On the Road*, it is in the later novel that Kerouac specifically focuses his attention on the subject of spiritual enlightenment. *The Dharma Bums* portrays Kerouac's thinly disguised alter ego Ray Smith's struggle to understand and assimilate both theoretical and practical aspects of Buddhism whilst engaging in a series of retreats into the American wilderness. This chapter will begin by discussing the ways in which Kerouac's Catholic upbringing influenced his experimentation with religious imagery and language in *On the Road* and how this experimentation informed the metaphysical content of *The Dharma Bums*. The chapter will then go on to focus on the influence of Buddhism on the writing of *The Dharma Bums,* specifically exploring the ways in which wild spaces develop into sacred spaces as Smith's spiritual quest leads him to discover 'the actual warmth of God' (*TDB*: 9) in the "blessed night" (*TDB*: 113).

To Be, or Not To Be

Kerouac was something of a spiritual chameleon, moving in adulthood from Catholicism to Buddhism and back again. A French Canadian by decent, he was brought up a Catholic in Lowell, Massachusetts. Although during the time in which he wrote *On the Road* (1948 to 1951) he still retained a measure of belief in some aspects of Catholic doctrine, the former altar-boy and prospective candidate for the priesthood was increasingly moving toward a position of disillusionment in relation to the Catholic Church. One of his main criticisms was his belief that the Catholic Church had developed a greater interest in organisation than in spirituality (Nicosia, 1994: 594). He also claimed that it systematically excluded joy, a belief not dissimilar to that held by the Controller in Huxley's *Brave New World* who claimed that religion is not compatible with universal happiness since it involves sin and guilt (Huxley: 1969). Kerouac also argued that the Catholic Church enslaved people due to its promotion of the idea of deferred gratification with a posthumous heavenly reward for earthly suffering (Nicosia, 1994: 86). Although Kerouac indulged in an excess of earthly gratification during his own life, dying of alcohol-related disease in 1969, this particular criticism may have been the impulse behind a passage in the closing chapter of *On the Road* where the novel's focaliser Sal Paradise (another thinly-disguised alter-ego) meets a mysterious shrouded figure who, in a Sophoclean acknowledgement of inevitable human suffering, advises him to "*go moan for man*" (*OTR*: 306).

Kerouac's philosophical relationship with Jesus Christ was often volatile and subject to constant revision. In a letter to fellow Beat Neal Cassady dated 28 December 1950, he claimed that, although he believed that Christ was the son of God, he was not "jealous of Jesus to the point of madness like Mr Nietzsche" (Kerouac, 1995b: 251). His belief did not preclude direct criticism: at one point he accused Christ of being a political egomaniac (Nicosia, 1994: 464). If, claimed Kerouac, in one of his more antagonistic moments, Christ had familiarised himself with Buddhist beliefs, Christianity would not have become "the dualistic greed-and-sorrow Monster that it is" (Nicosia, 1994: 464).

At the time of writing *The Dharma Bums,* Kerouac still retained the same faith in a higher force that he had during the writing of *On the Road* where, in response to a discussion of the Nietzschean claim that "God is dead",[3] Paradise's travelling companion Dean Moriarty "out of his mind with real belief", retorts "no one can tell us that there is no God . . . everything is fine, God exists" (*OTR*: 120). In *On the Road*, Kerouac's definition of God is opaque to say the least. In the final chapter, for example, Sal Paradise enigmatically suggests that "God is Pooh Bear" (*OTR*: 309), a cryptic definition which would locate heaven somewhere within A. A. Milne's Hundred Acre Wood. The God which manifests itself in *On the Road* significantly diverges from the traditional Christian image of the Divine Being. In its place Kerouac offers what seems to be a pantheistic, Romantic representation of the Creator as nature itself: for example, as Dean and Sal traverse the Colorado–Utah border, they come to see the natural world as a sacred space. In a precursor of the way in which Kerouac would explore the concept of revelation through contact with nature in *The Dharma Bums,* Sal describes how he "saw God in the Sky in the form of huge gold sunburning clouds above the desert", clouds that seemed to say, "pass here and go on, you're on the road to heaven" (*OTR*: 182). This passage highlights Kerouac's belief that the concept of sacred space, like the concept of God, is fluid, and that it should not be exclusively related to the fabric of religious buildings or ruins. This refusal to specifically locate sacred space may have been influenced by fellow Beat writer and spiritual guide Gary Snyder who argued that "inspiration, exultation, and insight do not end when one steps outside the doors of a church".[4] It was Snyder who, in addition to encouraging Kerouac to consider Zen Buddhism as a way of life, and accompanying him on a number of his trips into the mountains, promoted the idea of the natural world as a sacred space, as a potential catalyst for spiritual development: "the muse", he wrote, "is the voice of nature herself, whom the ancient poets called the great goddess, the *Magna Mater*", a voice which he claimed was "a very real entity" (Snyder, 1974: 107). It is this concept of sacramental geography that informs the relationship between spirituality and nature in *The Dharma Bums*.

In spite of his belief in some form of God, after becoming increasingly interested in Buddhism in the period between the writing of *On the Road* and *The Dharma Bums*, Kerouac agonised over whether to leave the Catholic Church. Although he did turn his back on Catholicism for many years, Gary Snyder was convinced that he would eventually return to Catholicism and that, ultimately, he would desire Catholic last rites on his deathbed (Nicosia, 1994: 490). Snyder was right.

The Dharma Bums depicts Kerouac's flirtation with Buddhism, a flirtation that proved to be relatively short-lived for, unlike fellow Beats Snyder and Allen Ginsberg who remained devout Buddhists, when his retreat into nature inevitably came to an end Kerouac became disillusioned with the teachings of the Buddha. As early as June of 1959 he told Philip Whalen that the *Dharma* was "slipping away from [his] consciousness" and that he struggled "to think of anything to say about it anymore" (Kerouac, 1999: 206). Although he did manage to find something more to say about Buddhism, writing a series of meditations on Buddhist spirituality which became *The Scripture of the Golden Eternity*, the novel *Desolation Angels* (1965), which included reflections on Buddhist teachings and a number of other works which were published posthumously, by the turn of the decade the attraction of Buddhism was starting to fade.[5] In February of 1961, again in a letter to Whalen, Kerouac wrote,

> I dreamed I was dying suddenly and screaming for help but no sound came from my voice and suddenly I gave in, gave myself up to God . . . I gave in, gave myself and soul up utterly. (Kerouac, 1999: 281).

Evidence of his gravitation back towards Catholicism can be found in *The Scripture of the Golden Eternity* where references to Catholic saints and "innumerable holy ghosts" invade the text. Subsequently, just as Snyder had predicted, Kerouac increasingly inclined towards his early faith, coming to label himself a "Catholic Conservative" (Kerouac, 1999: 283), keeping a crucifix above his bed and professing a belief in "order, tenderness and piety" (Kerouac, 1999: 455). During the writing of *The Dharma Bums*, however, it was Buddhism, and in particular Zen Buddhism, rather than Catholicism which was to be his main influence, and it is this association, and the way in which it informed Kerouac's relationship with sacred space that will be the focus of the remainder of this chapter.

Hippie Zen

In January 1958 Kerouac suggested to Philip Whalen that that year was going to be "*Dharma* year in America" and that "everybody [would be] reading Suzuki on Madison Avenue" (Kerouac, 1999: 97). Kerouac's claim was of course hyperbole but, nevertheless, a significant number of Americans from both the old-guard Beat Generation and from the embryonic hippie movement did begin to look to Buddhism for spiritual direction towards the end of the 1950s when, as Rick Fields points out in *How the Swans Came to the Lake*, "Zen talk" was a staple of every middle-class cocktail party (1992: 247). What Kerouac termed the "rucksack wanderer" (*TDB*: 83), became part of a rebellion against what many young people considered to be the vapid conformism and standardisation of the Eisenhower years (1953–61). A steady stream of "drop outs" became "bards of old desert paths", turning on and tuning in to psychedelic "Zen lunacy" (*TDB*: 83), and experimenting with mind expanding hallucinogenic substances. As the West Coast intelligentsia became increasingly influenced by the exoticism of Zen philosophy as expounded by Buddhist priests such as Shunryu Suzuki-roshi, Yasutani-roshi and Harada-roshi, San Francisco became the centre of the Bay area Zen movement. In *The Dharma Bums* Japhy Ryder, Kerouac's fictional representation of Gary Snyder, predicts:

> a world full of . . . *Dharma* Bums refusing to subscribe to the general demand that they consume production and therefore have to work for the privilege of consuming., all that crap that they didn't really want anyway such as refrigerators, TV sets, cars . . . a system of work, produce, consume, work, produce, consume, work. (*TDB*: 83)

He has, he says "a vision of . . . thousands or even millions of young Americans wandering around with rucksacks, going up to mountains to pray" (*TDB*: 83). In practice, however, such idealism proved somewhat naïve. Barry Miles, confidant to the counterculture's major movers and shakers during the 1960s, cynically suggests that "for a while every Bohemian with a beard and a set of bongos . . . claimed to be a Zen Buddhist" and that "Zen became yet another excuse for existential disengagement". Very few of these "Bohemians", he snipes, ever did any "serious" meditation (Miles, 1998: 236).

Kerouac's interest in Zen Buddhism was further stimulated by the writings of other Zen evangelists such as philosopher Alan Watts whose *Beat Zen, Square Zen and Zen* influenced a large number of potential Bohemian mystics after its publication in 1958.[6] After his "conversion" Kerouac appears to have developed a genuine intention to immerse himself in Buddhism, a movement which he described as "the word and the way [he] was looking for" (Kerouac, 1995b: 430). In a letter to Neal Cassady dated October 1957, Kerouac claimed that he had promised Buddha that he would "go meditate [a] whole month in Mountain solitudes . . . praying for all living creatures" (Kerouac, 1999: 73). True to his word, with Snyder's help and encouragement he did seek out the solitude of mountains. As Roderick Nash has argued, "the solitude and total freedom of the wilderness" creates "a perfect setting for either melancholy or exultation" (Krakauer, 1998: 156): during his meditative experiences in nature Kerouac was to experience both emotions. Sometimes with Snyder and on numerous occasions alone, he undertook "monastic" retreats into the more remote mountainous areas of Lake Tampalais State Park, Yosemite National Park, Mount Baker National Forrest and Cascades National Park where, in the words of Barry Miles, he sought to "leave the common errors of the world . . . far below" in his search for "a new sense of pure material kinship . . . with earth and sky" (Miles, 1998: 235).

To the Woods

There has traditionally been an extensive interest in wild spaces in American literature. Kerouac's "dream of the 'Great Northwest'" (*TDB*: 35) and his attraction to the meditative possibilities of engagement with the natural world were directly influenced by the works of Snyder, by naturalist and environmentalist John Muir[7] and by transcendentalist Henry David Thoreau. In a letter to Gary Snyder dated 15 January 1958, Kerouac described how he had "dream'd of Thoreau" and "my boy [John] Muir", describing them as "two of the same cloth" before citing his admiration for both, "what men, what men" he wrote (Kerouac, 1999: 106). In *Walden, or Life in the Woods (*Thoreau, 1983: 264), Thoreau describes his experiments in transcendentalism, of how he sought spiritual enlightenment in periods of solitude in the woods near Concord, Massachusetts: "all nature", he wrote, "is your congratulation, and you have cause momentarily to bless yourself", and in *Ktaadn* he asks the reader to "think of our life in nature . . . daily to come into contact with it, rocks, trees, wind on our cheeks! The solid earth," he argued, *is* "the actual *world*" (Thoreau, 1985: 646). After reading *Walden*, Kerouac told the *New York Post* journalist Al Aronowitz that he would "cut out from civilisation, and go back and live in the woods like Thoreau" (Aronowitz, 1959: 22). Thoreau's notion of the natural world as a form of spiritual library was shared by Kerouac who argued that "the closer you get to real matter, rock air fire and wood . . . the more spiritual the world is" (*TDB*: 172).

The word "nature" comes from the Latin *natura*, which can be defined in relation to the concept of birth. In his retreat into a series of natural spaces where he is able to practice mindfulness and ponder the grand narratives of life and death, Ray Smith experiences a form of spiritual rebirth. For example, the intimate relationship between man, spirituality and the natural world is highlighted in *The Dharma Bums* when Ray, having discovered one of the many wild spaces described in the novel, relates how on "an early spring morning" as he moved through the four progressive states of Jhâna meditation[8] he saw "the truth . . . the world as it is" (*TDB*: 120), an experience which illustrates the Buddhist claim that when a meditator emerges from Jhâna he or she is able to penetrate previously subterraneous "truths" relating to the human condition.

Lonely as a Cloud

When reading works of fiction it is often dangerous to conflate the implied author (the author created by the text), with the actual author, but in the case of *The Dharma Bums* it is safe to say that we can, for the most part, equate Smith's experiences with those of Kerouac himself. Like Ray Smith, Kerouac in his meditations specifically sought to follow *The Diamond Sutra*'s call for the negation of all arbitrary conceptions about the nature of selfhood. He increasingly came to assimilate the idea that the separate self is an illusion and that there is no external self apart from interaction with the world. This epiphany is re-presented in *The Dharma Bums* when, immersed in the pastoral surroundings which he increasingly came to regard as sacrosanct, Ray ecstatically describes his integration into emptiness:

> It really started late in January, one frosty night in the woods in the dead silence it seemed I almost heard the words said: "Everything is alright forever and forever and forever." I let out a big Hoo, one o'clock in the morning, the dogs leaped up and exulted. I felt like yelling it to the stars. I clasped my hands and prayed, "O wise and serene spirit of Awakenhood, everything's all right . . . thank you thank you amen" I felt free and therefore I was free . . . I'd run these words through my mind to train myself: "I am emptiness, I am not different to emptiness, neither is emptiness different from me; indeed, emptiness is me." (*TDB*: 117)

In *The Dharma Bums* Kerouac tells of how he sought an escape from "the profound ignorance of the modern world" (Kerouac, 1995a: 453), a world he described as "beautiful" yet "sad" and "ungraspable", a world "dominated by consumerism"; America, he argued, had lost its spirituality and its soul (Nicosia, 1994: 595). The novel allowed him to retell the story of how he discovered sacred space in the wilderness of mountains, space in which he could practise *Dharma* and experience the mystic ecstasy of pure being. A significant contribution to this hierophantic quest was his communion with the natural world. It is not so long since our ancestors spent their days working the land, land which to them was sacred in the sense that its fertility or sterility controlled their lives. Since the industrial revolution and the subsequent demographic shift from rural to urban living, a pronounced desire to commune with nature has developed amongst many city dwellers. In *The Dharma Bums*, this Romantic sensibility can be observed in the narrator's descriptions of the landscape. Take this passage for example, where Ray Smith engages in Wordsworthian laudation when describing his interaction with the forest:

> One afternoon as I just gazed at the topmost branches of those immensely tall trees I began to notice that the uppermost twigs and leaves were lyrical happy dancers glad that they had been apportioned the top, with all that rumbling experience of the whole tree swaying beneath them making their dance, their every jiggle, a huge and communal and mysterious necessity dance, and so just floating up there in the void dancing in the meaning of the tree. I noticed how the leaves . . . looked human the way they bowed and then leaped up and then swayed lyrically side to side. It was a crazy vision in my mind but beautiful (*TDB*: 150–151).

Once isolated within this monasterial wilderness, Smith, just as Kerouac himself had done, turns his attention to the practice of *zazen.*[9] "When there is practice", wrote Zen priest Shunryu Suzuki-roshi, "there is enlightenment".[10] (1967: 71). Although like many American converts Kerouac found *zazen* easier to begin than to continue, his experience of *satori* (a state of sudden indescribable enlightenment) did develop through practice. Sitting (uncomfortably) each day on his makeshift *zafus*, his meditation led him to a place where he was able to comprehend the Buddhist notions that "all life is a dream" (Kerouac, 1995a: 413), that a thing exists "because it is", that "it doesn't exist because it is a dream", that it "neither is, nor is not", that "it partakes of no reality and partakes of non-reality", that it is "merely a vision, a phantasm, the moon shining on the lake, an evanescent dew, a flash of lightning, a shadow" (Kerouac, 1995b: 421). The idea of life as an ephemeral "flash of lightning" led an inquiring Kerouac to contemplate the concept of impermanence. The Buddha-*Dharma's* Third Truth states that whatever is subject to arising is also subject to ceasing, that everything we see, hear, feel and cognate is subject to continuous change. In *The Dharma Bums*, Ray Smith articulates his understanding of the relationship between existence and change acknowledging the fact that "things come but to go", that "all things made have to be unmade", and that "they'll have to be unmade simply *because* they were made" (*TDB*: 122). He goes on: "everything's gone, already come and gone . . . there isn't any finding of the farthest atom . . . things are just empty arrangements of something that seems solid appearing in space, that ain't either big or small, near or far, true or false, they're ghosts pure and simple" (*TDB*: 122).

Alone on the mountain, isolated from contemporary American society, a society once described by Kerouac as the "great World Snake" which wormed its way "up from the middle of the world . . . excrescing dirt" (Kerouac, 1995b: 250), Smith engages in a contemplation on the meaning of suffering (*duhkha*): "looking up at the splendorous night sky", he observes "Avalokiteśvara's ten wondered universe of dark and diamonds"

(*TDB*: 10), and proceeds to meditate on Sakyamuni's noble truths, specifically on the idea that all life is suffering and that as "there's nothing in the world but the mind itself . . . all's possible including the suppression of suffering" (*TDB*: 14). Later he imagines going "prowling in the wilderness" hoping to experience "the ecstasy of stars" (*TDB*: 35), a desire which would later be replicated by "stardust" hippies looking to get "back to the garden". Walking through the forest, Smith is transfixed by "the sound of the creek, the gurgle and slapping talk of the creek", he sees "the stars begin to flash", he feels the mountains to be "Buddhas and our friends", and he hears "the roar of silence . . . like a wash of diamond waves" as he ponders "the Milky Ways of eternity" (*TDB*: 61–62).

Another example of the dynamic relationship between transcendental experience and the natural world occurs when Ray, alone in the "moony countryside" on what he feels to be "a blessed night", falls "into a blank thoughtless trance" in which his body sinks into "a blessedness surely to be believed" (*TDB*: 114). He feels himself to be "completely relaxed and at peace with all the ephemeral world of dream and dreamer", and he thinks of "all living and dying things . . . coming and going without any duration or self-substance" (*TDB*: 114). "When your spirit is not in the least clouded [and] the clouds of bewilderment clear away", suggests sixteenth-century Japanese philosopher Miyamoto Musashi, "there is the true void" (Musashi, 1974: 95). Now Ray's spirit is free of cloud and he experiences one of many spiritual epiphanies engendered by the contemplative benefaction of the natural world; "we can't possibly exist" he marvels, "how strange, how worthy, how good for us" (*TDB*: 114). Here Ray comes to appreciate the interrelationship of the parts of Zen form that result in the concept of emptiness: "form is emptiness" states the Heart Sutra of the Prajnaparamita, and "emptiness is form".[11] At this point Kerouac's protagonist feels that he fully comprehends the nature of reality and the necessity of mortality. "What a horror it would have been", he opines, "if the world was real [because then] it would be immortal" (*TDB*: 114). Later, when, "pacing in the cold windy darkness" feeling "tremendously depressed", he prostrates himself on the ground crying "I'm gonna die!" at which point he experiences "the tender bliss of enlightenment" (*TDB*: 115). The "truth" he now understands is "realizable in a dead man's bones", a truth that is "beyond the Tree of Buddha as well as the Cross of Jesus" (*TDB*: 115). With "the diamond light" in his eye, free from the materialist props which normally allow us to hide from ourselves, Smith finds his "truth" – "that the world is an ethereal flower, and [yet] 'ye live'" (*TDB*: 116).

Later in the novel Ray discovers a new sitting place "under a twisted twin tree by a little opening in the pines and a dry stretch of grass and a tiny brook" (*TDB*: 119). Here, looking around at "new little birds . . . the dogs yawning and almost swallowing [his] *Dharma*" (*TDB*: 120), Ray believes that he has perceived a mystical "truth" in one of his sacred spaces: "here this is *it*", he exults, "the world as it is, is Heaven. I'm looking for Heaven outside what there is [but] it's only this poor pitiful world that's Heaven": after his revelation he promises to devote his meditations to "the awakening and the blessedness of all living creatures everywhere" (*TDB*: 120).

As the sun sets on his final sojourn into the mountains, Ray acknowledges his spiritual debt to the sacred space he has discovered in the natural world, space where he concedes, "I learned all" (*TDB*: 204). His retreats into solitude have facilitated a series of spiritual epiphanies, and by the time he comes down from the mountain he claims to have "fallen in love with . . . God" (*TDB*: 204). Exactly what he means by "God" at this point is difficult to ascertain, and the problem is further complicated when, cryptically, Kerouac describes Ray's spiritual experiences as "Blah" (*TDB*: 204), a description which is impossible for the reader to decode. While we may never know the answer to the "Blah" question, Kerouac closes the novel with the claim that the mountain "would understand what [it] meant" (*TDB*: 204).

The Dharma Bums presents a narrative rooted in the spiritual. After tentatively exploring links between nature and the sacred in *On the Road*, Kerouac presents a novel which offers a serious reflection on what he sees as the symbiotic relationship between sacred space and the natural world. The text operates as a *bildungsroman*, a right of passage narrative which sees Ray Smith move through a series of profound spiritual experiences toward a face to face meeting with "the serene spirit of Awakenhood" (*TDB*: 117).

Notes

1 Kerouac, 1991. All subsequent quotations are taken from this edition. Hereafter cited as *OTR*.
2 Kerouac, 1994. All subsequent quotations are taken from this edition. Hereafter cited as *TDB*.
3 See Ansell and Large, 2006: 245–291.
4 See <http://home.clara.net/heureka/art/snyder.htm>.
5 *Some of the Dharma* (1995) and *Wake Up: A Life of the Buddha* (2008) were published posthumously.
6 See *Chicago Review*, summer 1958. On close inspection Watts' philosophy can

be seen to be closer to Taoism than to Buddhism.

7 See for example Muir, 1998.

8 The Jhânas are said by the Buddha to be conducive to a pleasant abiding and freedom from suffering, as the mind becomes free from the five hindrances – craving, aversion, sloth, agitation and doubt.

9 In the context in which the term is used here, I utilize Gary Snyder's (1990: 11) definition of "wilderness" – "A large area of wild land with original vegetation and wildlife, ranging from jungle or rainforest to arctic or alpine".

10 *Wind Bell* 6(2–4):71.

11 See Simpkins and Simpkins, 1999: 53.

References

Aronowitz, A. 1959. 'The Beat Generation', *New York Post*: 22.

Fields, R. 1992. *How the Swans Came to the Lake: A Narrative History of Buddhism in America.* Boston. Shambhala Publications.

Huxley, Aldous. 1969. *Brave New World.* London. Penguin.

Kerouac, Jack. 1960. *The Scripture of the Golden Eternity.* San Francisco. City Lights.

Kerouac, Jack. 1965. *Desolation Angels*. New York. Coward McCann.

Kerouac, Jack. 1991. *On the Road.* London. Penguin.

Kerouac, Jack. 1994. *The Dharma Bums*. London. Flamingo.

Kerouac, Jack. 1995a. *Some of the Dharma*. London. Penguin.

Kerouac, Jack. 1995b. *Selected Letters 1940–1956* ed. A. Charters. London. Penguin.

Kerouac, Jack. 2008. *Wake Up: A Life of the Buddha*. London. Penguin.

Krakauer, Jack. 1996. *Into the Wild.* London. Pan.

Leland, J. 2007. *Why Kerouac Matters*. New York. Viking.

Miles, B. 1998. *Jack Kerouac King of the Beats*. London. Virgin.

Muir, John. 1998. *The Wilderness Journeys*. London. Canongate Press.

Musashi, M. 1974. *The Book of Five Rings*. Woodstock, NY. Overlook.

Nicosia, G. 1994. *Memory Babe: A Critical Biography of Jack Kerouac*. Berkeley, CA. University of California Press.

Pearson, Keith Ansell and Large, Duncan (eds), 2006. *The Nietzsche Reader*. Oxford. Blackwell.

Simpkins, Alexander and Simpkins, Ann-Ellen. 1999. *Simple Zen: A Guide to Living Moment by Moment*. Dublin: Newleaf.

Snyder, Gary. 1974. *Turtle Island.* New York. New Direction.

Snyder, Gary 1990.*The Practice of the Wild.* New York. North Point Press.

Thoreau, H.D. 1983. *Walden and Civil Disobedience*. London. Penguin.

Thoreau, H.D. 1985. 'Ktaadn', *Thoreau*. New York: Library of America.

Watts, Alan. 1958. 'Beat Zen, Square Zen and Zen', *Chicago Review*, Summer Edition. Watts, Alan. 1997. *Zen and the Beat Way*. Boston. Charles E. Tuttle.

Website:

http:/www.home.clara.net/heureka/art/snyder.htm – accessed 7 September 2008.

Contributors

Rina Ayra is a senior lecturer in art history and theory at the University of Chester. With an academic background in the history of art (BA, University of Leicester) and theology (MA from the University of Leeds and PhD from the university of Glasgow) she has published in the areas of art and spirituality. She is particularly interested in the role of the sacred in secular culture and the possibility of thinking about religion after the death of God. She has published papers on various aspects of the art of Francis Bacon, including his use of religious iconography. Her e-mail address is Rinaarya77@yahoo.co.uk.

Mark Barrett is a Benedictine monk of Worth Abbey, Sussex, where he has taught literature, theology and media studies. He is Chairman of the English Benedictine Congregation Monastic Theology Commission. He is the author of *Crossing: Reclaiming the Landscape of our Lives* (Darton, Longman and Todd, 2001).

He is currently engaged in research into the work of Augustine Baker, the seventeenth-century Benedictine teacher of "mystical theology". His e-mail address is jmbarrett@worth.org.uk.

Caroline Bennett is a Senior Lecturer at Liverpool Hope University. Her research areas include the works of Isabel Allende, Ian McEwan and Kazuo Ishiguro. She is presently conducting research into the ways in which Christian spirituality is represented in art, architecture and literature. Her e-mail address is bennetc@hope.ac.uk

Steve Brie is a Senior Lecturer in English Literature at Liverpool Hope University. He has published works on Poetry, Film, Television Drama, Theology, History and Popular Music. His research interests include: the poetry of Charles Bukowski; the novels of Jack Kerouac; British and American television drama and popular music. His e-mail address is bries@hope.ac.uk.

Jan Brown is a Senior Lecturer in Marketing at Liverpool Hope University in the United Kingdom. Her research interests include service marketing, experiential consumption, consumer culture theory and branding in complex environments. She has published in the academic and practitioner press. Her e-mail address is brownj@hope.ac.uk.

Jenny Daggers is a Senior Lecturer in Theology and Religious Studies at Liverpool Hope University. She is author of *The British Christian Women's Movement: a Rehabilitation of Eve* (Ashgate, 2002) and co-editor of *Sex, Gender and Religion: Josephine Butler Revisited* (Peter Lang, 2006). Jenny has also published a number of articles on feminist theology and women's history. Her e-mail address is daggerj@hope.ac.uk.

Mark Godin is a researcher in the University of Glasgow's Centre for Literature, Theology and the Arts. His research interests lie in Reformed theology, liturgy (specifically sacraments), the body, story and poetry. He is an ordained Minister of Word and Sacraments in the Presbyterian Church in Canada. His e-mail address is markagodin@googlemail.com.

Pepa Grundy is a Lecturer in Academic Skills and a Learning Support Tutor working for Liverpool International College, affiliated to the University of Liverpool. Her research interests include the role of religion in society and in education. She is currently engaged in a study of Sufi influences in the Balkan Peninsula and Primary Religious Education. Her e-mail address is 07012908@hope.ac.uk.

Ron Geaves is Professor of the Comparative Study of Religion in the Theology and Religious Studies department of Liverpool Hope University. He is currently Chair of the Muslims in Britain Research Network and advisor to the Preventing Extremism Unit at the Ministry for Communities and Local Government. His principal publications include *Islam and the West post 9/11* (Ashgate, 2004), *Aspects of Islam* (Darton, Longman & Todd and Georgetown University Press, 2005), *The Study of Religion* (Continuum, 2007), *Saivism in the Diaspora: Contemporary Forms of Skanda Worship* (Equinox, 2007), and will shortly publish *Sufis in Western Society : Global Networking and Locality*. Routledge Sufi Series, 2009). His e-mail address is geavesr@hope.ac.uk.

Robin Hartwell is a Senior Lecturer in the Department of Music at Liverpool Hope University. He is active as a composer and music analyst.

He has previously published on rhythm in the music of Anton Webern and on postmodernism in music. He has composed works for many different mediums including solo voice (Heartsounds, 2008) orchestra with choir (Jubilee, 2007), chamber orchestra (Unequal Division, 2006) and electronic music with visuals (Venice Postcards, 2004). His e-mail address is hartwer@hope.ac.uk.

Vish Maheshwari is currently undertaking his PhD research in "Place Branding and its sustainability" on a full-time basis at Liverpool Hope University Business School. His research interests include destination marketing, place marketing and analysis of brand building models. He is an active member of various professional bodies such as the Academy of Marketing Science, USA, the British Academy of Management, UK and the Chartered Institute of Marketing (CIM). His e-mail address is maheshv@hope.ac.uk.

Pascal Mueller-Jourdan is a Lecturer in Ancient Philosophy at the Université Catholique de l'Ouest. His main research area is Physic and Logic in late antiquity. His latest publication is *Une initiation à la philosophie de l'Antiquité tardive* (Paris. Cerf, Vestigia, 2007). His e-mail address is pascal.mueller-jourdan@uco.fr.

John Phillips is a Senior Lecturer in the Business School at Liverpool Hope University. After a career in senior management in the public and voluntary sector he began teaching in higher education. His research interests include organisation theory and leadership and interdisciplinary areas of study, such as culture and identity. His e-mail address is phillij@hope.ac.uk.

David Torevell is Associate Professor in Theology and Religious Studies at Liverpool Hope University. He is the author of *Losing the Sacred: Ritual, Modernity and Liturgical Reform* (T&T Clark, 2000), *Liturgy and the Beauty of the Unknown, Another Place* (Ashgate, 2007) and joint editor with Clive Palmer of *The Turn to Aesthetics: An Interdisciplinary Exchange in Applied and Philosophical Aesthetics* (Liverpool Hope University Press, 2008). Among his research interests are contemplative theology and spirituality. His e-mail address is toreved@hope.ac.uk.

David Weir is Professor of Intercultural Management at Liverpool Hope University, Visiting Professor in Management Development at Lancaster University and Affiliate Professor at the ESC Rennes and Distinguished

Visiting Professor at the ETQM College in Dubai. He has written extensively on management in the Arab Middle East including several chapters on the region in the *Regional Encyclopaedia of Business and Management*. He is the founder and Chair of the Editorial Board of the International Journal of Islamic and Middle Eastern Finance and Management. He is currently engaged on cross-national research with colleagues in the United States, the Netherlands and India into the interface between spirituality and management. His e-mail address is weird@hope.ac.uk.

Index

Abramovic, M. 116–19, 121
acoustics 106–10
Afghanistan 162–65, 170–71
Agamic and non-Agamic religion 129, 132–36
Altizer, T.J.J. 115
ambiguity 50
Andrew, Patricia 158
Anglican Group for the Ordination of Women 98
Aristotle 30
Arkell, Andy 12, 13
art 9–10, 35, 146, 182
  see also icons; performance art; singing; statues
Artaud, A. 120
Arthur, Ann 94
Association for Inclusive Language 88
astrology 140 n5
a-theology 123
Augustine of Hippo 30

Bachkovo Monastery 146–48, 154–55
background music 104
Bacon, Francis 122–23
Ballard, Roger 140–41 n10
Balthasar, Hans Urs von 28
Bamiyan Buddhas 162–65, 170–71
Bataille, G. 118
Batak, St. Nedelia church 150–52, 155
Baudelaire, Charles 158–59
Baudrillard, J. 34, 161, 165
Bauman, Z. 43, 50
beauty 28–29
Beck, U. 50
being 32
Belk, R.W. 59, 73–74
Belle, Carl Vadivella 135
Benares 58
Benedict XVI (Pope) 32
Berger, Peter 3
Bollywood 64–65
branding 57–58
Brock, Rita Nakishma 94
Brown, David 161
Buddha statues 162–65, 170–71
Buddhism, Kerouac's flirtation with 189–90
Bulgarian Orthodox Churches 144–55
business management 40–41
Byron, Robert 163

Called to Full Humanity 100
Campbell, L. 168
Casey, Michael 13, 19
cathedrals
  acoustics 106–10
  Coventry 168–69, 172
  Liverpool 104, 106
  Moscow 165–67, 173
Catholic Women's Network 88, 91–92, 95, 100

Catholic Women's Suffrage Society 98
choral singing 107
Christian feminism 93–95
Christian Feminist Newsletter 90, 100
Christian Parity Group 88, 98
  Newsletter 89
Christian Women's Information and Resources 99
church conversions 160
cities, noise in 12
Cixous, Hélène 110
Clothey, Fred 130
communalism 63–64
communism 153
consumerism 34, 60
consumption 36, 55–75
contemplation 30, 35
contemplative pedagogy 33
Cornis-Pope, Marcel 44
Coventry Cathedral 168–69, 172
cricket 61, 70–73
culture 34
CWIRES project 99

David, Ann 141–42 n35
Davie, Grace 10, 14
death 16
decision-making 40–41
democracy 34
Denmark, Tamil rituals in 134
Derrida, Jacques 109–10
desert spirituality 27–28
Diamante, Fra 157
Diogenes Laertius 83
disenchantment 158
Diwan 41, 45–50
Docherty, T. 34–36
domains of consumption 59, 61, 63–73
Dowell, Susan 89
Durand, William 157–58
Durkheim, Emil 6, 56, 74, 115

Ecumenical Feminist Trust 99
education 35
  see also universities
Eliade, Mircea 6, 39, 44, 55, 79–80, 81, 159, 161
Enlightenment 3

Fageol, Suzanne 95
fellowship 20
Feminist Theology Project 100
festivals 127–39
Fibiger, Marianne 134
Fides et Ratio 31–32
Field, Jackie 99
Filkin, C. 40
film industry 64–65
Fitzpatrick, G. 25–26
football 60, 61, 65–70
Foucault, Michel 82

Garcia, Jo 99
Geertz, C. 49
Ginsberg, Robert 158
Gourmont, Jean de 157
Greenham Common 92–93
Groning, Philip 14
Guigo II 30
Guttmann, A. 60

Hadot, Pierre 31
Hanlon, P. 56, 57
Hartlebury weekends 89–90
heart
  inclusive 25–26
  in monastic spirituality 25–28
  purity of 16, 28, 31
heritage industry 161–62
Herzberg, F. 56

heterogeneity 74
Hetherington, Kevin 181
Hetzler, Florence M. 163
Hill, R. P. 74
Hillsborough disaster 66, 67
Hinduism *see* Shaivism
Holbrook, M.B. 74
Hopkins, Gerard Manley 28–29
Howe, J.-M. 26–27
Hurcombe, Linda 89

icons 147–48, 149
images 26
  see also art
inclusive heart 25–26
inclusive language 95, 101 n.1
India 61, 63–65, 70–73
insight 33
Insoll, Timothy 161
Into Great Silence (film) 13, 14
Islam
  in Bulgaria 149
  see also Taliban

Jacobsen, Knut 133
Jenner, Judith 100
John Paul II (Pope) 31–32

Kaiser, A. 61
Kannan, R. 131
kavadi 128–39
kenosis 117
Kerouac, Jack 187–96
Keskinen, Mikko 103, 109–10
knowledge 30–32, 35
koinonia 20
Kostadinov, Peter 151–52
Krishnan, Gauri 136
Kroll, Una 88–89, 98

Lathrop, Gordon 177, 184
Le Corbusier 145
League of the Church Militant 98
Leclercq, Jean 18–19
lectio divina 18–19, 30–31
leisure 29–30
Li Tim Oi 89, 95
liminality 6, 41–44
liturgy
  intonation 106
  as map 184
  and sacred buildings 144
  women's 5, 87–97
Liverpool 57–58, 64
  Alma de Cuba restaurant 160
  Anglican Cathedral 104, 106
logos 83, 84
Louth, A. 29–30
lunar mansions 140 n5

McClatchey, Diana 89
Macgahan, Januarius 150–51
MacGregor, Neil 9–10
Maitland, Sara 93
Malaysia, Tamil rituals in 135–36
management 40–41
  in the Middle East 44–45
Marcus Aurelius 82
Maruyama, Magoroh 40, 49
Maslow, A. 56
'Mass' (nightclub) 64
Mauritius, Tamil rituals in 135
Mayfield, J. 149
meditation 33
Merton, Thomas 24
monasteries 10–21
  Bulgaria 146–48, 154–55
The Monastery (TV series) 13–14
monastic life 2–3, 5, 23–24
Moore, S.D. 122

Morley, Janet 90, 95–96
Moscow, Cathedral of Christ the Saviour 165–67, 173
Movement for the Ordination of Women 89–90, 99
Muir, John 192
Murugan (Hindu deity) 128–29, 131, 132–33, 135–36
music 103–13
myth 39

Nakshatras 140 n5
National Gallery 9–10
Nature 82–84, 192
Newman Association 91
Nietzsche, Friedrich 188
night stairs 16
nightingales 12
Nitsch, Hermann 123
noise 14
  in cities 12
  see also silence
Norway, Tamil rituals in 133

Ostwald, Conrad 161
Otto, Rudolf 159, 161
Oxford Catholic Women's Group 99
Oxford Christian Feminists 99
Oxford Christian Women's Group 91
Ozymandias 157

Pachomius 20
Pane, Gina 115–16, 119–20
Panikkar, R. 32
partying 64, 65
Peiper, J. 31
performance art 114–24
pets 74
Peychinova, Ekaterina 150
Picard, David 127
pilgrimage 128, 130, 131
Poulton, Jane 103–4
Pratt, Ianthe 88
Punjabi religion 140–41 n10
purity of heart 16, 28, 31
Pushya 128

Quaker Women's Group 92, 100

reading 18–19, 30–31
rebranding 57–58
religious art 9–10
Remnick, David 167
Robinson, Mike 127
Roman Catholic Feminists 99
routine 17–18
ruins 157–73
Rule of St. Benedict 15, 16, 17, 20, 23, 24
Russian Orthodox Church 166

sacraments 178
sacred
  in antiquity 159
  and consumption 59–60
  defined 39
  modern understanding 161
  and profane 44, 55, 115–18
Said, Edward 45
St. Hilda Community 90–91
St. Joan's International Alliance 98
St. Nedelia church 150–52, 155
Savage, Andrea 23, 24, 29
Scarry, E. 118
Schalk, Peter 133
SCM 99
Scruton, R. 39, 49
Seeing Salvation (exhibition) 9–10
Shaivism 130, 132–36
Shankly, Bill 69

Shelley, Percy Bysshe 157
shopping 62
silence 14, 23, 24, 26, 27–28
Simpson, David 35
Singapore, Tamil rituals in 135
singing 103–13
Smithson, Robert 182
Snyder, Gary 189, 191, 192
Society for the Ministry of Women in the Church 98
Somum, Khesaven 135
soulscape 27
spatial deconstruction 40
Sri Lanka 132–36
statues 162–65, 170–71
Stoicism 82, 84–85
Strawberry Hill conference 100
Student Christian Movement of Britain and Ireland Women's Project 99
Subramaniyam, S. 134–35

Taliban 163, 164
Tamil diasporas 128–39
Taylor, Donald 132–36, 137
Taylor, Mark C. 123
Taylor, Peter (Lord Justice Taylor) 66
Taylor, Rogan 66–67
Thomas Aquinas 144
Thomas, Sophie 159
Thoreau, Henry David 33, 192
Tomkins, S. 60
tourism 58, 127–28, 130, 140, 153, 163
Tumarkin, Maria 166
Turner, V.W. 42–43
Twain, Mark 58, 160

Unitarian Women's Group 92, 100
universities, medieval 29
Urquhart, Jane 176–84

Van Gennep, A. 41–42
Varanasi 58
Vergine, L. 120
vicarious religion 14
virtue 82

Watts, Alan 191
Weber, Max 158
Weil, Simone 34
Weir, David 40
Wilson, B.R. 74
Windsor Great Park 159
Womanspirit movement 88–97
women
  liturgies 5, 87–97
  ordination 87, 89–90
  singing voice 103–13
Women in Theology 89, 90, 100
Women's Training for Ordination Project 100
work 31
Worlock, Derek 66
Worth Abbey 12, 13

Xuanzang 164

Zajonc, A. 32–34
Zen Buddhism 190–96